Teaching in the
Real World
Strategies to Survive and Thrive

Dan Zukergood
Springfield College

Anne Marie Bettencourt
Springfield Central High School

Merrill
is an imprint of

Upper Saddle River, New Jersey
Columbus, Ohio

Library of Congress Cataloging-in-Publication Data

Zukergood, Daniel.
  Teaching in the real world: strategies to survive and thrive /
Daniel Zukergood, Anne Marie Bettencourt.
    p. cm.
  ISBN-13: 978-0-13-159052-6
  ISBN-10: 0-13-159052-9
  1. Teaching 2. Classroom management. 3. First year teachers—
    In-service training. I. Bettencourt, Anne Marie. II. Title.
  LB1025.3.Z85 2009
  371.102—dc22   2007052557

Vice President and Executive Publisher: Jeffery W. Johnston
Executive Editor: Darcy Betts Prybella
Editorial Assistant: Nancy J. Holstein
Project Manager: Sarah N. Kenoyer
Production Coordinator: Roxanne Klaas
Design Coordinator: Diane C. Lorenzo
Cover Design: Diane Ernsberger
Operations Specialist: Susan W. Hannahs
Director of Marketing: Quinn Perkson
Marketing Coordinator: Brian Mounts

This book was set in Times by S4Carlisle. The book and cover were printed and bound by
R. R. Donnelley & Sons Company.

Pearson Education Ltd.   Pearson Education Australia Pty. Limited
Pearson Education Singapore Pte. Ltd.   Pearson Education North Asia Ltd.
Pearson Education Canada, Ltd.   Pearson Educación de Mexico, S.A. de C.V.
Pearson Education–Japan   Pearson Education Malaysia Pte. Ltd.

Merrill
is an imprint of

10 9 8 7 6 5 4 3 2 1
ISBN-13: 978-0-13-159052-6
ISBN-10:   0-13-159052-9

This book is dedicated to all current and future teachers who strive daily to give their students the tools and knowledge to become wise, powerful, and compassionate citizens of the world.

What many teachers quickly realize once they enter the classroom is that some of the issues they are dealing with in their new schools were never covered in any of their education courses. This is particularly so with teachers who have been placed in an urban school (often very unlike the schools they were educated in) in which many suburban, middle-class, pre-service teachers have had little or no experience.

In fact, approximately 90% of our nation's students preparing to become teachers are white and middle class, and were brought up in rural or suburban households and schools. Yet, approximately 40% of the students they will teach during their student teaching placements or in their first classrooms will not be white or middle class, and they will attend an urban school. As a result, many teachers are ill-prepared to deal with the issues they will face in these schools. They will rightfully complain about their lack of preparation to teach in a setting in which they know nothing more about their students than the stereotypes they have seen in movies and on television shows.

Not only will they experience the typical stress faced by most student teachers, such as dealing with lesson and unit planning, and classroom management, they will also have to deal with the stress of learning how to function effectively in a very unfamiliar setting.

It is impossible for even the best schools of education to fully prepare pre-service teachers for the myriad of events that could take place in a typical school day in any kind of school. The question that departments of education must ask is, "How can we best prepare pre-service teachers for urban, suburban, and rural student teaching experiences so that they are most quickly able to meet the challenges of teaching in these schools?"

That's where this book will help. *Teaching in the Real World: Strategies to Survive and Thrive* is a collection of reflective journal entries sent via e-mail by Miss B, a 23-year-old, white graduate student doing her student teaching in an urban high school in Springfield, Massachusetts, to her college supervisor, Professor Z, a faculty member of the Springfield College Education Department and a veteran secondary school teacher. For easy identification, Miss B and Professor Z's e-mails have each received unique fonts. In these e-mails, the reader witnesses the transformation of Miss B from a passionate but struggling student teacher who is sometimes stymied by the challenges posed by her students to a teacher who has found her voice and the confidence to achieve her dream of improving the lives of her students.

Appropriate for Student Teaching/Practicum Seminar courses, and Methods, Urban Education, or Introduction to Teaching courses, this book introduces and discusses issues that teachers will be confronted with in today's classrooms.

By reading this book, pre-service teachers will be able to "experience" urban student teaching *before* actually getting into the classroom. Students already in their student teaching placements will be able to read about issues that they may not have encountered yet, but will be more prepared for after reading how Miss B reacts to each situation.

Since nearly all teachers are asked to write a daily reflection/journal, this book will serve as a model of what good reflective teaching/learning looks like. Miss B's e-mails set an excellent example for what a reflective practitioner looks for in seeking to improve his/her teaching. Finally, after reading about Miss B's experience within a situation, readers will see the response by Professor Z, and get an experienced teacher's suggestions on how to deal with the specific situation.

What is extraordinary about this book is Miss B's ability to re-create the student teaching experience and inform the reader what it is like to student teach in today's urban schools in a very honest, compassionate, inspiring, thoughtful, and humorous way. Readers will experience the joys, frustrations, fears, and compromises they will likely confront when they are doing their own student teaching. They will learn about the student teaching experience from a peer who can describe teaching in today's urban schools in a way that a professor might not be able to do.

Miss B struggles with issues of discipline, and with students who don't seem to care about school or see any relevance to it, students who are angry or sad, and students who just seem to need a hug and someone to say good morning to them. She attempts to teach students who are homeless and hungry, and who come from family environments too awful to imagine. She listens to the voices of bright and enthusiastic students who are chastised by their peers for being "good students." She also struggles to develop lessons that motivate students to learn as well as have her students see the importance of learning. In the process, Miss B makes lots of mistakes that set her back and many decisions that move her forward. In each case, readers will be thinking about how *they* would have dealt with that particular situation.

Professors using this book in their courses will find it to be an excellent tool to promote discussions on contemporary critical issues that pre-service teachers should be aware of. It provides an opportunity for students in pre-service programs to think about, discuss, critique, and problem-solve situations that are likely to arise during their student teaching or first classroom placement, whether they are teaching in an urban, suburban, or rural school. Many of Professor Z's comments are backed up with the latest research in teaching and are cited in each chapter for further reference.

Since the book is written chronologically, readers will be able to see Miss B's growth and discoveries during her placement. They will be able to envision more clearly how their teaching experience might seem like an endless series of mistakes and breakdowns that can, if reflected on constructively, lead to successes and breakthroughs.

Additionally, the book provides features in each chapter that students can use to plan for and monitor their own efficiency in different aspects of teaching. At the end of each chapter, readers will find:

1. *Discussion Starters:* Questions that will have readers react to key topics discussed in the chapter in greater depth.
2. *Professor Z's Tips, Strategies, and Relevant Data:* Great ideas for dealing with issues student teachers will face in the classroom, such as
   a. How to effectively teach critical thinking skills
   b. How to incorporate constructivist teaching into your lessons
   c. How to prepare for your first week of student teaching
   d. How to write good objectives
   e. How to create effective classroom routines
   f. How to create a good working relationship with your students
   g. What are the causes of discipline problems and how do I handle them
   h. How you and your cooperating teacher can work closely with parents
   i. How to effectively manage your classroom
   j. What you need to know about cooperative learning
   k. How to deal with the stress of student teaching
   l. How to get a class quiet—stopping the action
   m. Why you should use student feedback: the positive effects of soliciting feedback from your students
   n. How to create the vision for your future classroom
   o. How to work effectively with your cooperating teacher
   p. How to create a teaching portfolio
   q. How to write a resume
   r. How to prepare for getting a teaching job
   s. How to get more involved in the teaching profession
3. *Professor Z's Student Teaching Checklist:* These pages can be cut out and/or reproduced and hung on the wall as daily/weekly/monthly reminders that will prepare the student teacher for his/her placement and keep them on track once they are teaching. These topics include
   a. Getting YOUR Act Together
   b. Getting Your CLASS Together
   c. Classroom Management
   d. Effective Teaching Methods
   e. Things to Remember to Do During Your Placement
   f. Teaching in Urban Schools
   g. Post–Student Teaching Activities

Plus, as a result of having both a chronological table of contents and a thematic table of contents, professors and students will be able to quickly find sections of the book that deal with specific classroom issues.

This book is a discussion starter as well as a resource for student teachers on how to handle the many different situations they will have to respond to in their classrooms. It takes them deep into the classrooms of today and allows them to experience the "joy of victory and the agony of defeat." It will make them laugh, cry, and think. This is a book that can make them better teachers.

ACKNOWLEDGMENTS

Many people supplied support and guidance to this project. We are grateful to the wonderful staff at Merrill for their expertise that helped us create the book we truly wanted. We would particularly like to thank Debbie Stollenwerk for recognizing the possibilities of this book. When we submitted the "final" copy of our book, we thought we were nearly done. But the wonderful editing by Christina Robb added to a better "final" submission, for which we are very thankful. We want to thank Darcy Betts Prybella, our latest editor, for her enthusiastic endorsements and ideas.

Additionally, we thank the wonderful reviewers who were not only enthusiastic about the book, but who were able to make excellent suggestions on how to make the book better. Many of these are reflected in the final manuscript. The reviewers are Linda F. Balog, SUNY Brockport; L. Carole Byrd, Florida Community College at Jacksonville; Carrie Dale, Eastern Illinois University; Lois K. Draina, Marywood University; Andrea McLoughlin, Long Island University— C.W. Post; Timothy J. Richards, McKendree College; and Kathryne Van Til, Grove City College.

We would like to thank the many friends and family who helped in numerous ways:

Professor Z: Of course, without the fine job done by Anne Marie in her daily journal, there would never have been a thought about writing a book like this. She has always wanted to be a writer and have a book published and I am thrilled that she allowed me to "discover" her. The fact that I have co-authored a book with a favorite student and a woman who I know is going to make a huge difference in the lives of all her students makes this project all the more enjoyable.

My sincerest thanks go to my wife, Laurie, for being my soulmate and such a fabulous source of love and support for, not only this book, but for everything I do in life. Thank you, Hoot, your support and Meghan for being the greatest kid in the universe. I am not sure that our book would have been considered by the publishers had it not been for the marvelous initial editing done by Lisa Kent. Her love, support, and numerous other contributions to this book are deeply appreciated. More thanks go to Susan Seigel, April Huckaby and Amanda Johannson for their fine research and editing skills.

A million thanks go to Bill Paglia-Scheff for his consistently great coaching and friendship. I am forever grateful to all the wonderful friends who support me unconditionally and keep reminding me how lucky I am to have them as my friend—Lara Kramer, Deb Sheehy, Barry and Vicky Elson, Fay Kelle, Jack Mallan, Beth Spong, Southside Johnny and the Flashbacks, Ava, Cheryl Randall, and those fabulously cool cats, The Forrestos (Rich Michelson, Steve Schechter, Bill Mermelstein, and Stu Mellan). Thanks to my colleagues at Springfield College for their always uplifting and kind words ☺ and for making work seem so much like play.

Thank you Abbe, Mike, David, Paul, Caren, and Fred and all the kids for being such a wonderful family. Thanks to all the Singers and Levins. Finally, my thanks to my mother, father, and Seth who I am so happy to make proud as their son, "The Author."

Anne Marie: First and foremost I want to thank Brent for his guidance, his patience, and his ability to set high expectations for his students and his student teachers. Thanks for taking me on. Thanks to the students and staff of Providence Summerbridge including Rameka Blakey, Ashely Duffault, and Tim Charon. If it weren't for you all, I wouldn't have realized my true passion for teaching in the first place. Thanks to all my friends for listening to me rant and rave about my experiences, and for bouncing ideas off me during my student teaching. To Drew, my brother, who supports everything I do, no matter how big or small. I love you very much. Thanks for always being there. I want to thank Dr. Z for his belief in creating *great* teachers, because "we have enough mediocre ones out there already." I hope to inspire my students the way you have inspired me. I see now why all the seminar students raved about you before I met you. Last but certainly not least, my mom. You were the best teacher of all.

He who dares to teach must never cease to learn.

ANONYMOUS

BRIEF CONTENTS

CONTENTS

ABOUT THE AUTHORS

Daniel Zukergood

As an Associate Professor of Education at Springfield College in Springfield, Massachussetts, Dr. Dan Zukergood has been fortunate to realize his passion—that of helping to make his students extraordinary teachers—for the past twelve years. He believes that the world can be transformed, one great teacher at a time. His other passions include being an active democratic citizen (and teaching this to others), ending the current standardized testing madness, and rocking out with his band, The Rummagers.

He earned his BA at the State University College of New York at Oneonta and spent twelve years in junior and senior high school classrooms teaching social studies. He earned his MA and PhD at Syracuse University.

Anne Marie Bettencourt

Anne Marie Bettencourt is a seventh grade English teacher at Chestnut Accelerated Middle School in Springfield, Massachusetts. At Syracuse University, she ran and volunteered for several youth and educational programs for inner-city children. Her summer teaching experiences with Providence Summerbridge in Rhode Island fueled her passion for teaching, and she went on to graduate with her M.Ed from Springfield College. She spends her summers teaching outdoor skills to campers at Camp Massasoit. Yeah, she really, really loves kids.

INTRODUCTION

Pre-Student Teaching Reflections:
The Day Before My Practicum Starts . . .

From: Anne Marie Bettencourt

To: Mom

Subject: Pre-Student Teaching Reflections

Dear Mom,

Thanks for speaking with me the other day about my concerns regarding starting student teaching. I thought you might want to read my diary for today, which deals with many of the topics we spoke about.

Lots of love,

Anne Marie

THE DAY BEFORE MY PRACTICUM STARTS . . . WHAT DID I GET MYSELF INTO?

After eight hours in our first practicum seminar, my only thought is why ANYONE would want to be a teacher given all the hoops and hurdles we have to jump through and over. No wonder people quit the field so early! I am amazed that after an entire day of the Three R's (Rules, Regulations, and Red Tape) no one said, "Screw this! I'm outta here!" Around the room, you could see confusion and panic on everyone's faces. If it wasn't evident on my face, it was certainly noticeable from the teeth marks on my pen cap that I had been gnawing on while Dr. D was overloading us with information.

As I paper-clipped together the pink, yellow, and white forms; booklets for curriculum standards; and a folder full of articles with

tips on how not to bumble your student teaching experience, a ban-
ner of thoughts from today's lecture was flashing through my brain:
"Turn in the pink one to your professor, the yellow one to me, and
keep the white one for yourself . . . teaching portfolio needs to have
assessment pieces in it . . . make your daily journals interesting . . .
miss school only if you are dying. . . ." My head was spinning with
all the paperwork and all the things I had to remember on top of my
actual job of teaching.

Then again, the seminar is only one of the things adding to my
nervousness. I have spent weeks planning how I want my classroom to run. I have checked and rechecked my binders for my
classes, making sure I have the tabs aligned, have all the forms,
rules, letters of expectation, student surveys, etc. I have spent late
nights jotting down thoughts and ideas of what my classroom "culture" is going to be, what rules I want, how many I want [tip from
Dr. D: More than 5 rules is too many], etc. And I haven't even
touched the unit plans and curriculum outlines for the actual subject I am teaching.

Looking over the articles we got today, I thought to myself,
"Hmm, this isn't right. We are missing crucial information here."
For instance, there is not one line in any of the paperwork that
I received today that tells us, "Student teachers should be prepared
to teach classes on five hours of sleep, because that is what you will
have when you are done planning lessons and worrying about
whether or not your kids are going to eat you alive."

My situation is a little better than that of other student teachers. I have been in the same school since September (I can't believe
it is already January). I know the classes I will be working with, the
kids know me, the staff knows me, and I have a pretty good idea of
which bathrooms are clearly off limits no matter what time of day
it is and how bad you have to go. I was fortunate to start my academic year in our college's Americorps service program, where I
have been working with Mr. B (the ninth-grade teacher whose
classes I will be taking over) as a classroom tutor and aide. Since
we had to do pre-practicum assignments last semester, I got to test
out some of my lessons, and I have gotten to know some of the students. The other student teachers are not so fortunate. They will be
stepping into their school and their classrooms for the very first
time tomorrow. They don't know their students, their supervisor, or
anything about the school's culture.

But still, I am worried. What if they laugh at me tomorrow
when I am going over the rules? What if they know more than I do
about what I am teaching? What if I can't answer a student's
question?

What worries me most is the risk of failure. For months, I have taken courses on methods, good and bad assessment, what color ink to use when grading, etc. My professors have tried to get us hyped up about what amazing teachers we are going to be, how great it will be to finally experience the things we've talked about, blah, blah, blah. Now, tomorrow, I will look straight into the eyes of 30 students knowing that I am responsible for each and every one of them.

I have to say, my confidence was much higher before tonight. Now I am wondering, "What if I can't do this? What if I don't connect and my class is a joke? What if I stink at teaching? Then what do I do with my life?"

I am wondering if these thoughts will be evident in my eyes tomorrow. I wonder if my students will know that I am not sure of myself. I mean, I wouldn't take me seriously! I forget to turn the stove off and the dryer on, and I eat blue raspberry candy just because I like sticking my blue tongue out at people. This is who they are putting in charge of ninth graders? I love my T-shirt and jeans, and now I am stuck wearing dress pants five days a week. And somehow, tomorrow, I have to act like I have been doing this my whole life, that I love dress pants, that school is never tedious and boring and that I am an adult capable of handling anything these ninth graders can throw at me.

I can't laugh when one student mocks another, even when I'm thinking, "That's a good one! I'll have to tell my friend Nicole that!" I have to enforce some rules that I know don't make any sense and turn a deaf ear to students ranting about teachers that I personally can't stand. After today, only one thing is certain—I am going to need way more paper clips.

~ Anne Marie

WEEK ONE

"The mediocre teacher tells. The good teacher explains. The superior teacher demonstrates. The great teacher inspires."

WILLIAM ARTHUR WARD

Day 1: Josh/My First Day of Student Teaching (What They Don't Teach in Behavior Management Courses)

Building Relationships with Students, Classroom Management, Student Behavior, Teacher-Student Relationships, Motivating Students

Day 2: The Moat/Funding for Urban Schools

Dealing with Funding Realities, School Resources, Injustices in Our School System, The Politics of Education

Day 3: Covering Your Butt and Covering the Material

Testing—Too Much to Cover, School Politics, Curriculum Restraints, Standardized Testing, Teacher Responsibilities, Lesson Planning, Constructivist Teaching

Day 4: Black Man, White Man, Don't Give a Damn

Uncovering Racism, Sexism, and Classism; Teaching Methods; The Effects of Poverty and Race on Student Learning

Day 5: Good Luck, Miss B!

Faking Confidence, Teacher Issues (Attitude, Fear, Confidence), Classroom Management

---

Discussion Starters for Week One
Professor Z's Student Teaching Checklist

Topics Discussed This Week

In this chapter, you will learn

1. How to deal with the physical and emotional problems of students.
2. How to motivate students to do their work (and do it well).
3. How to become an effective advocate for educational change.
4. How to become an effective constructivist teacher and still prepare students for standardized tests.
5. How to get students to become effective advocates for causes they believe strongly in (racism, poverty, etc.).
6. How to survive your first day of teaching.
7. How to deal with fear and confidence issues.
8. How to create a well-managed classroom.
9. How to create good working relationships with students.
10. How to work in schools that do not have adequate resources and materials.

DAY 1

From: Anne Marie Bettencourt

To: Professor Z

Subject: Week 1, Day 1—Josh/My First Day of Student Teaching (What They Don't Teach in Behavior Management Courses)

"What's up, Miss B?" It was a quiet voice that called my name—so quiet, in fact, that he had to call my name twice before I realized he was talking to me. I turned around to see Josh, one of the students in my E period class, leaning against the brick wall with his girlfriend, Sarah. Josh is one of those students that I am going to be agonizing over the entire semester.

I first met Josh when I was doing my Americorps program here at the school last semester. He is very bright and insightful, but not motivated. I became interested in Josh after a parent conference that my supervising teacher and I had with his mother. I learned that Josh had not been turning in work, and his grades were dropping fast. His mother informed us that Josh was frequently depressed and sometimes prone to fits of anger at home. She mentioned that he loved two things: his girlfriend and his guitar. Unfortunately, Josh had smashed his guitar a few weeks ago and could no longer play. A light bulb went on in my head . . .

I called Josh up to my desk at the end of class one day and mentioned that I had heard he played guitar quite well. Surprised, Josh replied that he did but that he no longer had the guitar around to play. I put on my, "Huh, no kidding?" face and asked, "Well, was it acoustic or electric?" I mentioned that I had an acoustic guitar that I was clueless at playing. Perhaps he could give me lessons? I struck a deal with him that every Wednesday I would let him jam on my guitar, if he would give me lessons and complete his class work.

Through our after-school sessions, I learned a lot about Josh. I learned that he hates his home life, that he feels uncared for and unloved by his mom, and that he misses his brother terribly, since he moved to Colorado. I learned that he despises his father, but gets along with his stepdad. Josh's stress at home caused him to create burns on his arm with a hot wrench. He also cuts himself. We discussed ways to handle the situation, but I tried to listen rather than analyze or advise him. Since the guidance counselor already knew of the situation, I merely tried to be an ear for Josh.

A few weeks after our sessions started, Josh came to me one morning with tears in his eyes and asked to speak to me alone. I pulled him into a vacant teacher's lounge and sat him down. Josh rolled up his sleeve to reveal 25 fresh, bleeding cuts on his forearm that he had made with a thumbtack and his nails minutes before in his science class. He said that his mom had yelled at him for something he did not do and had punished him unfairly. Then, he discovered he had to serve office hours as a punishment in a class he thought he was improving in. This caused his stress to overflow and to cope, he had cut himself.

Now, inside my head I was thinking, "OK, they haven't taught us about this in *any* class I have taken. What do I do? What *do* I do?" I became a spectator. I saw myself look at the thin streams of blood coming from Josh's arm. I saw my mouth open and heard it say gently, "Well, we need to clean that up, so I think a trip to the nurse is a good idea." I looked up and saw tears streaming down Josh's face as he nodded. I just hugged him tightly for a moment and said, "It's going to get better, Josh."

I spent that day in the nurse's office with guidance counselors, crisis counselors, adjustment counselors, etc. I didn't talk much, because I was figuring out how to untie the knot in my stomach. I watched Josh withdraw from each person who attempted to talk to him except me. I was a wreck by midday and left Josh with the crisis counselor and his mom, unsure of how to continue the relationship I had built with him. He was out of school for a week and I did not call, though I thought of him whenever I looked in the direction of his vacant desk. Each day after school I drove home thinking, "I wonder how you are, Josh, and when you are coming back; *if* you are coming back." Should I have called him?

Before I left for break, Josh and I had a few more jam sessions where he talked of finding new ways to deal with his pain. He had started keeping a notebook that he drew and wrote in. I have never seen such grotesque, yet creative, pictures in my entire life.

I was happy I had built a relationship with Josh that allowed him to talk to me. That is what most student teachers are drilled to do: "build relationships with your students . . . show them you care." But no one ever tells you the end of that sentence, which is "but don't care too much."

The adjustment counselor warned me to be careful: "You can build a relationship with Josh, but remember that if he becomes dependent on you, when you leave, and you *will* leave, then he has nothing to fall back on, and he will crash and burn." I fully agreed with her, but now I am perplexed as to how to continue. I get stellar work out of Josh. Whenever we have our Wednesday guitar sessions, he talks to me and we work out strategies for dealing with problems, but I am afraid of him becoming dependent on me, or worse, wrecking the student-teacher boundary I am trying to keep.

I would appreciate any ideas on how to proceed without damaging our relationship or Josh's progress. I know that finding a balance between my relationships with students will be one of my greatest challenges this semester. I tend to bond easily with them, and I empathize with many of their issues outside of the classroom. I want them to know that I am concerned and that I care, but I don't want to be viewed as a peer, or get walked on in the classroom. I am still figuring out where the line is that separates the students from seeing me as a teacher, or as a friend. Suggestions?

~ Anne Marie

From: Professor Z

To: Anne Marie Bettencourt

Subject: Week 1, Day 1—Josh/My First Day of Student Teaching (What They Don't Teach in Behavior Management Courses)

I have been teaching for over 30 years and have never gotten a first journal entry like this one from a student teacher. Most student journals are only a fraction of yours in length and do not reflect on school situations in such depth. I applaud you! I am a true believer that the better a teacher is at reflecting on his/her teaching, the better the chances are that he/she will become an extraordinary teacher (which is my goal for all my students). You are a truly gifted writer. I can visualize the entire situation with Josh quite clearly.

You are dealing with very significant issues in your first week of student teaching! I appreciate your honesty and your willingness to engage with these difficult issues. With the depth of reflection and effort you put into your journal, you leave me little choice than to respond in kind!

Before I start, and since we have never met each other, I suggest we set up the context for our communications. In my responses to your journal entries, I'll try to shed light on the issues you are dealing with and suggest ways for you to effectively address them. Remember that my suggestions may or may not work for you and your students. Many factors come into play that make each student-teacher interaction unique. What works for me might not work for you. What works for one student might not work for another. So, as many a teacher has probably told you in response to a "How do I do this?" question, the answer usually is, "It depends."

> **MINI TIP**
>
> Each student-teacher interaction is unique. Do not assume that any two students will react the same in any given situation.

Think of me as a shoe salesman. I'd like you to try on my suggestions like they were shoes. If they fit, wear them. If not, try on another pair or find another pair from another "store." However, if there is something you are doing that is hurting you as a teacher, I might insist that you wear a pair of corrective shoes for a while. Ultimately, my job is to help you find a wardrobe of shoes that you can wear to meet the different needs of your students.

Here are some comments on the points you raised:

1. *Josh—Students in physical or emotional trouble:* You did the right thing by immediately reporting that Josh had cut himself. Teachers are legally responsible to notify the proper school authority when students are self-destructive. While I appreciate

> **MINI TIP**
>
> Teachers are legally responsible to report self-destructive student activities to the proper authorities.

the adjustment counselor's warning that Josh might become dependent on you and burn when you leave, I'm not sure that staying away from him will be any better. He needs you now!

   However, you must keep boundaries clear. *Do not* give him your home phone number, have him visit your home, or allow him to miss other classes to talk with you. *Do* find some time each day when the two of you can talk. You can create a dialogue with Josh and help him find ways of dealing with his problems after your student teaching ends. I think you are handling him well. Just keep the line very clear regarding what is appropriate and what is not.

2. *Josh—Motivating students who need a helping hand:* Josh's motivation problems are typical of students who have home-life problems. How can a student concentrate on English or algebra when he feels unloved at home

and unsupported by his parents? Possibly the best you can do is to just be there for him and to listen to what he has to express. It could be that you are the only person in the world he is opening up to!

By establishing this relationship, there is a much better chance that his schoolwork will improve, at least in your class. Once he starts doing better in your class, you can work with him on doing the same in other classes. You can collaborate with the adjustment counselor on what advice to offer Josh, and whether the advice improves Josh's home and school lives.

3. *Outside the Box Methods of Motivating Students:* One of the most important things a good teacher does is motivate ALL students to learn—even the ones who don't seem to care. While there are traditional means of motivating students (see any methods textbook), you often need to think outside the box to meet the needs and grab the attention of your not-so-ordinary students. In fact, only classroom management ranked ahead of the motivation of students as the major concern of new teachers.[2]

I remember one of my eighth-grade students who moved to our town in the middle of the year and would not do anything in my class. He just sat there, not participating in the lesson, not speaking to other students—a real shut-down loner. He wore T-shirts each day that had the names of rock bands on them. One day, as the class was leaving, I dropped a copy of *Rolling Stone* magazine on his desk and told him, "I thought you might like this." I did not wait for a thank-you. I did not want him to feel beholden to me, to see this as a bribe, or to think that I expected a thank-you from him. I just walked away.

While he never thanked me, he did start doing his homework and seemed to be paying more attention in class. When I finished reading the next issue of *Rolling Stone* (I had a subscription), I put it on his desk and walked away. This time, I got a "Thanks" as he left the room at the end of the period. While he never did speak in class and never participated in small or large group work situations, he did his work, passed his tests, and passed the course. A big win? No. A small win? Yes. Since then, I have used *Sports Illustrated* and *Rolling Stone* with students who I couldn't seem to reach in any other way. At best, this method got some students involved. At the very worst, it got them reading something!

One of the best ways to motivate students is to get them to see that you are interested in them. Once they see this, they will want you to like them and will work hard to seek your continued interest and approval. After all, you have the intelligence to like *them* and find *them* interesting, so you must be a good teacher! You are doing this well with Josh.

Another way you can motivate students is to "mix it up" with them whenever you can. During recess, go to the gym and watch them shoot basketballs while making comments like, "I dare you to make two in a row," "Good shot," etc. Join a game if you can play and talk to some of the students just hanging out, particularly if you see someone not talking to anyone.

Get to know students' families whenever possible. Students will be more motivated to work for you if they know that you are in contact with their parents. Attend as many parent-teacher meetings as you can. Send letters home to tell parents when the student has done something good in your class, not just when he/she has done something bad. Good notes home can motivate students just as well, if not better, than negative notes. Increased motivation results in improved student attitudes about learning, fewer classroom management problems, and greater satisfaction with school for both teachers and students.[4]

Whew! I just want you to know that I have *never* written such a long response to a journal entry before. But your journal was so good and you are thinking so deeply about such important topics that you have motivated me to respond in this way. I hope you find my responses helpful!

Best wishes,

Prof Z

Tips, Strategies, and Relevant Data

How to Show Students That You Care About Them[5]

1. Learn student's names quickly.
2. Call on students by their first names.
3. Greet each student and get to know them as individuals.
4. Make eye contact with students when speaking to them.
5. Smile when speaking to them.
6. Demonstrate relaxed body language when speaking to them.
7. Use "we" and "our" in reference to class activities and assignments.
8. Spend time with students.
9. Demonstrate respect for students as individuals.
10. Get involved in activities that students are involved in.

DAY 2

From: Anne Marie Bettencourt

To: Professor Z

Subject: Week 1, Day 2—The Moat/Funding for Urban Schools

Hey Dr. Z! After reading over your suggestions, it seems we are on the same page about Josh. He will be out of school for a week, but I did not give him my phone number and I think I will continue those jam sessions with him and see where it goes. His girlfriend came in today and mentioned that he is doing all right and that he is still excited to play the guitar with me on our regularly scheduled Wednesday sessions. Crossing my fingers on this one! So, on to today's issues . . .

Have you ever seen a moat? You know, the kind that surrounds castles, with a dragon in it, or a serpent lying in wait, or maybe one containing just plain old acid. Usually you need a drawbridge to cross it. Or a valiant knight shoots a rope from his arrow and bravely climbs, hand over hand, to the tower on the other side. Well, that is what our school parking lot was today—a moat. It happens every rainy day and you can tell it's a rainy day just by looking at how cars are parked in the lot. The periphery of the lot is filled with cars, even cars parked illegally behind other cars, while the center is either empty or contains a few cars whose owners were foolish enough to think that the water, which is now up to the middle of their tires, wasn't that deep.

There is no way around the moat, so the students and the teachers wade (with water past our ankles) across the moat to the school on the other side. On rainy days, parking becomes like NASCAR, with contestants vying for the outermost spaces. Students spend rainy days wandering the halls with sopping pant legs. Teachers have called numerous times about this problem, including calls to both the media and the superintendent, but apparently fixing a moat isn't top priority around here.

Having enough books to go around to all students isn't a top priority either. At my first faculty meeting last semester, the principal announced that we were all making too many copies: the budget allotted us 3 million total copies for three years, and we had already made 2 million in three months. We were told that we would have to cut down. The irony of this was that we (150+ teachers) had just received six packets of paper, none of which was double-sided, from the administration with the school plan, agenda, and various useless information on them.

For every student to read the same material, we were advised to make transparencies for every other chapter of the books, since there aren't enough books for all classes to read the same novel at once or even for one class to read the same novel. So today I went up to make copies, and as I was hunting around for transparency sheets, I was informed that there were none. We had to buy our own! We also have to buy our own art supplies, and the kids have to pay for their own field trips, because there isn't a budget for any of those things.

If I had any political clout at all, I would drag proponents of No Child Left Behind down here and demand that they explain how no child was getting left behind in a school like this. Days like this irritate me when I think of the unequal opportunities poorer districts are given. There are no field trips, no books to write in or keep as their own, and no art supplies. Yet our students are supposed to get the message that education is important and it will take them places? I think the message being sent to these kids is that nobody really cares that much if they get an education or not, that they are losers and that the rich kids will get all the goodies instead of them.

Education is most definitely segregated! And yet, everyone is expected to pass these high-stakes tests with flying colors, and have the same outcomes, regardless of funding. One of the teachers I spoke with pointed out that perhaps our government was simply trying to privatize education.

Why isn't anyone getting as upset as I am about it and writing letters, making noise, and storming Congress? Perhaps they are jaded or working three jobs to support their family, or both. What's going to happen to these students if no one speaks up? And what can I, a newbie teacher, do to change it?

Eventually, I want to start my own school, similar to Deborah Meier's Central Park East schools for city kids, to prove that public education can succeed. It just needs to be restructured, that's all. Other people have done it and it has worked. So why aren't we jumping on the bandwagon and changing our system? I feel like the field of public education is a forest fire, and the teachers have been handed Dixie cups of water and told, "Put it out."

~ Anne Marie

From: Professor Z

To: Anne Marie Bettencourt

Subject: Week 1, Day 2—The Moat/Funding for Urban Schools

Dear Anne Marie,

Many of my pre-service teachers say they do not get involved with politics. They believe our political system is a corrupt one and is filled with poor leaders. They believe that their one vote does not make a difference. They do not think that they can make a difference, and they don't think that their elected officials will listen to them. They also say they wouldn't know what to do even if they wanted to try to make a difference. They feel powerless and try to ignore politics. They also believe that by being a teacher, they don't need to get involved in politics, because their job simply is to teach kids. How wrong they are!

> .... **MINI TIP** ....
>
> Politics is involved in every aspect of teaching. The purpose of politics is for people to solve society's problems together. If aspects of society do not meet your expectations (poor condition of schools, lack of books, and poor technological resources), then it is your responsibility as a teacher to advocate for your students so they all receive a quality education.

Politics is involved in every aspect of teaching. Political decisions made at the school and at the local level affect the number of students in your class, which students you get, which classroom you are assigned, the amount of supplies you get, the number of field trips you take, how much you get paid, the books you use, what kinds of benefits you get, the number of aides in your classroom, the number of children with special needs you have, the disciplinary practices you use, the food served for lunch, and whether you get rehired each year.

Political decisions made at the state and federal levels affect the amount of money your district has to operate the school (which affects many of the items just listed), the curriculum you teach, the number of standardized tests that children must take each year as well as numbers of state and federal mandates that must be met.

The truth is, that whether they like it or not, teachers are deeply involved in politics. But many refuse to admit this. They put their heads in the sand and complain to other teachers that they have too many kids in their class, not enough supplies, too few aides, and so forth. And while they might have strong views on such issues, they do nothing constructive to change the situation. When I've asked, they admit that they have never contacted any of their elected officials who *do* have the power to make constructive changes in the way we run our schools.

For example, the vast majority of teachers I have met are against the way high-stakes standardized tests have taken over our schools. They see how it not only has hurt the students who fail the test, but how it has negatively affected every student and teacher in some way.

For example, many states now use just one test to determine whether a student should graduate from high school. Teachers know that you cannot measure what a child has learned after 12 years of schooling by taking one multiple choice test. They know that these tests are biased and invalid. Even the testing companies say that more than one determinant should be used to decide whether a student should graduate or not. However, most states have ignored this wisdom.

Teachers know that hundreds of millions of dollars are spent on these tests, while they still have large class sizes and don't have enough books and computers for all of their students. And what have we really learned from all this testing? We've learned that wealthy kids who speak English and don't have any learning disabilities do better on standardized tests than poor children who do not speak English well and who have disabilities! Very deep! I would have told them this for the price of a cheeseburger!

Also, in preparing for the tests, some districts have done away with art, music, physical education, and in some cases, even social studies (the social studies test is usually the last to be developed, so why waste time on it if kids won't be tested?). So much for a well-rounded education! Let's not forget to mention the emotional toll for the many kids who are not good test takers and who might not like having negative labels attached to them. But, the state probably figures, "Why worry about them when they'll probably just drop out anyway when they realize they won't pass the test." What a terrible way for a school system to act if they really are committed to leaving no child behind!

Sadly, while most teachers deplore the points mentioned above and the fact that they have become glorified test-preparation experts, they have done nothing to change the situation. Imagine if every teacher and parent met with their elected officials to insist upon a better use of these hundreds of millions of dollars. I guarantee that tremendous changes would be made

Even with limited time, teachers can take small actions that can achieve big results. One year, several of my students and I went to Boston and testified before the Health and Human Services Committee (along with several other organizations) on the topic of increasing the budget for the universal school breakfast program. We were concerned about the number of children who came to school hungry each day as a result of living in food-insecure homes. As teachers, we knew it would be very difficult for a child to learn to the best of his/her ability if he/she were hungry. We succeeded in getting $3 million added to the universal breakfast budget, raising it nearly 50%!

Teachers need to speak up to the people who can change these conditions, not

MINI TIP

Be in touch with your elected officials. See *How to Communicate with Your Elected Officials* in today's Tips, Strategies, and Relevant Data section.

just complain about them in the faculty room! They need to organize meetings with representatives. They need to get other people involved! We have no choice as to *whether* we want to play politics in education. We already do. The question is whether we want to learn how to play politics in a way that will improve conditions for both teachers and students or just let things continue the way they have been.

Regarding the moat—Has anyone written letters to the Board of Education, taken pictures of it for the media, or invited elected officials to come down and see it? Sometimes, students can be the most effective lobbyists. All it takes is one teacher, parent, or student to make the moat a classroom advocacy project (having people sign petitions, speak to the media, etc.).

Now, with all this said, do I think that as a student teacher you should be front and center on this issue? No! I think you now have your hands full learning how to be a good classroom teacher. While I am sure there are some small projects that you could take on politically at this point, keep your eyes on the prize—becoming an excellent classroom teacher! Take on big political projects after you get a job!

Maybe it is something your cooperating teacher would be interested in taking on. Certainly, creating a well-written petition and letters to elected officials or local media sources (Letters to the Editor) would be excellent English projects. Plus, I am sure most students are sick of the moat and would be very motivated to get credit for trying to get rid of it.

Regarding the lack of supplies—Have you spoken to other teachers who also see the irony of the administration wasting paper while teachers do not have enough themselves? Possibly a group letter would be appropriate. Again, I would suggest you work with your cooperating teacher as there is less risk of you sticking out. Remember, you will be looking for a teaching job next year and you do not want to be labeled a "troublemaker." You can do excellent political work behind the scenes and not jeopardize your employment chances for next year.

Good luck!

Prof Z

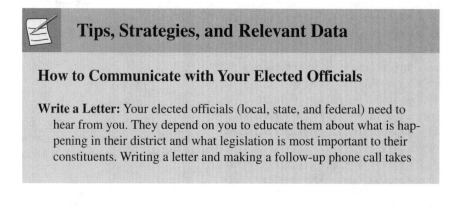

Tips, Strategies, and Relevant Data

How to Communicate with Your Elected Officials

Write a Letter: Your elected officials (local, state, and federal) need to hear from you. They depend on you to educate them about what is happening in their district and what legislation is most important to their constituents. Writing a letter and making a follow-up phone call takes only a few minutes of your time, but it ensures that your representatives know how you want to be represented.

Be sure to include all of your contact information so your Congressperson's office can reply. Here is an example of how to write an effective letter to your elected officials:[6]

Engage   Dear Senator_____,

As a mother of two small children, I was shocked to find out that more than 100 million primary-school-aged children around the world are not in school.

Problem   Can it be that the only thing standing in the way of these children having access to a brighter future are school fees often as little as $50 a year? I've recently learned that the number one barrier for poor, vulnerable, and orphaned children in getting an education is school fees.

Inform About the Solution   How can we expect any country to develop to its full potential when its children are not getting educated? Not one developed country has been able to do so without first making education free and compulsory for its children.

When school fees were dropped in Kenya over 1.2 million new children showed up for school.

Call to Action   Please become an initial cosponsor of H.R.1406, legislation calling for the elimination of school fees with a $250 million incentive fund for countries to draw upon to help defray the costs of hiring new teachers, building new schools, and providing all children with a quality education. I look forward to your reply on this issue.

DAY 3

From: Anne Marie Bettencourt

To: Professor Z

Subject: Week 1, Day 3—Covering Your Butt and Covering the Material

OK Dr. Z, while I love your political stance and '70s activism, you are going to have to nudge me on this one. First of all, Mr. B does *not* get involved in politics. He prefers to do his thing and let the tide pass. I think he views things more as phases and is waiting for this whole budget thing to pass. Besides, I have talked with other teachers about the moat thing, and apparently they have called the media in before only to have the school department reply, "Yeah, about that . . . money's tight, sorry." And the ones who *do* make a fuss don't seem to be high on the principal's list and a few have even gotten "relocated" to other districts. Any websites you can give me on covert politics in the educational field? For now, I am just going to observe and talk to the renegade teachers and when I get a job, at least I'll know who to go to for ideas and plans of action!

Well, today I was in the teacher's room chatting with other student teachers from UMASS Amherst when I came to this realization. Katie, a history teacher, was grumping that her cooperating teacher sprung the "you-have-to-give-a-midterm-now" talk on her. Apparently, Katie was already "behind" according to curriculum standards. She was not covering content "fast enough," and was frustrated that the midterm was going to slow her progress and would not be meaningful for her students.

Jake, an English teacher and one of my great buddies for ideas, also complained that it was impossible (and I agree) to do an "Open Response" question for MCAS (MA standardized test) every two weeks and keep up with curriculum. An Open Response every two weeks? It takes my students one week just to digest the paragraph and understand the prompt! Jake's kids didn't even know what a prompt was, never mind rewording it and then writing about it! I have no problem teaching writing, and critical writing for that matter, but I do have a problem cramming knowledge into my students for the sake of "covering" all the things they are supposed to know.

First of all, my two classes work at different paces. My E period class, the college prep one, flies through short stories, so we are into the Harlem Renaissance already. They get ideas and concepts a little quicker than C period does. C period is a little "behind," because they love to talk, which I actually prefer because it makes discussion enjoyable and easy compared with pulling E period through the mud to answer a question.

We are required to teach two novels, a packet of roughly eight short stories, and poetry and fiction from the Harlem Renaissance, and somehow squeeze in grammar to boot. Now the student teachers and I have figured out this means that we have exactly enough time to teach it all, if the students "get it" the first time around, and if we skim the short stories without going over the rich language, imagery, and themes. (Not like it's important to discuss literature, right?) So, if by chance we have to reteach something, there is no way to get through it all, and give our students an appreciation of literature and its richness, as well as improve their writing skills with workshops and long essays, because we've got to stick to the schedule! Needless to say, we were all wondering what good this is for the students. They won't be able to remember it all, so why not just focus on critical thinking skills and let the teachers work the curriculum in such a way that the students get the skills instead of cramming them with 80 stories a year?

Liz, my writing lab teacher, devised a course that was to be taught in conjunction with history. She developed an entire syllabus that focused on topics for world history and corresponding books that would be taught in English class. I thought, "What a wonderful idea! The kids will understand the themes, and have it reinforced in two classes . . . excellent!" The school turned it down.

I want to know who is in charge of making this curriculum, and why we can't demand to have it changed so that kids are focusing on themes or critical questions around maybe three topics a year instead of eight. I know in other countries, students do better than ours, and research has shown that they study fewer topics but in greater depth, thus gaining a better understanding and grasp of the material. That's common sense.

Perhaps I am talking from a lack of experience. But I can tell you that I remember a lot more from my college courses, where we focused on a theme or a question for a semester, than from my high school courses, where I can barely tell you what I read, never mind what I was supposed to have learned. My goal is to open my own progressive school for citizenship (you will probably hear me talk about "in my school" a lot, sorry!), and I wonder if I can make a curriculum that is skills-based and theme-based, rather than content-based. I wonder if there are schools out there that already do that. I wonder also, why we aren't given a wand and cape with our plan books and (eek) red pens, so that we can magically teach our students everything they are supposed to learn in one year's time.

~ Anne Marie

From: Professor Z

To: Anne Marie Bettencourt

Subject: Week 1, Day 3—Covering Your Butt and Covering the Material

Dear Anne Marie,

Great job on this journal entry.

One of the main purposes of public schooling in the United States is to create good citizens.[7] Good citizens are those who have content knowledge and who can reason—both important things to have in a democracy, where it is the people who lead. The problem is that we emphasize the content part so heavily that we "don't have time" to teach kids how to reason (think critically). Standardized testing makes many teachers feel that they must just cover the material. If they do, and their students don't do well on the test, they can say that it is not their fault because they "covered" the material.

Unfortunately, *covering* the material does not necessarily mean that the students are *learning* the material. Teaching is not really about *covering* material. It is really about *uncovering* it so the student has a good understanding of it.

Yet, most teachers try to cover the material by relying largely on lecture, a strategy that does not typically result in high levels of knowledge retention. As research shows, we retain very little of what is lectured to us. I have included the learning pyramid to show you how little is retained by students when you lecture to them and how much is retained when they are active participants in their own learning.

Many teachers use vast amounts of time putting notes on boards or overheads,

MINI TIP

The best way for kids to truly understand the material is for them to use higher critical thinking skills such as teaching, comparing/contrasting, analyzing, synthesizing, and hypothesizing in contexts that are authentic, experiential, and relevant to their lives. See *How to Effectively Teach Critical Thinking Skills* in today's Tips, Strategies, and Relevant Data section.

People Generally Remember

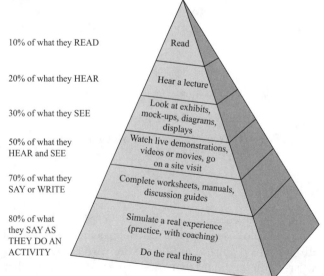

An Important learning principle, supported by extensive research, is that people learn best when they are actively involved in the learning process. The "lower down the cone" you go, the more you learn and retain.

10% of what they READ	Read
20% of what they HEAR	Hear a lecture
30% of what they SEE	Look at exhibits, mock-ups, diagrams, displays
50% of what they HEAR and SEE	Watch live demonstrations, videos or movies, go on a site visit
70% of what they SAY or WRITE	Complete worksheets, manuals, discussion guides
80% of what they SAY AS THEY DO AN ACTIVITY	Simulate a real experience (practice, with coaching)
	Do the real thing

Adapted from *Audio-Visual Methods as Technical.* Editor Dale Devden Press, N.Y. 1864 p. 43.

having the students copy those notes, and then testing them on Friday. By the time they go over the test on Monday, it is apparent that the students have already forgotten much of the material. This is not good teaching. Yet, this is what many teachers believe they must do to cover the material and cover their butt.

I wish I could blame the standardized testing movement for this sorry state of affairs. Unfortunately, many teachers have been using the lecture approach forever. Why? Because besides making it easier to cover your butt and cover the material, it is an easy way to teach! You can use the same notes and tests year after year. You are sure of the material, and there is little risk that a student will throw you with an unusual or creative question. We all have done this at times, including myself and it is sometimes necessary and logical to use a lecture approach. However, teachers should not use it as the only method.

The alternative is to teach using a student-centered approach, in which you become the "guide on the side" as opposed to the "sage on the stage."[8] In this approach, your classroom becomes a laboratory of learning. The teacher's job is to give the students activities (experiments/performance tasks) in which they will have to use their prior content knowledge and critical thinking skills to find solutions to the issue at hand.

The term for this is *constructivist education*. It is all about what the student accomplishes. In this approach, teachers need to be prepared to learn right along with their students and not have the idea that their job is to "fill those empty vessels" with the knowledge that you want them to learn. Instead, you teach students how to learn. At the end of the year, I would rather say that I have created motivated lifelong learners than to say that I simply covered the material for a standardized test.

With all that said, it is certainly possible to teach in a creative manner and cram for the test when the time comes. It requires good planning. Every year, I would need to prepare my students for

MINI TIP

Constructivist teaching can be a very effective means of achieving student understanding. See *How to Incorporate Constructivist Teaching into Your Lessons* in today's Tips, Strategies, and Relevant Data section.

the NY State Regents exam. As we learned different topics throughout the year, I would tell them to put an "R" next to certain topics that I thought had a good chance of being on the Regents. I just refused to make passing the Regents exam the overall goal for the year.

I want to be clear that I feel it is very important for students to learn the content and pass the standardized tests. I just think that the methods used by too many teachers simply require students to memorize material that is quickly forgotten. By using more constructivist approaches, students will more likely understand the material and retain it for a longer period of time.

Did I always cover all the material in depth? No. It is nearly impossible to cover every topic in the curriculum in enough depth to insure deep understanding. There is simply not enough time to give each topic the depth it deserves. However, there are certain topics that seem to be tested each year. Be aware of these by reading study guides to the tests and make sure students are very familiar with them. It is important to not beat yourself up for not teaching everything in depth, but to try your best to be a good planner. Much of this comes with experience.

Hopefully, your cooperating teacher is one who uses a student-centered approach. If he/she doesn't, observe other teachers in the school who do. There are numerous websites filled with excellent examples of constructivist teaching. Plus, all major book companies have teacher's guides and activity packages with the texts. Many departments or districts have access to videos and supplemental materials. Ask your cooperating teacher if you can look at these.

I used to prepare to teach each topic by reviewing two or three of these activity packages from different book companies. I would use the ideas that I liked and those that helped me meet my objectives. I have found some tremendous materials in these packages. Many student teachers try to only use lessons that they have personally created. This is a tough thing to do when you are a new teacher. You don't need to re-create the wheel. Find existing lessons and get used to the many resources that are available to help you. There are numerous websites in which you can find wonderful lessons. Use them!

Finally, as a student teacher, you must remember that you are still a visitor of sorts in the cooperating teacher's classroom. You might not have the opportunity to do things as you want to do them. Some cooperating teachers will insist that you lecture, cover the material, and do all the things I just railed against. Unfortunately, as a student teacher, that is just the way it goes. However, cooperating teachers are always hungry for new lesson ideas. It is possible to persuade them to let you try some of your new ideas. You will get your chance to use all of your ideas when you get your own classroom.

Prof Z

Tips, Strategies, and Relevant Data

How to Effectively Teach Critical Thinking Skills[9]

1. Build a community of trust in your classroom so that students feel comfortable sharing and offering different opinions.
2. Have students collaborate with each other. Students retain the most information when they teach each other.
3. Teach students to look beyond the obvious. Hand them a simple object such as a rock or peanut and ask them to study it. Have students share with classmates what they have discovered. You will be amazed at how many different answers you will get from your students.

4. Offer students games, puzzles, and riddles for warm-ups, homework, extra-credit, etc. to stimulate their thinking.
5. Encourage your students to deal with real-world issues often.
6. Incorporate critical thinking into daily lessons by having students do the following:[10]
   a. Give reasons for their answers.
   b. Generate their own problems.
   c. Offer multiple solutions.
   d. Elaborate on their answers.
   e. Relate the lesson to their own lives.
   f. Relate the lesson to other classes.
   g. Combine ideas from different sources.
   h. Evaluate each other's work.
7. Use Bloom's Taxonomy and the Task Oriented Question Construction Wheel[11] to help you prepare questions that will stimulate critical thinking.

Task Oriented Question Construction Wheel Based on Bloom's Taxonomy

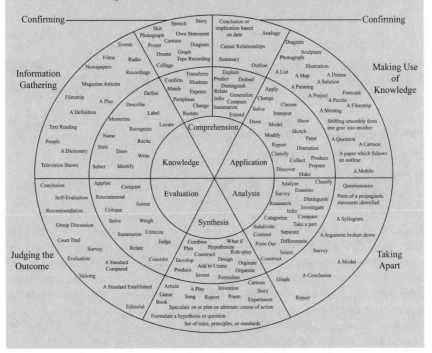

©2001 St. Edward's University Center for Teaching Excellence. *http://www.stedwards.edu/ cte/bwheel.htm*

How to Incorporate Constructivist Teaching into Your Lessons

1. Have learners construct their own understandings rather than telling them yourself. Be the "guide on the side" rather than the "sage on the stage."
2. Have your lessons build upon what they already know. This is one reason why it is so important for you to assess what students know before teaching them anything.
3. Once you assess students' prior learning, review the basic content that you are expecting to build upon in the lesson. In other words, make sure everyone is with you before you go forward. New learning depends on prior understanding and knowledge.
4. Create lessons in which students need to interact with each other. Learning is enhanced by social interaction.
5. Have students work on real-world tasks, problems, and situations whenever possible. Authentic learning tasks promote meaningful learning.[12]

DAY 4

From: Anne Marie Bettencourt

To: Professor Z

Subject: Week 1, Day 4—Black Man, White Man, Don't Give a Damn

Talking about racism with urban kids is like talking about the effects of drug use at a rehab center. Both groups are going to give you the, "No kidding, that really happens? Gollllllllleeee, you don't say" attitude. So, today when we dealt with racism in our lesson on pre-Harlem Renaissance material in C period, I should not have been surprised at the level of apathy I got from my students.

Mr. B and I made some transparencies of minstrel shows, blackface, and song lyrics from minstrel shows. He also had the students watch Part I of the Jack Johnson documentary, which

I had never seen and was really interested in. I had presumed all the students (white, black, and Latino) would have been outraged at what happened to Johnson, and at the blatant racism African Americans experienced in 1908, but to my surprise, the students sat there either bored or yawning.

OK, I thought, perhaps that's because it's a video, and it's in black and white. Surely the minstrel stuff will get them riled up. Again . . . apathy. So now I am wondering, what did we do wrong? Why aren't these ninth graders fired up about racism, and demanding to make changes to eliminate it? Then I thought of what the students were trying to tell us, ever so politely. "Miss, this is our life. You're not telling us anything we haven't experienced already." Duh.

Akeem, a black student, pointed out that "it's everywhere you go, Mister (to Mr. B), and a student would be stupid to say racial stuff in front of a teacher so of *course* you wouldn't hear it." Janisa, a Latino student, just shrugged her shoulders and said, "It happens." So now I am the one getting outraged (inwardly of course). It just happens?! No, it does *not* just happen! I am wondering if my students have just had so much dealt to them over the years that they have almost come to expect racism, or to see it as a way of life, rather than a disease for which we have not yet found a cure.

It's as if they've come to accept it, and I'm not sure why. Martin Luther King's generation didn't accept it, and I don't think it's a whole lot less blatant than it was back then. Schooling is actually more segregated, or unequal, now than it was then. But perhaps the students don't see it that way.

How can I teach them about social injustices and not get apathy in return? I want to show them that this is not OK, it's not just "the way it is," and they should not be used to it. And since Akeem so honestly pointed out that a student would indeed, be stupid to say something in front of a teacher, now I wonder what goes on behind my back that I don't see with my students. What racism am I missing? What else am I missing? Is there a way I can see it, or have I crossed a line so that I am no longer "in the know" because I am a teacher, and not privy to students' lives and discussions?

How can we understand what we don't see, but the students do? It's almost two different worlds in one building—the students' world and the teachers' world, and neither side has full access to both. So now I am wondering how I am going to structure my lessons so that I get some passion out of my students, some energy, and maybe some desire to change things. Any thoughts, Prof Z?

~ Anne Marie

From: Professor Z

To: Anne Marie Bettencourt

Subject: Week 1, Day 4—Black Man, White Man, Don't Give a Damn

Dear Anne Marie,

I have this funny sense that instead of watching TV tonight, I am going to be writing a long response to you. That's why they pay me the big bucks! ☺

It is tragic that students leaving our public school systems will, in my opinion, likely be more racist, more sexist, more classist, etc. than when they entered. Maybe it is because our society is very oppressive, but surely the way we do schooling in the United States contributes to this.

This is a difficult topic, one in which teachers are in different stages of understanding and development. Most student teachers are white, middle class, speak English, and come from suburban environments. Most of their urban students are none of the above. It is imperative that student teachers strive to develop their multicultural awareness, knowledge, skills, and actions.

> **MINI TIP**
>
> Be acutely aware that the effects of oppression are everywhere and are affected by the actions we all take as teachers. See *What You Need to Know About Poverty* in today's Tips, Strategies, and Relevant Data section.

While there is oppression in every school, the effects of it are felt much stronger in poor urban schools. Many students, in urban schools, face problems that suburban kids would never dream of. For example, approximately 20% of these students come from food-insecure homes. Middle-class students worry about *what* is in the refrigerator. Poor students worry *if* there is food in the refrigerator. Sometimes there is none.

Our educational system is extremely classist and racist. Look at where the money goes, and at who has the power and who doesn't. Poor students many times do not have health insurance and sometimes go without medication, glasses, hearing aids, etc. because their parents cannot afford them. Poor students go to schools that are typically old and have poorer and more dated materials, fewer certified teachers, fewer working computers, larger class sizes, poorer student services, poorer athletic facilities, etc. Poorer students are sick more often than wealthier ones and typically miss more school as a result. Poorer students do not get the extra school help, tutors, aides, and out-of-school prep courses that wealthier students take for granted.

Students know what is going on. Students in poor schools can see that their schools are different from the ones on "the other side of the tracks." They see that most of their teachers do not look or live like them. They see that the administrators and the politicians do not typically look like them and don't seem to have their interests as a high priority. They see how many of their teachers are not certified in the subjects they are teaching and how they are lacking books, materials, and a safe learning environment. They see how they are tracked differently than others at an early age. They see that for some kids, vacations mean a trip to some other part of the world, but they may not have even left the town they were born in. They do not see many role models who look like them, and they are not encouraged to succeed like other students are.

While all teachers need to be aware of issues of oppression and privilege and their effects on students, urban teachers will likely be teaching children who do not have many of the privileges that students in suburban schools have. Teachers in suburban schools will typically deal with children who are white, who are middle to upper class, and who hold economic, social, and political privileges. This makes a huge difference in virtually every aspect of a student's life, and teachers need to be able to respond effectively to these differences.

Besides being aware of issues of institutionalized racism and classism, teachers should be aware of the personal biases and privileges they carry around and how these might get in the way of providing each one of their students with an excellent education. For example, these biases may lead to assuming things about their students that are not true as well as raising or lowering expectations for certain students. Our expectations play a huge role in how we act towards students. We must be careful not to base our expectations on race, skin color, class, language spoken, gender, or sexual orientation.

Author and educator Ruby Payne writes about the "hidden rules" that exist in every economic class.[13] She points out that when people in positions of power come from classes in which rules are different from those of the people they work with, understanding and communication can break down. Thus, when a middle-class teacher works with students who live in poverty, he/she often expects the class to behave in middle-class ways and is perplexed when they do not. This may create tremendous miscommunication, leading to poor instruction and a lack of achievement on the part of the students.

In fact, in my Multicultural Education class today, nearly the entire class admitted that they would have higher expectations for students from a local school in an affluent neighborhood than for students from an inner city school. Many of my students are very passionate about creating a more just educational system. But these biases are part of the reason it is so hard for minority groups to improve their lot in the system we have created. In fact, my students could be part of the problem rather than the solution if they do not improve their multicultural awareness.

> **MINI TIP**
>
> Teachers should be aware of the personal biases and privileges they carry around with them and be clear that they are not acting out of them.

In fact, study after study has shown the harm that is spread when teachers have low expectations of students based simply on their economic or racial status.[14] For example, a common stereotype that many student teachers (as well as many veteran teachers) accept is that African Americans are not good students. Many teachers buy into these stereotypes at some level and do not expect as much from African-American students as they would from Asian-American students, for example.

This affects how each student is treated in class by the teacher. The African-American student is not called on as frequently and is not encouraged as much as the Asian American. This, in turn, affects how the student perceives him/herself and the stereotypes actually become internalized within that student. As a result, the African-American child may, in fact, not do as well as others through no fault of his/her own.

Additionally, the African-American student may not be expected by his/her teachers to go to college. Thus, they are not treated and pushed the same as other students who are expected to go to college based simply on their color and wealth. Minority students who do continue their educational pursuits after high school typically do so in spite of the system, not because of it! Much work is needed to transform this oppressive system and the players in it (teachers, administrators, elected officials, etc.) in order to have a system that works for *all* students.

All teachers, but particularly urban teachers, need to not only be aware of the effects of oppression on their students but also aware of how to fight it. All teachers need to be part of the solution of changing patterns of exclusion, harassment, discrimination, rejection, and violence instead of acting in ways that keep the system in place. If teachers do nothing to make change, they are unconsciously helping to reinforce the system as it is.

Since many teachers have political, social, and economic power due to their class, race, and other factors, they have great power to be change agents. They also need to empower their students on how to do the same. When these two groups work together, change has the best chance of occurring.

You ask what we can do about this. Of course, this is the million dollar question, and I don't have *the* answer. But I do have some ideas that will help make our schools more effective and equitable:

1. Study the topic of privilege and oppression. Become very clear about the privileges you have as a white, middle-class, English-speaking, mentally and physically able person. Learn about the biases, stereotypes, and prejudices that you bring to your classroom. Learn about the costs of oppression to *all* of us and do what you can to create an educational environment that affords all students the same privileges. Have appropriate expectations of *all* of your students based on the child's abilities, not the social, economic or racial group he/she belongs to. Do not "go easy" on kids due to their race, class, gender, etc. Push them all to do their best.

2. Show genuine interest in your students' lives. Learn more about what their lives are like living without the privileges you may have. Be in contact with parents and guardians. By showing interest in their lives and giving them

your respect, you can also help change some of the assumptions they have about you.

3. Try to help end the apathy among students. One method I have used is to ask my students how many will probably be having kids of their own at some point. Then I ask them what kind of world they would like their kids growing up in. Would they like a world that is sexist, so that their daughters do not have the same privileges as men? Would they like a world that is racist, in which their children are discriminated against because of the color of their skin or because they choose to date/marry someone of another race? Would they like a world that is homophobic, so that if their child is gay, they will grow up being persecuted as a result? When students look at world problems from the point of view of a parent, I find they are much more willing to do something for "their kids."

4. Teach them how change happens. Teach them that their actions and comments are important. As Beverly Tatum says, "Teachers should be honest about racism and prejudice so as to empower their students, encouraging them also to engage in social justice to combat it."[15]

Whew! Another novel! Well, we both got some good rants in on this entry, didn't we? There are no easy solutions to the issues you bring up here, Anne Marie! However, I commend you for the depth of your reflections and the commitment you have to having your kids learn. Keep up the good work!

Prof Z

Tips, Strategies, and Relevant Data

What You Need to Know About Poverty

Consider the following statistics on poverty and differences in the socio-economic status of students.[16]

1. Eleven percent of U.S. families fell below the poverty level in 2002 (defined as an income of $18,100 for a family of four). The percentage has increased since then.

2. The incidence of children living in poverty is considerably higher among minorities and single-parent families. The rate of childhood poverty in the United States has risen every year since 2000, more than in all other industrialized countries.

3. The majority of the poor are white (65 percent) since the majority of Americans are white, but the incidence of poverty in other ethnic groups is higher.

4. Low income fourth graders were twice as likely to fall below basic levels of reading on National Assessment of Educational Progress tests as students who were not low income (58 percent versus 27 percent) and were much less likely to achieve at the proficient level (13 percent versus 40 percent).

5. Dropout rates for students from the poorest families in the United States exceed fifty percent. When compared with students whose families are in the highest income quartile, students in the lowest quartile are two and a half times less likely to enroll in college and eight times less likely to graduate.

DAY 5

From: Anne Marie Bettencourt

To: Professor Z

Subject: Week 1, Day 5—Good Luck, Miss B!

I could not have had a more nervous, yet exciting day today. I took over my first of three classes. They are all mine, C period, for the next seven weeks. Not only did I toss and turn all night, finally getting up at 5 AM to finalize seating charts and go over my rules and procedures for the fifth time, but I also sweated out half the day worrying. I prayed to the teaching gods not to let me screw this up. I spent the day doing the "what ifs." What if they don't move when I ask them to, what if they glare at me all day, what if they laugh in my face, what if they don't read, what if they don't learn! This was my biggest fear, and it still is.

I put on my best poker face all day. I survived the fire drill that sent my writing lab students and me out into the freezing cold. I countered Murphy's Law and grabbed my own stapler when the copier ran out of them. I cheered through B period's Acting I class as Mr. B and I cast all the parts for our May play, Aristophanes' *The Wasps*. Then the bell rang, signaling the end of B and the start of C. It felt like that movie moment when everything slows down, and suddenly, all you can hear is your heart pounding. I took a deep breath, gave myself a fast pep talk about how I could do it, and be strict, be strict, be strict. Then I had the best moment ever when I walked into the classroom and glanced up at the board.

Jeremy had written, "Good Luck, Ms. B" on the board in bright blue dry-erase marker. The students waved good-bye to Mr. B, and they LISTENED to me! They listened as I changed their seats, they listened and nodded as I went over rules and procedures, and they actually did what I asked them to! I know this sounds trivial, but I really didn't believe they would take me seriously. I just pretended like I did. And, I think I learned that pretending is what counts.

You can, indeed, fake confidence, and fake that you believe everything that you are saying, even if inside your head, you're thinking things like, "OK, put on your serious face. They are going to hate you but cross your fingers and lay down the law and pray they don't get up and walk out." It's the teaching persona that counts. I have to walk into that class and psych those students into believing that I think grammar is amazing. I have to be excited about Thoreau (even though I think he can be dry) and about teaching adverbs. I need to do this because if I show the slightest shred of doubt, they will sense it.

Now this acting thing is actually easy because, fortunately for me, I am excited about most literature and writing, and fascinated by it. But I also think I learned how exciting self-discovery and application really is. I was ecstatic that the tricks I had learned in my methods class actually worked and that I was experiencing what mentor teachers had told me about classroom presence, tone, and personality. And I was excited by the end of the class that I was actually DOING IT!

Really, it's all about attitude and sticking to your guns. I am prepared for them to test my rules. This is what students do, right? But I am also prepared to be excited and spread it around. I did break one cardinal law of teaching. I smiled. But don't worry. It was after I went over the rules and consequences. And besides, Jeremy smiled first.

~ Anne Marie

From: Professor Z

To: Anne Marie Bettencourt

Subject: Week 1, Day 5—Good Luck, Miss B!

Dear Anne Marie,

It's Showtime! Fake it till you make it!

You seem to have come up with (and are living by) one of my favorite sayings in teaching (and in life) . . . Even if you are not positive that what you are doing is correct, "fake it till you make it!" Unless you are visibly scared (hiding behind the teacher's desk, hugging the chalkboard, sweating profusely, voice quivering), many students wouldn't have a clue that you are panicking inside. To them, you are an adult and a teacher, as long as you present yourself as a "teacher," not as a "student teacher."

I believe that student teachers need to think of themselves as teachers and act as teachers if they expect to receive the same respect as teachers. If you present yourself as a student teacher,

MINI TIP

Fake it till you make it.

you will be treated as such. The minute the cooperating teacher leaves the room, the students will act as if there is no teacher in the room. However, when student teachers take on the role of teacher and act like teachers, it will not be acceptable for students to treat him or her any differently than they would any teacher. I think you must send the message that even though you are doing your student teaching, you are still a teacher and will act as such and expect to be treated as such. How else can you learn to fit into the role of "teacher?"

Of course, students will test you to see if you will be acting like a student teacher or a teacher. Therefore, as you point out, you must stick to your guns. You must know what the rules for the class are and must enforce them consistently. Once you show that you are consistent, students will not test you very often. Thus, it is important that you stay focused and not let things slide. This is not an easy thing to do. Teaching is quite exhausting, especially when you are just learning. Sometimes you will think it is just easier

MINI TIP

Once you show that you consistently act like a teacher, students will no longer test you as often. See *How to Prepare for Your First Week of Student Teaching* and *How to Have a Successful First Week of Student Teaching* in today's Tips, Strategies, and Relevant Data section.

to let things slide. It isn't! You create new problems and dig yourself into a hole each time you are not consistent about enforcing the rules. *Be consistent.*

In addition to this, a strong and confident attitude is extremely important in showing students that you are in charge of the classroom. As stated earlier, I think student teachers need to take ownership of their classrooms. They need to be very aware of why they are teaching what they are teaching, and of the benefits it will bring to the students. Once convinced that what they are doing is important, good teachers will not let students fall through the cracks or get in the way of other students' learning. They will not tolerate classroom disturbances.

Why? Because if kids are going to go anywhere in life, they had better know how to read and write, know about themselves and others, know how to think critically, know how to work with others, and know how to be lifelong learners. And if you don't teach them, they may never learn these things. Therefore, you should allow *nothing* to get in the way of your teaching. Kids need to see this passion and commitment and understand why it is crucial for them to learn the material. Once you have shown them, they are yours!

"Don't smile until Christmas" is an old teacher saying (and the name of a book on teaching). I don't buy it. Students need to know that you are a human being. And human beings smile. You can

MINI TIP
You can still uphold the rules with a smile.

still uphold the rules with a smile ("Bill, I'm sorry dude but I gave you your last warning. You obviously don't feel like learning today, so I'll see you tomorrow. Here's your pass to the office. We'll talk later."). Smiling is good for everyone. It can indicate to your students that you are happy to see them and that you believe learning can be fun. It can show that you are confident and relaxed with them. This is all good and makes for a comfortable learning environment. So, keep the smile but uphold the rules consistently.

Similarly, I think it is good to be friendly with your students. However, the line must be clear that you are their teacher first and a friend second. Many new (and experienced) teachers are so concerned that their students like them that they do things that weaken their position as a teacher. Students want and expect teachers to act like teachers, not pals. They want and expect teachers to keep peace in the classroom, to discipline kids who are not following the rules, to be knowledgeable of the content, etc. When a teacher lacks these skills and fails to do these things, students lose respect for him or her. The real measure of success is not whether they like you as a person but whether they respect you as a teacher.

I have seen many student teachers admit to their classes that they are "a little nervous." Bad move! Very bad move! Students will take advantage of this. Remember to fake it till you make it! Work out the

MINI TIP
Do not admit to the students that you are nervous.

jitters in your voice before school by cranking the music in your car and singing (Springsteen works for me). Do some nonobvious stress relaxing exercises (isometrics, something to squeeze in your hand, etc.). Then use teaching techniques that take the pressure off you—come into class asking questions of the students—that puts the pressure on *them.*

Finally, I think the key to good classroom management is to be very clear with your students about what the rules are and what the consequences for breaking them are and to be consistent in enforcing them. Since you came in during the year, Mr. B has already set these rules down and has been enforcing them throughout the year. But it wouldn't be a bad thing for you to go over them with your students so they know what rules you have and what the consequences are.

Bottom line—it sounds like you have gotten off to a great start, which is very important. Student teachers who do not hit the ground running discover that they have dug themselves into a hole that they need to get out of at some point. As the saying goes, you only make a first impression once. And I think the messages that you sent today are ones that will support your work during your placement. Great!

Also, excellent job on this journal, Anne Marie! Keep up the good work. I am truly enjoying this dialogue we have created. I am learning much from it and hope you are as well.

Prof Z

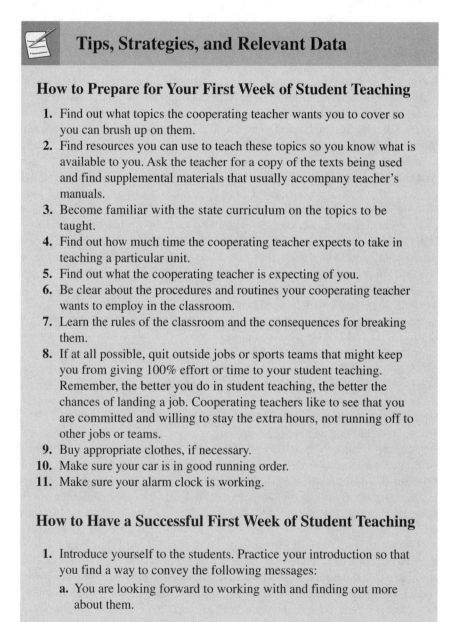

Tips, Strategies, and Relevant Data

How to Prepare for Your First Week of Student Teaching

1. Find out what topics the cooperating teacher wants you to cover so you can brush up on them.
2. Find resources you can use to teach these topics so you know what is available to you. Ask the teacher for a copy of the texts being used and find supplemental materials that usually accompany teacher's manuals.
3. Become familiar with the state curriculum on the topics to be taught.
4. Find out how much time the cooperating teacher expects to take in teaching a particular unit.
5. Find out what the cooperating teacher is expecting of you.
6. Be clear about the procedures and routines your cooperating teacher wants to employ in the classroom.
7. Learn the rules of the classroom and the consequences for breaking them.
8. If at all possible, quit outside jobs or sports teams that might keep you from giving 100% effort or time to your student teaching. Remember, the better you do in student teaching, the better the chances of landing a job. Cooperating teachers like to see that you are committed and willing to stay the extra hours, not running off to other jobs or teams.
9. Buy appropriate clothes, if necessary.
10. Make sure your car is in good running order.
11. Make sure your alarm clock is working.

How to Have a Successful First Week of Student Teaching

1. Introduce yourself to the students. Practice your introduction so that you find a way to convey the following messages:
    a. You are looking forward to working with and finding out more about them.

    b. You know the subject matter.

    c. The subject matter is important to learn and relevant to their lives.

    d. You are capable of managing the classroom.

    e. You are a teacher and expect to be treated like one.

    f. You will handle discipline problems quickly and consistently.

    g. You are not afraid of them and are fully in charge of the classroom.

2. Remember that many of the messages mentioned in #1 can be sent without actually speaking them. How you speak to them (such as voice, body language, confidence, eye contact, and movement around the classroom) will convey whether you are confident or not. What you say and how you say it will convey whether you are passionate about your subject and will give clues as to what kind of teacher you will be. The trick is to be prepared with an introduction that sends the right messages.

3. Learn your students' names as quickly as possible.

4. Introduce yourself to administrators, staff (secretaries, janitors, lunch room workers) and other faculty whenever appropriate.

5. Attend all required teacher's meetings.

6. Become more familiar with teaching materials, audio-visual equipment, and services you have access to (local libraries, film libraries, etc.).

7. Dress professionally.

8. Be proactive. Do not wait to be told everything. Do what a teacher would do.

9. Learn the names and get to know other teachers. Shyness is not a good thing at this time!

10. Do not gossip or say anything negative about any students or teachers to anyone.

11. Keep confidential information about students to yourself and discuss only with appropriate faculty.

12. Remember that you are being watched and judged by everyone in the school. Be professional at all times.

13. Learn the fire drill procedures.

14. Observe the teaching techniques of your cooperating teacher and as many others as you can to see which ones your students respond to best.

15. Make fully detailed lesson plans for each of your lessons.

16. Think and act like a teacher, and you will be treated like a teacher. Think and act like a student teacher, and you will be treated like a student teacher.

17. Do whatever you can to make life easier for the cooperating teacher.

18. Establish good control of your classes immediately.

Discussion Starters for Week One

1. How would you deal with Josh, the student who cut himself? Would it be similar to or different from the way Miss B handled it?

2. When you begin your student teaching, will you consider yourself to be a student teacher or a teacher? How will this affect your classroom, methods, etc.?

3. Prof Z is obviously against high stakes standardized testing. In what ways do you agree/disagree with Prof Z?

4. How do you feel about Prof Z's views on lecturing as a teaching strategy?

5. Prof Z suggests that teachers and students should get involved in communicating with their elected officials to solve local, state, national, and global problems. He points out that one of the main purposes of public schooling in a democracy is to create good citizens and that this requires them to work with their elected officials. What do you think?

6. In what situations do you think it is acceptable for teachers to make their positions on controversial issues known?

7. Should students have to hand letters to their elected officials in to their teachers, who will then know what their students' positions are on these issues? What are the pros and cons for each argument?

8. Prof Z says that all teachers need to be political advocates for children. Do you agree? When was the last time you communicated with your elected officials? Do you know who your elected officials are? What steps would you have to take to become educated on this issue?

9. Why is it so important for you to know *why* the subject you are teaching is so important? How would you respond to a student who asks you, "Why do we have to learn this junk?"

10. How do you feel about the idea that you should not smile until Christmas?

11. Professor Z states that one of the most important things a student teacher should know on his or her first day are the rules of the class and the consequences for breaking those rules. What are your thoughts on this? What are the consequences for not being prepared for this? What rules will you have in your classrooms?

12. Professor Z writes that, "The measure of success is not whether they like you as a person, but whether they respect you as a teacher." What are your thoughts on this?

13. Most people, if they really looked, could probably find biases they have against people who seem to be different from themselves. What biases do you

hold against people of other races, classes, sexual orientations, cultures, abilities, etc.? How might this get in the way of your giving a student from that group the same quality education as every other student?

14. Make a list of the absolute *worst* things you could do to get off to an absolutely *terrible* start as a student teacher.

15. In what ways is teaching in an urban school different from and similar to teaching in a suburban school? A rural school?

☑ Professor Z's Student Teaching Checklist

Getting YOUR Act Together: Class Give some thought to each of these questions. If you need to work on some, think about what you must do to be prepared.

1. ___Have you adjusted your frame of mind to act like a teacher, not a student teacher?

2. ___Are you clear about your philosophy of education? It is essential for you to know what your goals are and why what you are teaching is important.

3. ___Are you ready to fake it till you make it? When you are not sure about what to do in an unusual situation, you might have to think about how an experienced teacher would react and then do the same.

4. ___Are you clear that it is okay to make mistakes? It's how you learn! Don't beat yourself up!

5. ___Are you ready to act professionally? Have you given thought to your dress, demeanor, language, and answering machine message; punctuality; what to do when you are sick; getting to know your colleagues; and so forth?

6. ___Have you created a good positive attitude towards your student teaching placement? Are you mentally prepared to teach and give 100% to this endeavor?

7. ___Are you prepared to be a good role model? Students learn from all of your actions (good manners, poor manners, etc.).

8. ___Do you have appropriate professional clothing for your placement?

9. ___Are you in good physical condition? Student teaching is stressful and time-consuming. You will need to take good care of yourself. Eat well, sleep well, get exercise, and put into your daily calendar time to do things that relieve your stress. Time management is not only important in the classroom, it is also important in creating an effective lifestyle while you are student teaching.

10. ___Are you prepared to introduce yourself to the secretaries, janitors, administrators, and other school personnel? Learn more about them. Thank them for letting you student teach in their school.

11. ___Do you have a quiet place at home where you can work? Work this out with roommates who might not have the same schedule or responsibilities that you do.

12. ___Do you own a reliable alarm clock? If not, buy one!

13. ___Is your car in good running order?

14. ___Are you clear about your responsibilities to your college (assignments, journals, etc.)?

15. ___Have you filled out all of your paperwork and made sure that your cooperating teacher has all the paperwork he/she needs from the college?

16. ___Do you have all relevant phone numbers and e-mail addresses of your cooperating teacher, the school, your supervisor, etc.? Make sure they have all of your numbers and addresses.

17. ___Do you know the procedure for getting lesson plans to your cooperating teacher in case you are absent?

18. ___Have you thought about the expectations, biases, and judgments you have about the school you will be teaching in? The students? The teachers? The parents of the students? The area that the school is located in? Are there any prejudices that show up in your thoughts that might get in the way of giving each student a quality education? Are any of your thoughts racist, classist, homophobic, sexist, etc.? Aim for positive and high expectations for all of the students in your school regardless of the color of their skin, their economic status, their sexual orientation, religion, language, dress, etc.

19. ___Have you spoken to other student teachers to get their advice on how to balance your life as a student teacher, to get hints on working with particular supervisors and cooperating teachers, and such?

20. ___Have you read over your student teaching handbook?

21. ___Have you created personal goals for your student teaching experience?

22. ___Have you looked at what extracurricular activities you might be able to help out in?

23. ___Have you read the mission statement of the school, the history of the school, facts about the teachers and administrators who work there, etc.?

24. ___Have you created a teaching portfolio in which you can collect artifacts like photos, copies of student work (minus names), lesson and unit plans, awards, and recommendations throughout the semester?

25. ___Have you gotten to know the community? Walk around it, shop in it, go out to dinner in it, etc.

Endnotes

1. Brophy, J. (2004). *Motivating students to learn* (2nd ed.). Boston: McGraw-Hill.

2. Veenman, S. (1984). Perceived problems of beginning teachers. *Review of Educational Research, 54* (2), 143–178.

3. Osterman, K.F. (2000). Students' need for belonging in the school community. *Review of Educational Research, 70,* 323–367.

4. Brophy, J. (2004). *Motivating students to learn* (2nd ed.). Boston: McGraw-Hill.

5. Alder, N. (2002). Interpretations of the meaning of care: Creating caring relationships in urban middle school classrooms. *Urban Education, 37* (2), 241–266; Osterman, K.F. (2000). Students' need for belonging in the school community. *Review of Educational Research, 70,* 323–367; Wilder, M. (2000). Increasing African American teachers' presence in American schools: Voices of students who care. *Urban Education, 35* (2), 205–220. Found in Kauchak, Donald P., & Eggen, Paul D. (2007). *Learning and teaching: Research-based methods* (5th ed., pp. 120–121). Boston: Pearson, Allyn & Bacon.

6. RESULTS.org; Activists Info: Making it Happen.

7. National Council for the Social Studies Position Statement, NCSS.org.

8. McKenna, J. (1998, March). The wired classroom, from now on. *The educational Technology Journal, 7* (6).

9. Bruning, R., Schraw, G., Norby, M., & Ronning, R. (2004). *Cognitive psychology and instruction* (4th ed.). Upper Saddle River, NJ: Prentice Hall; Perkins, D. (2001) Wisdom in the wild. *Educational Psychologist, 36,* 265–268 (found in Kauchak and Eggen book).

10. Thompson, J. (2002). *The first year teacher's survival kit.* San Francisco: Josey-Bass.

11. St. Edwards University Center for Teaching Excellence. (2001). http:/www.stedwards.edu/cte/bwheel.htm

12. Kauchak, Donald P. & Eggen, Paul D. (2007). *Learning and Teaching.* Boston. Pearson, Allyn, & Bacon.

13. Payne, Ruby K. (2001). A framework for understanding poverty. Highlands, TX: Aha Process Inc.

14. Bamburg, J. (1994). Raising expectations to improve student learning. Oak Brook, Illinois: North Central Regional Educational Laboratory.

15. Tatum, B.D. (1997). "Why are all the black kids sitting together in the cafeteria?" and other conversations about race. New York: Basic Books.

16. Kauchak, Donald P., & Eggen, Paul D. (2007). *Learning and teaching: Research-based methods* (5th ed.). Boston: Pearson, Allyn & Bacon. pp. 45–46.

WEEK TWO

"Security is mostly a superstition. It does not exist in nature, nor do the children of men as a whole experience it. Avoiding danger is no safer in the long run than outright exposure. Life is either a daring adventure or nothing. To keep our faces toward change and behave like free spirits in the presence of fate is strength undefeatable."

HELEN KELLER

Day 1: Lessons After School Part I

Engaging Multiple Intelligences, Teacher-Student Relationships, After School Activities, Teaching Methods, Constructivist Teaching

Day 2: Writing Right

Planning Clear Objectives and Effective Routines, Lesson Planning, Giving Good Directions, Teacher Expectations, Motivating Students, Being a Reflective Practitioner, Classroom Routines, Bloom's Taxonomy

Day 3: Miss, Why Are You So Mean?

Choosing Your Battles, Student Behavior, Classroom Management, Teacher Issues (Philosophy of Teaching)

Day 4: The "Tag Team" and "The Buzz"

Engaging Disengaged Students, Student Behavior, Classroom Management, Teacher Issues (Attitude and Confidence), Lesson Planning

Day 5: Standardized Testing Stinks!

Teaching in a High Stakes Testing Environment, High Stakes Testing, Politics of Teaching

---

Discussion Starters for Week Two
Professor Z's Student Teaching Checklist

Topics Discussed This Week

In this chapter, you will learn

1. How to create good working relationships with your students.
2. The importance of managing your time.
3. More reasons why constructivism is an effective method of teaching.
4. The characteristics of an effective teacher.
5. How to give clear directions.
6. Whether you should give extra homework as a punishment.
7. How you can create lesson plans that are relevant to your students.
8. What to do when students cut class.
9. How to prepare students for standardized tests.
10. How to create good classroom routines.

DAY 1

From: Anne Marie Bettencourt

To: Professor Z

Subject: Week 2, Day 1—Lessons After School Part I

I did not intend to stay after school today. But of course, as I was walking out of the teacher's room, jacket on, gloves on, keys in hand, Kareem had to walk up to me and say (with his adorable broad grin that makes saying "no" virtually impossible) "Hi, Miss B! You aren't leaving now are you?" This was followed by, "Our dance team needs an advisor to watch while we practice after school. It will only be until 3:30 or so." So, being the strong-willed teacher that I am, I said, "OK."

I said OK for a couple of reasons. The first is that I am a firm believer that the extras like dance team, football, drama, etc. are what keep kids that ordinarily hate school coming back every day. So, I am going to do anything I can to help out the few we have left. Second, it was *Kareem* asking me. Kareem is a role model student who stuns people because he spends his lunch hour in the library reading, and he is (gasp) black! ☺

Kareem is the one who came after school every day and begged Mr. B and me to let him have the role of the sandpiper bird in the play our acting class is working on, after auditioning for it three times in one class. He also now knows the majority of his lines, and he just got his part today (the sandpiper, of course). I couldn't say no to Kareem!

Marissa, a student I have in my E period and in acting class, is hysterical. She talked of being a flying monkey in *The Wizard of Oz,* and demonstrated her awesome flapping skills as our newly acquired Bird Priest. She then suggested that we do a scene where the birds sing and dance to the Hokey Pokey, but with changed lyrics, and on the spot, changed all the lyrics to match our play. I was impressed. Then there is Vangie, who has come up with several designs for our bird costumes and new ideas every day for colors, materials, and sketches.

So, as I drove home from school today, I thought, "Now *this* is what we need to do to get these kids coming to school." Why can't we have students create an adverb dance, or take on a character in a play and design a costume and a scene for him or her? Why can't they play a guitar to a poem they wrote? OK, they can, but why don't we as teachers encourage them to do so? Why are we so stuck on always writing essays, dissecting sentences, and letting the other talents go to waste? It would certainly mix things up and make class more interesting!

So I have decided to steal some of the things I am seeing in these so called "extras" and make them essentials in my classroom: motion, hands-on, music, movement, etc. First of all, the kids will freak because they are so used to sitting in their seats for 55 minutes that they won't know what to do. But then the creativity will flow (or so I hope). I can't wait to see the good stuff I get out of them once they become more comfortable taking their education into their own hands, the same way they do with their dance teams, their sports, their acting, and their instruments. I've never had so much fun staying after school!

~ Anne Marie

P.S. I can't wait to meet you! It seems we are on the same page when it comes to a lot of social issues, and you can help me figure out what I need to do to start my own school. Besides, we both appreciate a similar sense of humor (a little sarcasm, perhaps).

From: Professor Z
To: Anne Marie Bettencourt
Subject: Week 2, Day 1—Lessons After School Part I

Dear Anne Marie,

I want to commend you for your commitment to your students. For some teachers, teaching is a 9–3 job. However, some of my finest teaching moments came outside of normal school hours coaching basketball, watching students compete in different sports, attending plays, chaperoning dances, playing sports with them, teaching them how to play guitar and drums, and sitting at my desk after school and simply talking to kids who needed someone to listen. The number one question that kids have

.... **MINI TIP** ....
Get involved in your students' lives outside your class. See *How to Get Involved with Your Students Outside of Class* in today's Tips, Strategies, and Relevant Data section.

about you is whether or not you are really there for them and whether you care about them. Once you have passed that test, you are much more likely to get more out of them in class, as they will want to please you.

During my first year of teaching, I had tremendous disciplinary problems with two classes. However, I started showing up at their basketball and soccer games and would greet each student at the door the next day and tell them how much I enjoyed their game, what a great three-point shot they made, what a great save they made, etc. I had proven my interest in them and had far fewer discipline problems!

Once my students saw that I was interested in them, they became more motivated to do the work than to act up and make the new teacher cry. Plus, the athletes were now my allies and would tell the other students to be quiet or stop acting up. I was now a "good guy"—someone for whom you should do your best work. Demonstrating my interest in my student's lives made my first year easier than it would have been if I had never gotten these kids "on my side."

Your willingness to be an advisor for the dance team shows them that you care about them and that you are willing to go the extra mile for them. This can only help you in the classroom. Plus, you get to learn more about them. And you can certainly incorporate these things into your lessons, as you suggested. Good job!

Another thing I am impressed with is that you are not making the typical student teacher mistake of thinking that you have to be up front and center (and lecturing) for learning to occur. As I've said before, a good teacher should be a "guide on the side," not a "sage on the stage." Your students are the ones who should be doing all the work, not you! The teacher's job is to create a "laboratory of learning" for the students and give them appropriate "experiments" from which they will learn. So, I commend you on the types of lessons you are creating. Keep it up!

.... **MINI TIP** ....
Make learning fun and relevant to the students' lives. Make sure you are able to convey to the students why the material is important to learn and how it can help them in their lives.

One of the keys to successful teaching is to make learning fun. I loved it when students would leave my classroom, and I could overhear them saying that all we did in class was have fun, even though I knew that I had achieved exactly what I wanted to with them. Learning should be fun. And after you have taught for a while and have gotten the basics handled, teaching becomes this wonderful game of trying to create the perfect lesson—one that is fun and relevant, that builds on their content knowledge as well as their critical thinking skills, that meets the standards and that gets them motivated to learn more.

I like your idea of creative methods to get your students to learn. Incorporating music, dance, poetry, acting, and other fine arts into your lessons will surely increase student motivation and participation. The more multiple intelligences that you have students incorporate into their learning, the better it is for all concerned.

Prof Z

Tips, Strategies, and Relevant Data

How to Get Involved with Your Students Outside of Class

1. Go to their games. Wish them luck before the game. They will be thrilled that you came to watch them, and it might actually get them to play harder! Make sure you attend both men's and women's games.
2. Attend plays they are acting in. If possible, stop in after the play and tell them how much you enjoyed seeing them perform.
3. Go to their concerts. Again, either wish them luck beforehand or congratulate them afterwards.
4. Join clubs. Most clubs can always use an extra hand. Help out with the newspaper, the yearbook, etc.
5. Become an assistant coach to a sports team. This is an excellent way to get to know kids.
6. Offer to assist the play director or the musical director.
7. If you are artistic, help the school develop brochures for upcoming events, help with the designs for the school play or help lead students decorate hallways, etc.
8. Offer to chaperone trips that different clubs sponsor.
9. Chaperone dances.
10. If you are musical, help stage and play in a concert featuring students from the school.

DAY 2

From: Anne Marie Bettencourt

To: Professor Z

Subject: Week 2, Day 2—Writing Right

Today I got a chance to look over my students' journal entries from my first day of teaching. I was excited. I had posted two topics on the board: "What is the most difficult choice you have ever had to make?" and "Are racism and poverty synonymous? Why or why not?" The students were told they could pick one topic and write about it. Most of them came into class, grabbed their journals, and began writing. I could not wait to see what brilliant thoughts my students had put on paper. I settled into Mr. B's office after school and eagerly stacked the colored folders on my desk.

Josh's journal was great. He wrote about how difficult his move here from Puerto Rico was and how he wished he could have spent more time with his grandfather before he died. Cassie's was also good. She wrote that yes, racism and poverty were synonymous, and that "most people pushed the blacks into places like the projects and the barrios." Then I got to Will's journal: "The toughest choice I ever had to make was between these two girls. One had a cute face, but the other had a cute face *and* a cute butt. It was tough."

It went downhill from there. I covered my face and groaned inwardly as I started to read the others . . . choosing a haircut or shoes, choosing which girl to date, or the infamous "I have never had to make a tough choice so I have nothing to write on." My one-paragraph entries became one-line entries. My teacher bubble deflated a little, I will admit.

How did this happen? I thought they were all writing! They were all quiet at least. Most of them were busy for the duration of the assignment (10 minutes—I use the time to do attendance and check homework). I told the students that I would be the only one reading their entries and that I wasn't grading content, merely that they were writing. I wonder if this was my first mistake, because then they took this as an excuse not to write much, and yet they could say they wrote *something*. I am telling you, these kids would all make great lawyers. They can find the loopholes in *anything*.

I was trying to get them to make connections between themselves and the main character of "The Man Who Saw the Flood" by Richard Wright. I wonder now if I should have been more explicit in my directions and given them more guidance. I think the abstract thought process is still fairly new to my ninth graders, and does not come as easily as I thought. (Duh, Miss B.) I forget that I am in grad school, and have had years of training on how to think "deeper" about topics and make connections, and that I couldn't just do it right off the bat.

Kara, another student teacher, gave me my next idea. She provided her 10th graders with a sample journal entry so they had an idea of what they were looking for. I think tomorrow I am going to be more explicit in my instructions and tell them they need to write at least a paragraph on the topic to get a good grade. In all honesty, I have to count the small victories. They didn't buck me on the journals, and they did write, albeit not much. They all stuck to the assignment, even though some were much closer to what I was looking for than others. And it was the first day.

They just need more guidance. And hey, at least it leaves *lots* of room for improvement over the next 6 weeks! So, today, I will try again, modifying my questions, explaining my purpose, and being tighter on what I am looking for. I cross my fingers and hope that now maybe only half of my journal entries will say, "I have no idea. Ms. B. Why are so you mean? Mr. B. would never make us write journals. I hate English." No, I am kidding. None of them wrote that, but I bet at least one of them will by the end of the semester.

~ Anne Marie

From: Professor Z

To: Anne Marie Bettencourt

Subject: Week 2, Day 2—Writing Right

Dear Anne Marie,

I think Kara had it right. You need to give clearer directions and be more specific about what you want. It is most important that you and your students all understand the objectives for the class. Were you certain in your own mind about what you wanted the students to achieve? If so, did you make it clear to them? Writing good objectives is not just a way of writing lesson plans. It is a way of making it very clear to yourself what you want the students to achieve during the class. Once it is expressed to the students, it enables them to better understand what they are to achieve and gives them a good sense of what would constitute success.

.... **MINI TIP** ....
Objectives should be observable, meaningful, and measurable. See *How to Write Good Objectives* in today's Tips, Strategies, and Relevant Data section.
....

New teachers sometimes are not specific in their planning. For example, they will write on the lesson plan as an objective that, "The students will understand the causes of the Civil War." While this might be a good purpose of the lesson, an objective should give a specific achievement that can be easily measured (i.e.: The students will be able to role-play the part of a southern plantation owner and list three reasons why they feel they should secede from the United States). Check your lesson plan and see if your objectives were specific enough!

I look at objectives as the lighthouse in the room for each lesson. My class and I are all in a boat and the job is to get closer and closer to the lighthouse. The teacher's job is to help the class navigate towards the lighthouse and get them back on track if they are going off course. This can typically be done by asking the class questions about what they are doing and whether they think they are going in the right direction. Again, success can only be achieved if both you and the class are clear about where they are going. Therefore, it is critical to be specific about your objectives and write them clearly on the lesson plan.

On another note, I want to applaud you for establishing a good classroom routine that makes effective use of the first few minutes of class—a time that should be used to get the students in work mode. It might surprise you, but the typical student teacher does not start the class by getting the students in work mode but spends the first three to five minutes taking attendance. And typically, it turns into a short- and long-term disaster.

The typical scenario has the teacher asking the students to say "here" when their name is called. First of all, the students have nothing to do during this time, so it doesn't take a brain surgeon to figure out that they are apt to talk to other students. Therefore, the teacher has to tell them to be quiet. But it is tough to keep a bunch of kids quiet the second after they have been running around the halls. Plus, they have been given nothing to do, which is the kiss of death for new and old teachers alike. If kids aren't doing something, they will simply talk!

.... **MINI TIP** ....
Establish a good routine in order to make effective use of the first few minutes of class. See *How to Create Effective Classroom Routines* in today's Tips, Strategies, and Relevant Data section.

So, while the teacher is trying to take attendance, the kids will typically talk and the teacher will typically yell out the names of students louder and louder so they can actually hear their names being called. When the noise level gets unbearable, the teacher will stop, wait, threaten, or yell at them to be quiet and then continue to take attendance. And the whole thing repeats itself!

Then, it all becomes a game. Instead of saying, "here," some kid will say "present" in a funny voice and all the kids will laugh. This, of course, causes more noise and gets the teacher more upset. Every threat, yell, and wait creates tension between the students and teacher. And if the teacher has already told the class what he/she wants them to say and a student says another word instead, the teacher is being tested to see if he/she will enforce what he/she asked the class to do. How do I know so much about this? Because it was one of the mistakes I made as a new teacher. I know better now, but it is a mistake many student teachers make before they see that there is a better way.

The best thing to do is to create a routine like you seem to be doing. Have an assignment on the board (in the same place every day) and have the students sit down and start doing the assignment as soon as they enter the room. Your job is to make sure they are working. During this time, take attendance, check homework, give back papers (only if you will be going over them in class, so it is not a distraction to them during class if they got a poor grade), etc. If you will not be going over the papers in class, give these back at the end of class as they are leaving.

By the way, unless you already know all the student's names, you might want to create a seating chart. It is the fastest way to take attendance. Students should know their seats and understand that they will be marked absent if they are not sitting in their correct seats when the bell rings. An even simpler method is to simply have students make nameplates to put on their desks.

.... **MINI TIP** ....

Unless you will be going over paperwork in class, wait to hand it back as the students are leaving. Otherwise, students might pay more attention to the grade they got on the paper than to the lesson you are trying to teach.

Again, the key is to make the best use of class time and get the students into an effective routine. It also helps to have interesting "warm-up" questions that will lead right into the lesson. Having good, relevant warm-up exercises will motivate your students to do good work. And that is a major job of a teacher—to be a motivator. I think that before you ask your students to do anything, you must get them excited about it in some way. Make whatever you are doing fun and interesting. Make it relevant to their lives. Make it a game, a dare, a challenge. Once you get them excited, learning is much more apt to take place.

For example, I have seen student teachers introduce a video by saying, "OK, we're now going to see a video" and then just turn the projector on. I think you need to set up the video by, for example, asking students what they would do in a specific situation. After discussing pros and cons of their ideas, tell them that they will be watching a video in which George Washington, for example, finds himself in the same situation and has to decide what to do. Ask them to jot down notes on Washington's actions and how they were different or the same as what theirs would have been.

I think you realize that it is not enough simply to get students to write during journaling time. But if you give them a sample entry and some good motivation to write about something they find exciting, you are more likely to get what you are looking for. Of course, much of this depends on how comfortable the students feel with you. Do they feel that they can be honest with you? Are they going to get in trouble if their views differ from yours? These factors will also come into play here.

I love your willingness to reflect on your teaching. Many student teachers would not be eager to analyze their teaching so closely, fearing to confront all the mistakes they are making. As I stated before, making mistakes is what it is all about. That is how you will learn. However, if a student teacher doesn't reflect deeply on his/her teaching, he/she is not likely to grow as a teacher. So, I commend you for the depth of your reflection and know that it will ultimately serve to make you a better teacher.

Prof Z

Tips, Strategies, and Relevant Data

How to Write Good Objectives

1. A good objective is very clear about what the student will learn and how success can be achieved. Take the objective, "The student will be able to write a sentence containing three nouns." It is very clear that the student will have to know what a noun is in order to include three of them in the sentence.
2. A good objective must be measurable. Take the objective, "The student will be able to list five causes of the Civil War." This is easily measurable. Either the student is able to list five causes of the Civil War or he/she isn't.
3. A good objective indicates understanding of a generalization, a concept, a skill, or an attitude.
4. Good objectives measuring a students' knowledge of a generalization:
   a. The student will be able to list five ways that the geography of a region affects the cultures of the people who live there.
   b. The student will be able to compare the lives of children living during the Revolutionary War period with their own lives.
   c. The student will be able to hypothesize why banks are more likely to lend money to people who have collateral.
5. Good objectives measuring a students' knowledge of a concept:
   a. The student will be able to state the meaning of technology in his/her own words.
   b. The student will be able to state three ways in which the technological revolution in the late 1860s was similar to the technological revolution going on today.
6. Good objectives measuring a student's knowledge of a skill:
   a. The student will be able to create a family tree going back at least three generations.

    b. The student will be able to organize data into pie charts.

    c. The student will be able to classify five items the Pilgrims might have considered a need and five items they might have considered a want.

7. Good objectives measuring a students' knowledge of an attitude or value:

    a. The student will be able to demonstrate respect for our nation by removing his/her hat during the National Anthem.

    b. The student will be able to empathize with a child who has little food by writing a diary entry as the hungry child might.

8. Use Bloom's Taxonomy[1] to help you form objectives based upon the level and type of critical thinking you want your students to use. Bloom lists verbs to include in your objectives that will help you determine what kind of thinking skills you want students to use in a lesson as well as the level of thinking you want the students to incorporate. He lists six categories of thinking:

- Knowledge (recalling information—names, dates, places, ideas, etc.)
- Comprehension (understanding information)
- Application (using information, methods, concepts, etc. in new situations
- Analysis (seeing patterns in how things are organized)
- Synthesis (using already-learned ideas to create new ones)
- Evaluation (comparisons between ideas)

The first three are considered lower-level thinking while the second three are defined as higher levels of thinking, which teachers should aim for their students to use during class.

9. Write objectives that incorporate the ideas of Howard Gardner's "Multiple Intelligences."[2] Your objectives should require students to demonstrate their understanding in multiple ways. This will insure differentiated instruction that will meet the multiple needs of your students. Have your objectives include student tasks that will allow them to demonstrate competencies using the following modes:

    a. Verbal/linguistic

    b. Logical/mathematical

    c. Visual/spatial

    d. Musical/rhythmic

    e. Bodily/kinesthetic

    f. Naturalistic

    g. Interpersonal

    h. Intrapersonal

How to Create Effective Classroom Routines

1. Create a plan to deal with common classroom situations such as
   a. **Classroom Entry:** What are students expected to do when they enter the classroom? Do you want them to put homework papers on your desk? Do you want them in their seats immediately? Do you want them working on a journal question when they come in? Do you want them quiet or can they speak softly to friends?
   b. **Bathroom Breaks:** What are students to do when they want to go to the bathroom? Do they need a pass? How long should they take?
   c. **Drinks of Water:** What are students expected to do if they need a drink of water? Do they raise their hands? Do they just leave?
   d. **Forgetting Supplies:** What are students to do if they forget their books or pencils?
   e. **Fire Drills:** What are students to do when there is a fire drill?
   f. **Absences:** What are students to do if they are absent?
   g. **Completion of Work:** What are students to do if they finish their work before the rest of the class?
   h. **Dismissal:** What are students to do at the end of the class in order to be dismissed?
2. Once you are clear about what you want the students to do, the procedures must be conveyed effectively to them. In some cases, it might be a good idea to rehearse some of them. Once they are effectively conveyed and rehearsed, students will begin to do them automatically. At that point, they become routines.
3. If a student does not follow the routine, it is up to the teacher to be consistent in enforcing the disciplinary procedure. In my classroom, there was one warning and then the student would be asked to leave the room. Be very clear what the rules and consequences are and make sure the class understands them.

DAY 3

From: Anne Marie Bettencourt

To: Professor Z

Subject: Week 2, Day 3—Miss, Why Are You So Mean?

Hindsight really *is* 20/20. After reading your response last night, I realized that yeah, I set really vague objectives for the journals and my intro to them had been incredibly dull. I think sometimes I forget that I already like this stuff (I spend my free time voluntarily in bookstores) and that I have many students who are not going to get as excited as I am without a little push. In other words, I need to plan better on how to make the journals relevant and exciting. So now I am staying up until 2 AM planning. No wonder the other student teachers look so tired!

OK, so here is today's update. The bottom line is that my plan is working perfectly. My students fell right into the trap I set and now I couldn't be happier: they hate me. OK, that's not entirely accurate. They think I'm "mean." In the past two days, at least four students have come up to me and told me, "Miss, we don't like your rules. Why are you so mean?" I am trying not to smile at this point (yes! I am thinking to myself, the teacher-as-my-buddy thinking is gone!) so I calmly respond that I think it is perfectly fine that they disagree with my rules. I even understand where they are coming from. But I am not changing my rules. Tough cookies!

Now this is where I try not to laugh. I ask which rules are really bugging them. I am thinking it is going to be the getting to class on time, or the journals, but NOOOOOOOO. The rule they are the most irate about? It's not even one of my five rules that I have posted. It's a tiny rule printed in 12-point type on the first page of the handouts I gave them that says: "You do not dismiss you. The bell does not dismiss you. I dismiss you, which does not happen unless you are in your seat and the classroom is cleaned up."

This is the rule, of all rules, that they chose to fight me on! I got an even better reaction when I told them that I was not going to write them passes for being late to class if they could not be in their seats when the bell rang. I can't help but think that Mr. B is right: if you fight the smaller battles, such as gum chewing, and apparently this bell-seat rule, then you don't get into bigger battles very often. The kids know what your limits are and will rarely push that far if they know you crack down on the little stuff.

Today was also the day, the students started testing rules, especially Keisha, the girl who goes back and forth between foster care and her grandmother and who has the biggest attitude problem I have ever seen in my life. I got the "death stare" when I told her that her seat had moved. At first, I thought "OK, I can deal with the death stare" but then Mr. B noticed and asked incredulously, "Why are you staring at her like that, Keisha? Are you that rude?" Upon which Tanissa (another of my students with an attitude) followed up with a very loud "What a b****!"

Of course, at this point I want to slap my forehead and groan (yesterday went so well!). Instead, I sternly tell Tanissa that she has detention with me after school for her inappropriate use of language. I know it wasn't meant for me to hear, nor directed at me, but I can't let that one slide! So, the problems have begun with the "Trio": Christina, Tanissa, and Keisha. They are the three most talkative and also the three with the most attitude in C period. I love them to pieces (secretly), and I think they are divas with wonderful insight and intelligence. But right now, they think I have it in for them.

This is good, and I wouldn't have it any other way. I am hoping by the end of my placement that they will have switched their adjective from "mean" to "strict" because they've realized the difference. Until then, I can deal with being mean, especially since being mean got them to stay in their seats until the bell rang yesterday and today. Mr. B was so right—it's the little things indeed.

~ Anne Marie

From: Professor Z

To: Anne Marie Bettencourt

Subject: Week 2, Day 3—Miss, Why Are You So Mean?

Dear Anne Marie,

I'm not sure that I agree with you and Mr. B about the "bell not dismissing you" rule. To me, it has always seemed like a big power play when teachers tell students they can't leave until they tell them they can. I actually think that the bell should dismiss the students and that teachers need to be prepared to have their lessons completed in time for the students to finish their work, get their homework assignment down, clean up around their desk, and so forth before the bell rings to end class. It is our responsibility to other teachers to let our students out in time to get to the next class. When kids don't have time to get to their locker to get books for the next class because you let them out late, it makes it difficult for the next teacher to teach. I agree that we must choose our battles. That is one I would not choose.

I love the fact that you did not let Tanissa's comment slide. It would have been easier for you to just ignore it. But it would have hurt you in the long run. The rest of the class saw your reaction and now know what you will put up with and what you won't. They got the message that you are not shy about keeping them after school. This is good!

You have to be like the character Fonzie from *Happy Days*. (I know. I am showing my age). He was the tough guy that everyone feared, yet he never got into a fight. His reputation kept him out of fights. By taking action like you did, you are creating a reputation that it doesn't pay to fight with you because you will always win.

I created something called the Red Light Theory. It basically states that if you ever see something going on in your classroom that you don't like, you don't just stand there thinking about whether you should do something about it, you just do it! I have seen many student teachers tell students that they must be respectful to one another and, at the same time, two students are talking right there in front of them. You can see the student teacher thinking, "I should get them quiet. It is rude to speak when I am speaking. But I don't want to say anything negative to them on the first day of student teaching. I don't want them to think I'm like Hitler. But I *should* do something. But I want them to like me...............blah, blah, blah." Red light theory states that when something happens that you know shouldn't be happening (kids talking when you are, for example), the "red light" goes on and you take action. I'll bet you will take the correct action 99% of the time. It sure beats allowing the kids to decide how your class should be run.

.... **MINI TIP** ....
Create a reputation that you consistently uphold the rules. Students will stop testing you if they see they cannot win. See *How to Implement Prof Z's Red Light Theory* in today's Tips, Strategies, and Relevant Data section.

All of the issues you mentioned today fall under the category of classroom management. I'm sure some would say they fall under the category of discipline. However, the key is to learn how to manage your classroom to avoid discipline problems. The better managed your classroom is, the fewer discipline problems you will have. That is why I suggest you let the bell dismiss the students and create procedures that will have everyone ready to go when the bell rings.

Classroom management includes all the things involved in managing your class, such as the set up of the desks, the routines you create and the rules and consequences for breaking them, the types of teaching strategies you employ, the way you group students, the way you work with parents, how you assess your students, how you meet the learning styles of your students, and even the books and materials you use.

It takes a lot of thought and organization to effectively manage a class, which is why it is so important that you continue to reflect upon these issues. An effective teacher creates a classroom that is a positive learning environment for his or her students, which in turn fosters student achievement.

Remember what I said the other day. It might be good to go over each classroom rule or procedure and the consequences for breaking each one. You might want to explain that these rules are there for them, as it would be very hard for them to learn if there was chaos in the room! They should know that you will allow nothing to get in the way of students who want to learn.

Prof Z

Tips, Strategies, and Relevant Data

How to Implement Professor Z's Red Light Theory

Students frequently test student teachers to see whether they will consistently enforce rules. Professor Z recommends that you do the following:

1. Whenever a student does *anything* that you are not comfortable with, your "red light" should go on. At this point, you need to take action.

2. Do not entertain any internal conversation in which you waver between whether you should do something or not. This train of thought is not helpful: "I know it is not right that a student is talking while I am. But I don't want them to think I am Hitler or something. But I really should do something. But I don't want them to hate me. Maybe I should let it go. But I really should do something." And so on and so on. . . .

3. When the red light goes on, look at the student and let them know that what they are doing is not appropriate. You can do this with a look, by your body language, by walking towards them, with a finger snap or with words ("Wait a minute. Bill, I am speaking. Please be quiet.")

4. If this doesn't work, follow the class rules. In my case, I would give the student his first warning ("Bill, this is your warning. If you speak again while I am, you will be asked to leave the room. It is your choice as to whether you stay or go. You talk, you go. You behave, you stay.").

5. If the student does not behave, do not hesitate to quickly and quietly (with as little distraction as possible) ask the student to leave ("Bill, you have already gotten your warning. Please go to the office.") or face whatever the usual punishment is for breaking that particular rule. Asking a student to leave the room might not be an appropriate punishment in many schools, so it pays to follow the rules of the cooperating teacher.

6. Be consistent! Whenever your red light goes on, take the appropriate action. Do not hesitate. This will send the message to students that it does not pay to test you.

DAY 4

From: Anne Marie Bettencourt

To: Professor Z

Subject: Week 2, Day 4—The "Tag Team" and "The Buzz"

I think we have met an "agree to disagree" patch in our conversations. I didn't pull the bell trick for a power trip. I end my lessons in time for the bell and, if not, I don't hold them because of my poor planning. The students are asked to stay in their seats when class is done until the bell rings. This is not only my rule, but Mr. B's as well. It keeps order and the students are allowed to chat with each other. If, however, everyone is *not* in their seat, then it is *they* who are making themselves late for class, not me.

Perhaps instead of holding the whole class, I will hold the individual student with the ants in the pants. But it *is* a rule we have set, and I feel, one made for good reason. If they want to test it, it's one small battle I will fight, because as Mr. B pointed out (and I still agree with him on this) it will prevent me from fighting bigger ones down the line because they will know they can't test me on this. I do understand your point but believe I need to support the existing rules of the class.

OK, so I had a few bummers today. Bummer number 1: Tanissa (the "What a b****!" girl) and Keisha (the death glare girl) decided to skip my class today. I was slightly annoyed because I don't think they would pull this stuff with Mr. B, and I am offended because I feel that they think my class isn't worth attending. I was more than happy to write them up today. (I shouldn't be spiteful to students I know, but I couldn't help it; I was honestly angry at being treated this way.) How *dare* they. . . act like rebellious teenagers bucking my new rules.

I should have seen it coming. Like Mr. B says, they aren't done testing me yet, but I got *tag teamed*. One girl skipping is bad enough. But *two*? Let's be reasonable . . . how much of a pushover could I possibly be? I know these two are friends so I know they skipped together. I have to say, the real reason I am upset is that I thought they *liked* my class . . . so secretly I am thinking, "Well you really only skip the dull classes, so am I dull then?"

Bummer number 2: I had to deal with the "buzz" today. This is that wonderful class that every teacher has after lunch where the students refuse to simmer down and pay attention. I had three to five students today who felt the need to show me their wonderful commentator skills. They would make fabulous sports broadcasters. I tried to focus on the individuals making the noise, but eventually I ended up doing what Mr. B calls "babysitting" and, of course, wore myself ragged trying to get them quiet. So Mr. B advised that I focus next time on the whole class and prepare to assign homework if the chatter doesn't stop. He said on a day like that, when the class is wired, I should be expecting to assign something extra.

Now, I have read that you shouldn't punish a class by giving them homework, because then they associate learning with punishment. But honestly, I have no idea what to do to get them to listen to me and respect my rules except threaten them with extra work. Do you have any suggestions or thoughts on this?

We were watching a video and I had asked them to write down a question for each section for a review game I was planning. Most of the class did this without complaint, but Christy, Quan, and Tony were my rat pack in the back that had something to say about every scene. How can I keep them quiet? Keep them after school?

Thank goodness it was, at least, a very productive class, with excellent journals and great questions from the video. Overall, my two concerns are: How do I approach Keisha and Tanissa tomorrow? And how can I keep order in my classroom during the after lunch "buzz?" Did I plan a quieter activity when I should have planned a more interactive one instead? I am not sure. Perhaps that is it. I should have planned for that after-lunch energy and saved the video for another day. Are there other alternatives though?

~ Anne Marie

PROFESSOR

From: Professor Z

To: Anne Marie Bettencourt

Subject: Week 2, Day 4—The "Tag Team" and "The Buzz"

Dear Anne Marie,

Ah, yes—the period after lunch! Dealing with the "after-lunch crowd" can certainly be challenging. I, too, can remember trying many different strategies to get them to do some work while digesting their food. Unfortunately, during my first years of teaching it didn't always turn out like I had planned. In fact, my first year, I had 35 students in my ninth-grade social studies class right after lunch.

Pot and angel dust were the drugs of choice at that time. The potheads would yawn and be mellow, and the angel dusters would be intense. I had virtually no control over them; my teaching methods were crude and traditional, and I was only a few years older than some of them.

Eventually, the principal took 11 of the worst kids out of class and had me teach them during our lunch period. They got to eat lunch during their regularly scheduled class and I didn't get to eat lunch until my free period later. For me, it was a double-edged sword. Yes, it did make the large class easier, but now I had another class to teach. It was exhausting! And depressing. And humiliating, as the entire school knew what was going on—I couldn't handle my class!

I tried everything. I tried being tough and giving detentions. I tried being nice. I tried making deals with the class ("If you guys work for the first half hour, we'll play a game the second half of class."). I tried different activities whenever I could.

But, looking back, I believe that I was not yet capable of creating lessons that the students would find relevant to their lives and that challenged them. I was a pretty traditional teacher in some sense—lots of notes, reading in class, worksheets when I could find them, some movies (even film strips!), etc. It was relatively boring stuff, given the way I was teaching it. I also had three entirely different preparations each day (two seventh-grade classes, one eighth-grade class and two ninth-grade classes). I was still learning the material myself and didn't have the skills to create exciting lessons every day. Computers weren't being used at this time, and I had few resources. And on top of all that, a good number of my students were high on drugs.

So, it took some time to be able to deal with the after-lunch crowd. As I developed more skills as a teacher, I was able to do more active activities that challenged them and had them see that what we were doing actually had some benefit to them.

Regarding Keisha and Tanissa, the key is to speak to them privately and find out what is going on with them. Create a good working relationship with them.

Ask a lot of questions and don't let your emotions take over. Respond to their behavior rather than reacting to it. Really listen to what is going on with them. See if there is a way for you to meet their needs while telling them what your needs are, and then shake on the deal. Hold them accountable and be accountable. If the carrot doesn't work, bring out the stick and have an appropriate punishment available.

Finally, regarding the issue of whether you or the bell dismisses the class, it is fine for us to agree to disagree. I am thrilled that you are willing to stand up for what you think is right. The only

> .... **MINI TIP** ....
> Getting to know your students well is an important part of becoming an extraordinary teacher. See *How to Create a Good Working Relationship with Your Students* in today's Tips, Strategies, and Relevant Data section.
> ....

> .... **MINI TIP** ....
> Respond to students' behavior rather than react to it.
> ....

time I will ever pull rank on you is if I am positive you are hurting yourself (and I probably would confer with Mr. B before saying anything to you). But I appreciate your consideration of my ideas and I respect your decision.

Prof Z

Tips, Strategies, and Relevant Data

How to Create a Good Working Relationship with Your Students

1. Respect your students.
2. Learn their names quickly.
3. Listen to what they have to say.
4. Acknowledge their ideas.
5. Let the students do the thinking. Don't do it for them.
6. Be kind, yet firm.
7. Get to know as much as you can about them.
8. Do not touch them while taking a disciplinary action.
9. Be genuine with them.
10. Don't always call on the first students who raise their hands. This will discourage others from participating. Wait!
11. Don't forget to smile. Show them you are a human being and someone who can create a fun and effective learning environment.
12. Be consistent in upholding rules.
13. Establish high, yet appropriate expectations for your students.
14. Don't say anything unless you mean it and are willing to back it up.
15. Use your "Teacher Eyes." Know what is going on in all parts of the room at all times.
16. Speak to your students at a level that they understand. Be appropriate.
17. Remember that you are here for your students.
18. Remember that you are being watched by your students at all times. Be a role model. Watch your language. Don't be negative or overly sarcastic.
19. Remember what your best teachers did to get you more interested in the subject.
20. Remember to create your classroom as a laboratory of learning, not an entertainment center. You are not there to entertain them. Being entertained makes them passive. You want them to be active learners, not passive observers. That is not to say that you shouldn't make your lessons fun or that you shouldn't be enthusiastic and fun. Just keep your eyes on the prize at all times—student learning!

DAY 5

From: Anne Marie Bettencourt

To: Professor Z

Subject: Week 2, Day 5—Standardized Testing Stinks!

I *hate* the MCAS test. I think that no matter what anyone says, I will hate it until the day that I die. I don't hate assessment, mind you, just this test created by people who don't seem to have ever set foot in a classroom. I can tell you all the reasons I hate it, and they're all about my students.

First of all, my ninth graders will tell you that they want to learn to write well so they can pass MCAS on the first try. I'm sorry. *What?* What happened to being a better writer so you can go on to college or write novels, or knowing how to write well so you can read well! And that goes for any subject matter they learn. If it can't help them pass the MCAS, I've heard, "I don't understand why we're learning this if it isn't on the test." I thought a test was a small piece of the educational process, and instead it has become these students' world.

Secondly, the test isn't even formatted well! Let's begin with Open Response, which we as teachers have to teach every other week now. A teacher commented the other day that not all interpretations of a piece of literature are right. I disagree. I think they are all right if they can be defended with proper evidence.

But our teachers are not even on the same page when they are teaching students how to go about writing responses to questions that ask for something based on textual evidence. So much for teaching students that multiple perspectives add to a discussion as long as you can defend what you say! So much for having students understand that a text can be open to many different interpretations.

Thirdly, some multiple choice questions are formatted incorrectly, some don't include a correct answer, and are worded so poorly or ambiguously that our students spend half the time figuring out what the test is asking, never mind what the answer is. Ugh! But if teachers protest against it, they can get fired. Students who refuse to take it get suspended or don't graduate. If these truly are critical skills that students need to have, then why don't private schools have similar tests, which oddly enough is where only more affluent people can afford to send their kids?

I don't understand why people who are not teachers, who are not in classrooms, are (a) making uniform tests for districts with unequal funding, unequal resources, and unequal opportunities, class sizes, etc., (b) creating acts like NCLB that are not properly funded and that penalize schools for failure without providing funds or materials needed to improve itself, and (c) creating ways for students to get *discouraged* about education, and hate coming to school everyday, instead of vice versa.

Worst of all, I have a hard time explaining to my kids that the world is bigger than this and that school is for more than passing the MCAS. Tell that to a kid who won't get a high school diploma because he or she failed it. The world, to them, will stop at the local Burger King where they will work because they couldn't get a decent job or have a shot at going on to college. I feel that if you are using something to "assess" performance, then great, but use it for what it was intended for. We said "assess," not "punish." Right?

I apologize for the rant, but I despise systems that set my students up to fail, and especially when those systems come from people falsely claiming to be interested in the well-being of students. It irritates me immensely. I am off to teach my students about Slam poetry, which will not be on the MCAS, but is a fantastic tool to promote social action through the power of spoken word. How is *that* for a reason to become a better writer . . . so you can liberate yourself!

~ Anne Marie

From: Professor Z

To: Anne Marie Bettencourt

Subject: Week 2, Day 5—Standardized Testing Stinks

Dear Anne Marie,

You are really going to get me going again on this one! The standardized testing craze that is currently going on is, in my opinion, the worst social experiment I have ever seen in my 30 years of teaching. For whatever good it is doing for us (and I haven't figured that out yet), it is doing way more harm. Politically it sounds good. We need *high standards*, and *standardized tests* to measure these *high standards.* And we won't let anyone graduate unless they pass this one test. Does it make sense? No! But it sounds good.

I don't think we can measure 12-years' worth of learning with one multiple choice test. Even the testing companies advise against using them in this manner! I believe that several criteria should determine whether a student should graduate from high school. Using a standardized test score along with the student's GPA and a portfolio score makes more sense. If the average of these three criteria is below a certain number, the student doesn't graduate. But don't base it solely on one score!

Plus, almost all of these tests are terribly biased. You know a test has problems when you can reliably predict a student's score simply by looking at a photo of his/her house! And, like you so wonderfully stated, it is not formatted well, does not emphasize critical thinking, and penalizes schools and kids who don't have the privileges that others do. In poor schools, almost 20% of the students come from food-insecure houses. Do you think they will be able to concentrate on calculus as easily as a kid from a wealthy home? Many kids in poor schools do not have medical insurance. Some need glasses and can't afford them. Some need hearing aids and can't afford them. Some need medications for disabilities or illnesses and can't afford them. Are we really going to punish them for not doing as well as a kid who has all these things?

Plus, everyone gets a label (failing school, succeeding school, etc.), the teachers teach to the test, the students believe that the purpose of school is to pass tests, critical thinking gets replaced by multiple-choice-type thinking, and other subjects such as art, physical education, music, and sometimes social studies (when there is no test in place) are forgotten in favor of more test preparation time! Now *there's* a well-rounded education! Why not just cancel lunch and breakfast so there is more time to study for these tests?

I agree with you that as citizens of a democracy, we need to get involved and fix these social injustices. I always incorporate political action into every course I teach because it is a skill that every American citizen (and surely every teacher) should be good at. When I taught grades seven to nine, five of my seventh graders wrote a letter to their member of Congress requesting that he cosponsor legislation dealing with world hunger. They got back a handwritten letter from the Representative saying that he had not intended to even vote in favor of the bill, but due to the persuasive argument the kids made, he was willing to cosponsor the bill. He then added a postscript—"Don't ever let anyone tell you that five seventh graders can't sway the vote of a Congressman!"

So, I figure that if five seventh graders can do that, so can I, so can my college students and so can all teachers. In fact, anyone can be a successful lobbyist. We just need to be aware of the issues, learn how to write strong letters, conduct effective meetings, and create a good working relationship with our elected officials. One of the best ways to do this is find organizations that support your cause. Many of them will teach people how to advocate on that issue. One that I strongly recommend is RESULTS.org, which explains how to be an effective advocate/grassroots lobbyist on topics related to poverty and children's issues.

It is time that teachers learn how to use the system to fight for better conditions for their students and themselves. It is unacceptable to have hungry students, students without health insurance, students without books, and overcrowded classrooms in the richest country in the world.

I also totally agree that we need to teach our students to be politically active. Whether it be a sit-down strike protesting the tests, a refusal to take the tests, or one

.... **MINI TIP** ....
Anyone can be a successful lobbyist.

million calls to their representatives, it needs to happen. Yet, we do not teach our students what their roles and responsibilities are as American citizens.

This is not surprising given the lack of role models in this domain. Most adults never communicate with their representatives! No wonder kids are never taught this. I would bet that the vast majority of teachers have never contacted their representatives over any issue, even ones they believe strongly in (like standardized tests). Again, that is why I teach civic education in all my classes—to show prospective teachers that teaching *is* political and that they *must* get involved! We live in a democracy. For it to succeed, we need an educated and active citizenry!

However, I would caution you about getting too involved in political school issues as a student teacher. While it might be fine to teach your students how to write letters to their elected officials as part of a social studies class, I would encourage you not to lead a fight to get students to boycott the MCAS while you are a student teacher. At this point in your career, you should be spending your time improving your teaching skills and lesson planning. Once you have a job and some experience (and optimally, tenure), then you can be that role model of an active citizen/teacher you always wanted to be.

.... **MINI TIP** ....
For teachers to be good role models as citizens, they must be aware of what is going on in the world (through newspapers and other sources of news), have good content knowledge for a deep understanding of world events, possess good citizenship skills (able to write a letter to or meet with their elected officials), and exhibit good civic character (take actions that will help solve social problems and make our country stronger). See *Evaluating Your Citizenship IQ* in today's Tips, Strategies, and Relevant Data section.

Thanks for your rant, and I hope you enjoyed mine!

Prof Z

Tips, Strategies, and Relevant Data

Evaluating Your Citizenship IQ

Take this citizenship quiz to see how strong you are in these different aspects of being a good citizen and in your ability to teach good citizenship to your students. Remember, being a good citizen involves a lot more than simply voting every few years.

Citizenship Quiz

I. *Skills*
  1. If eligible, did you vote in the last presidential election? YES   NO
  2. Have you, in the last five years, written or called a member of Congress or the president to voice your opinion? YES   NO
  3. List what you believe to be the two most important local, national, or global issues facing us today. Next to each, indicate what you have done, if anything, to help solve the problem.
  4. Have you ever influenced public policy on any issue that has affected your community, state, nation, or world? YES   NO
  5. Have you ever had a letter to the editor published in a newspaper? YES   NO

II. *Civic Character*
  1. What is the strength of your agreement with the saying, "Every vote makes a difference"?
     VERY STRONG   STRONG   SO-SO   WEAK
     VERY WEAK
  2. Do you feel STRONG, AVERAGE or WEAK in terms of how much difference you believe you can make in the world?
  3. Rate on a scale of 1–10 (10 being the strongest) the depth to which you show
       respect for individual worth and human dignity_____
       critical mindedness_____
       respect for law_____
       civility_____

III. *Community Service*
  1. Do you typically do more than an hour of community service each month?   YES   NO

IV. *Civic Knowledge*
  1. Do you feel you have a good understanding of the underlying ideals, founding political principles, and political institutions in our country today? YES   NO
  2. Could you teach a lesson right now on the role of civic life, politics, and government in our society today? YES   NO
  3. List the three branches of our federal government and state what each branch does.
     a.
     b.
     c.
  4. Could you now teach a lesson on checks and balances? YES   NO
  5. Could you now teach a lesson on how a bill becomes a law?
     YES   NO

6. Name the two senators who represent your state in Congress:
   _____and _____
7. How many states are there in the United States today?_____
8. Who is the current vice president?_____
9. Who is currently the speaker of the house?_____
10. What is the approximate population of the United States today?_____
11. What country has the highest population in the world today?_____
12. Approximately how many people in the world die each day from hunger and hunger-related diseases?_____
13. What two countries border the U.S. mainland?_____ and _____
14. Who is your representative in the House of Representatives in Washington, DC? _____
15. What is the overall purpose of the U.S. Constitution?_____

Discussion Starters for Week Two

1. Why is it important for you to participate in extracurricular activities? Which ones would you be most interested in?

2. How will you get students to trust you so that they can feel comfortable expressing themselves to you?

3. How do you feel about the "bell dismissing you" rule? Do you agree with Miss B? Prof Z? Do you have other suggestions?

4. Have you ever actually looked at a recent high-stakes standardized test in your state? How do you feel about what is being tested? What changes would you make to make it a better assessment tool?

5. What conclusions do you draw from the fact that most private schools do not require their students to take the state standardized test and do not base graduation upon passing this test?

6. Some states use just one test to decide whether a student should graduate from high school. Other states use an average of a student's scores on a standardized test, his/her GPA, and a portfolio to determine if a student should graduate. What are the pros and cons of using each method?

7. What methods did your high school teachers use in preparing you for standardized tests? Which methods worked best? Which didn't work well? Why?

8. To what degree are you willing to confront your mistakes? Are you apt to ignore your mistakes, focus on them too much or not focus enough? How can confronting your mistakes help you improve?

9. If two students were out in the hall talking about you as their new student teacher, what would you want them to say about you?

10. Do you believe you should use additional homework as a punishment?

11. What are the pros and cons of using Professor Z's Red Light Theory?

12. According to the cultural deficit theory, the linguistic, social, and cultural backgrounds of minority children prevent them from performing well in the classroom.[3] They lack the content, skills, and "cultural capital" that other students have. As a result, according to this theory, they do poorly in school. What are your thoughts on this theory? Do you agree? Do you think it blames the minority students and absolves the schools from responsibility for their success or failure? Explain.

✓ Professor Z's Student Teaching Checklist

Getting YOUR Class Together: Give some thought to each of these questions. If you need work on some, think about what you must do to be prepared.

1. ___Do you know what you will have to teach (standards, the units your cooperating teacher will be doing while you are there) and, if so, have you started researching these topics?

2. ___Have you found out what materials are available to you? Look for Teacher's Guides, material packets, textbook materials, websites, school resources, etc. Don't try to reinvent the wheel!

3. ___Have you learned how your cooperating teacher wants you to use the grade book?

4. ___Have you created professional goals for your experience? What are some of the teaching skills, planning skills, classroom management skills, and so forth that you would like to improve upon in this placement?

5. ___Have you observed your cooperating teacher in the classroom? Take note of things he/she does that are effective/not effective with the students you will be working with. Think about how you would do things similarly or differently.

6. ___Have you observed the students? What do they respond to best? What don't they respond to positively? Do you see any individual learning differences among the students? Who are the class leaders? Who is the class clown? Who are the students you will want to watch closely? How well do they work in groups?

7. ___Have you thought about how you will organize the classroom once you take over the class?

8. ___Have you made learning goals for your students? What will they learn during the time they have you as their teacher?

9. ___Have you been consistent in enforcing the rules of the classroom?

10. ___Have you thought about what rules you will have when you become the teacher in your own classroom?

Endnotes

1. Bloom, B. (1984). *Taxonomy of educational objectives.* Boston, MA: Pearson Education/Allyn & Bacon. Copyright © 2005, Counseling Services, University of Victoria found in www.coun.uvic.ca/learning/exams/blooms–taxonomy.html

2. Gardner, H. (1983). *Frames of mind: The theory of multiple intelligences.* New York: Basic Books.

3. Nieto, S. (2004). *Affirming diversity* (4th ed.). New York: Longman.

WEEK THREE

"How you deal with failure determines part of your success as a leader—not only in your own life but also in the lives of people around you."

KIM CLARK, *Dean of Harvard Business School*

Day 1: Discipline/All for One and One for All?
Gaining Respect through Being Consistent, Classroom Management, Student Behavior

Day 2: Low-Budget Learning
Teaching on a Tight Budget, School Resources, Teacher-Student Relationships, Student Behavior, Injustices of Our School Systems

Day 3: My First Observation/Da Bomb!
Being Observed for the First Time, Teacher Issues (Fear and Confidence), Lesson Planning

Day 4: Central High's Police State
Dealing with Police in the Schools, School Politics, Effects of Classism and Racism on Teaching, Time Management

Day 5: Tag Team's Back Again!
Making Class Relevant to the Students' Lives, Student Behavior, Teacher-Student Relationships, Lesson Planning

---

Discussion Starters for Week Three
Professor Z's Student Teaching Checklist

Topics Discussed This Week

In this chapter, you will learn

1. How to control unruly students.
2. How to create an effective relationship with your college supervisor.
3. The importance of being consistent in enforcing rules.
4. How to effectively discipline a student.
5. How Maslow's Hierarchy of Needs relates to students in urban schools.
6. How to deal with issues of race and class.
7. How to establish good relationships with your students.
8. How to deal with security issues in the school.
9. How to deal with a lack of teaching materials, supplies, and computers.
10. How to deal with being observed by college supervisors and cooperating teachers.

DAY 1

From: Anne Marie Bettencourt

To: Professor Z

Subject: Week 3, Day 1—Discipline/All for One and One for All?

Classroom management is clearly the Rubik's Cube of teaching. You have to try every possible combination before you find the one that fits—and of course, every class is its own unique cube. And when student teaching, I have fifty different people telling me what to do and what not to do.

C period, for instance, is my class full of energy and chatterboxes. They are lively, they are fun, and they are full of divas and guys who love to say, "Miss, you don't even KNOW," and "Wha'd I do?" I love them to pieces, because they bring instant energy to my class. I also struggle with them because they are a week behind E period, and it is hard to get through a lesson in a day. They ask questions and want to comment (mind you, it is relevant commentary) on just about everything we do.

Six of them—Quan, Tanissa, Christina, Keisha, Tony, and Will—won't be quiet unless I threaten them with detention, and then they *still* talk! One teacher suggested I mention constantly that they are being rude, to teach them that their behavior is not just wrong, but disrespectful and impolite. So I tried it. It kind of worked, but Mr. B railed me for it. "What are you hoping to accomplish by telling them that?" he asked me.

When I explained my rationale, he brushed it off and said "They don't care about that." He thought instead that I should give an extra homework assignment, such as three pages of writing if anyone else talks . . . to the *whole* class. Now I disagree with that on two levels. One, I agree with what you said last week about punishing the whole class when it is a small group of individuals who are causing the problem. I remember that from high school, and I hated it because I got screwed whether I behaved or not. It's simply not fair, and if nothing else, I aim to be fair. Two, I don't want to assign homework as a punishment, because then the students associate homework as negative rather than necessary and meaningful for learning. (Although they may associate homework with negative experiences anyway by now.)

So I am torn. Mr. B does things by raising his voice, being impatient, and threatening (then assigning) the whole group. I don't think things need to be done that way, and I have more patience than he does. I don't want a silent classroom. These are kids, and well, kids talk. I can tolerate a little bit of talking here and there as long as they are on task and doing what they are supposed to be doing. If they are not on task, then it becomes a problem for me. Mr. B wants silence, and comments every time he sees someone talking to another student, even though I explain that my assignments sometimes require group work and conversation.

A few of the teachers say, "Positive reinforcement, BAH! We'll do negative reinforcement and they will like it!" How's that for negative reinforcement! I think that since most students who act up seem to get slammed constantly for being "bad," it wouldn't hurt to let them know you "caught" them being good. Izzy for instance, is in my E period class. I love him, but he is constantly talking, or off task, or leaning so far back on his desk legs that I am expecting him to go flying any minute.

During our assembly, he was phenomenal. He was attentive. He clapped when he was supposed to and didn't make any extraneous noise. So I made sure to pull him aside and tell him how happy and impressed I was with his behavior. I know that doesn't guarantee that I'll have an angel tomorrow in class or at all for that matter, but I think it's a step in the right direction in letting him know I don't think he is a bad kid, and that I *do* take notice when he isn't acting up.

I constantly struggle with classroom management. I don't think I am horrible at it, but I know I can definitely use some pointers. On one side, an angel is saying, "Now Miss B, you were a student once too, and you occasionally talked to your friends, got your work done, and had your "off" days, so cut the kids a break. On the other hand is Mr. B, the other teachers, and a devil saying, "*GET EM!* Make them suffer, and above all else, NO MERCY." I understand structure, and I understand discipline, but I also want the students to be students and not soldiers at attention all the time. So I am still working out how to balance the two. If you could watch that when you observe me, it would help me tons.

~ Anne Marie

From: Professor Z

To: Anne Marie Bettencourt

Subject: Week 3, Day 1—Discipline/All for One and One for All?

Dear Anne Marie,

As I have mentioned before, the answer to many teaching questions is, "It depends." Everything depends on the specific kids, specific teacher, specific circumstance, etc. So, I again qualify all my following words of wisdom ☺ by saying that it all depends.

As I stated last week, I disagree with Mr. B on punishing the whole class and giving extra homework as a punishment. I think the first is unfair and the second negates the true value and meaning of homework—to learn more. Like you, I believe that much of the respect you will get or not get as a teacher is based on the fairness of your rules, your ability to consistently enforce them, your relationships with students, and your ability to plan exciting and relevant lessons.

Bottom line: I think that new teachers will be tested no matter who they are. Certainly, if students like and respect you, you have a better shot at getting their cooperation. But you first have to earn their respect by showing them that you care about them, that you know your content, that you are interesting and fun as a teacher, and that you know how to maintain a positive educational environment. Students *want* to know that you are in charge. They consider it to be your job to be able to manage the classroom. If you do not meet these expectations, it will be more difficult for you to get the respect you desire.

.... **MINI TIP** ....
Do not say anything that you will not enforce and take action on.

But it takes practice and patience. It takes making lots of mistakes and finding out what works for *you!* Basic rule—do not say anything that you will not enforce and take action on. If you tell them to be quiet, insist on it. Whatever the rules, enforce them consistently. I had only one rule—be respectful of others. This incorporated things like:

a. If someone is speaking, listen to them and do not talk while they are talking.
b. Do not curse or use derogatory words in my classroom.
c. Do not call out an answer unless I call on you.

d. Do not do anything that will disturb the learning of another student.

e. Do not put another student down for any reason.

I gave students one warning, and then they would be asked to leave the room. My thinking was that teenagers should only need one warning if they really wanted to stay in my room and learn. If they chose to break a rule for the second time, they were simply choosing to leave my room. Of course, I would later have conferences with the students to find out how we could remedy the situation for the future.

.... **MINI TIP** ....
Always discipline quickly so it does not interfere with the learning of the rest of the class.

One of the tricks of good classroom management is to discipline quickly. Do not allow it to interfere with the lesson. I would simply say, "Bruce, this is your first warning. Please don't speak while another student is speaking." If he broke another rule that period, I would say, "Bruce, I'll see you later. Please leave and go next door." And then I would turn away from him and go back to the lesson.

I had a great agreement with the teacher next door to me. He taught grades 10–12, and I taught grades 7–9. Whenever I kicked a student out, I would simply send him or her next door. He/she would not only get a zero for my class, but would face a certain amount of ridicule from the older students who knew why he/she was there: because they already had me as a teacher. Likewise, the other teacher would send his behavior problems to my room, where the older student would face a similar reaction from the younger ones. It worked and I did not have to deal with sending kids down to the office. I would handle the student immediately after class ended. I don't think this would work for you as a student teacher, but it might be something to remember when you get your own classroom.

The problem right now is that as a student teacher, you are pretty much a guest in Mr. B's room and are following his rules and routines. When you have your own classroom, you will have to think about what rules will help you create the learning environment that will best serve you and your students. I suggest you post them in your room and explain to the students why they are necessary for them to have a safe and comfortable learning environment. You should also post the consequences of breaking the rules and the rewards for following them. For example, if a student stands up and throws out a tissue without bothering anyone, I would have no problem with it. But, if they are noisy and obviously trying to get attention, I *would* have a problem with that. So, while I might not have a rule that a student couldn't stand up during class, I would have a rule that students couldn't disturb others.

From the moment you discuss the rules, you can count on students to test you on everything—including when it is okay to go to the bathroom, sharpen a pencil, throw out a tissue, shout out an answer, say something to another student, and stand up to borrow a pen from a friend, etc. You name it. They'll find a way to test you.

You should be ready to react to the obvious classroom situations, like what happens when a student wants to go to the bathroom, shouts out answers, forgets books or supplies, forgets homework, or chews gum. If the class has major problems with a rule, you might want to make some slight modifications. After that, your job is simply to enforce the rules consistently.

Failure to be consistent will create an awful learning environment and dig you into a deep hole. For example, as a new teacher you might face a situation in which a student breaks a rule by calling out and you do nothing about it. A little later, another student calls out and you give him/her a warning. That student will then have every right to say, "Why am I getting in trouble when Steve called out and you didn't give him a warning?"

Then, *you* are in trouble. The entire class will side with the student and for good reason. And then, you might get angry at *that* student for "talking back" and immediately kick him/her out of the class. Of course, by this time the entire class is angry at you because you have been unfair, and they have all witnessed it. That is how you lose respect! How do I know this situation so well? Because *I* was the teacher! I was not very good at being consistent when I first started teaching, and I paid the price. Believe me, it is not worth it. When students break rules, nail them! Phew, you can tell this brings up bad memories. ☺

····················· **MINI TIP** ·····················

Although it sounds simple, the key to successful classroom management is having fair rules with appropriate consequences and enforcing them consistently. See *What are the Causes of Discipline Problems and How Do I Handle Them?* in today's Tips, Strategies, and Relevant Data section.

··

Just be consistent, and you will be fine. If your rules and consequences are reasonable, students will accept them with little comment. Add this to creating good, fun, relevant, important, and exciting lessons that meet the needs of the students, and you will have a good chance of teaching in an excellent learning environment.

Prof Z

Tips, Strategies, and Relevant Data

What Are the Causes of Discipline Problems and How Do I Handle Them?

There are several significant causes of discipline problems as discussed by R. Curwin and A. Mendler in Discipline with Dignity (2000).[1]

Out-of-School Causes of Student Misbehavior

1. *Lack of a Secure Family Environment*: Many of your students may be growing up in poverty. Many are being raised by a single parent, who in many cases is experiencing economic and psychological problems brought on by the stresses of poverty. Because the number of people in poverty is actually increasing, more and more children are growing up in insecure family environments. Many live in unsafe homes where there is not enough to eat. As a result of this instability, the underlying conditions for behavioral problems at school are established.

2. *Limited Interaction Between Parents and Children*: The amount of time parents and children spend together has declined steadily in the past decade, especially in families with two working parents. Children typically spend more time with adults in school than with their parents. This often leads to a lack of parental influence on a student's behavior.

3. *Effects of the Media*: Research shows that watching hundreds of hours of television that includes numerous acts of violence affects children's behavior including that of your students. You may want to work with parents to help students learn to be discriminating in what they watch on television and help parents recognize the effects it can have on their children's education.

4. *Violence in Society*: Our daily newspapers and television news channels are filled with acts of violence taking place in our society. From the bombing of the World Trade Center and wars around the world, to murders and shootings in the local community and high-profile crimes, your students are constantly hearing about the behavior of adults. Since children learn by imitating adults, it is critical that we present positive role models that demonstrate better, nonviolent ways of settling disputes.

In-School Causes of Discipline Problems

1. *Unclear Limits*: It is essential that you develop effective classroom management skills that establish very clear limits as to what students may and may not do to allow the class to function in an orderly fashion. Students need to know the rules of the class and the consequences for not following them. The more unclear students are, the more they will test the teacher, thus creating more discipline problems.

2. *Student Boredom*: Many students create discipline problems because they are bored. It is important that teachers create exciting and significant lessons that students can relate to their lives.

3. *Sense of Failure and Attacks on Student Dignity*: Many students misbehave because they think that no matter what they do, they will not be successful in school. In many cases, these students have disabilities that interfere with their ability to learn. They see themselves as failures and act out to try to protect themselves from being hurt.

4. *Lack of Acceptable Outlets for Feelings*: Many students do not have anyone to whom they can express their feelings. As adolescents, they have many emotion-laden experiences. They tend to get hurt easily, they may feel left out or incapable in doing some of their school work, or they may feel alone and unwelcome at school. Children need to express these feelings and if they are unable to, they may become disruptive in class.

5. *Sense of Powerlessness*: Students often report feeling that they have no "power" or that their wants are not considered "significant" in school. As a result, they frequently rebel as a way of expressing dissatisfaction. Students who feel that schools are not meeting their needs and that they can't change how schools operate often don't want to be there and will sometimes cause discipline problems.

How to Create a Positive Classroom Environment That Will Help Prevent Disciplinary Problems

1. Be ready to hit the ground running on your first day of teaching. Know the procedures, routines, rules, and consequences for breaking the rules. Be sure that they have been clearly communicated to the students. Observe and uphold the rules that your cooperating teacher has been using.

2. Praise students and give them public recognition for work that is well done.

3. Get students working as soon as they enter the classroom.

4. Keep your school and classroom attractive, and decorated with student work, posters, and photos.

5. Create good relationships with your students. Go out of your way to get to know them and to talk with them when they seem to need a friendly ear.

6. Have all audio-visual equipment set up before class. Check to see that they are in working order. Check for blown bulbs in overheads. Make sure the DVD player is in working condition. Cue all videos to the beginning of what is to be shown.

7. Do not ever physically punish a student.

8. When disruptions do occur, handle them quickly.

9. Be consistent in enforcing all rules.
10. Show respect to each of your students.
11. Assigning homework on a regular basis is associated with better student achievement and behavior.
12. Begin your class on time.
13. Walk around the classroom to insure more student on-task behavior.
14. Do not end class until it is time to go. Do not give students free time in class. Use all the time you have for educational purposes!
15. Learn students' names quickly and call on them by name.
16. Encourage full student participation in all classroom activities.
17. Don't be afraid to smile and have fun in the classroom. Students will be more willing to learn when they feel safe with you, when they know you want to be there with them, and when they know that you are going to be fun to work with. Use your sense of humor whenever appropriate.
18. Make sure you have eye contact with your students when speaking with them.
19. Create lesson plans that are relevant to the students and that are fun, whenever possible.
20. If a student is punished, be sure to speak with him or her after class to ensure future success.

DAY 2

From: Anne Marie Bettencourt

To: Professor Z

Subject: Week 3, Day 2—Low-Budget Learning

Okay, so you are trying to tell me that I don't have to be Hitler and that consistency with discipline is being fair, which makes sense to me. I think sometimes as a new teacher trying to juggle paperwork, plan creative lessons, create interesting hooks, and deal with assemblies, testing, and MY OWN coursework, that part of me just goes, "Oh forget this, I'm too tired today to deal with these kids. And maybe it will be okay if I overlook it this ONE time. . . ."

BAD MOVE! If I do not deal with the problem, it will only get worse. You are right. Also, my confidence isn't there either, so it is contributing to my wariness in enforcing rules I am not sure about anyway. Teaching, while exciting, is also draining. I am going to request a caffeine I.V. for the student teachers at their first seminar next year.☺

Today was a weary day for me. I didn't teach, because my one class had an assembly and I don't see C period due to the rotating schedule today. So I was bummed out. Sad realizations came to me today. Akeem, a student of mine who I am constantly getting on for talking and being off task, gets corporal punishment at home. Wil (actually Wilfred) has divorced parents who take their anger out on him. Keisha is in foster care and is in a constant state of confusion. Josh, my guitarist, is insightful and a good musician, but is dropping out in three days and moving to another city. Christina came in today and high-fived me saying, "I got sleep last night, Miss!" and gave me a big hug. She doesn't see a lot of her mom because she works 3 to 11 to support her family.

These kids are bright, talented, and funny, and their home lives suck (to be blunt, sorry). I want to pick each and every one of them up and stick them in an environment of love and support with people who talk to them, pay attention to them, and discipline them in a nonviolent way.

I also got angry today. Our classrooms don't have the technology that would allow me to use PowerPoint, pull up websites, or do Web quests with the kids. We have three computer labs for 2600 kids. Each lab only has about 25 computers, and they are not all in working order. The Art Club just got cut because of budgetary problems. The library is small and meager and hard to get into with a class. Field trips are nearly impossible to take because there is no funding for them and the kids come from families that can't afford to buy them binders *and* lunch, *and* give them money for a trip. Heck, some of my students can't afford binders, so I bought them. The ceiling has tiles missing and some doors don't have glass in them. THAT IS NOT FAIR!!!!!

I know, I know, life isn't fair. Cry me a river. But these kids didn't ask for this. It isn't their fault. And I feel like they are being punished for being born. I understand why on some days they are unable to focus, and why they refer to school as a jail. How excited can you be about learning when your school looks like a prison? We do all this talking in our grad classes about ways to spice up lessons, integrate new books, and such. Well, that's a great theory, but what happens when your curriculum is so packed that your cooperating teacher tells you that there is NO WAY you are going to have room for multicultural poetry. And nope, that book can't be taught either because there isn't enough time to get the kids ready for the big standardized test.

How can I do PowerPoint when the projector I have doesn't even have an outlet for a laptop? Actually, the bulb just burned out too, so it doesn't even work at the moment. Can we please have a class about urban, low-budget classrooms? How about a seminar on places in and around Springfield where we can take our students that is inexpensive . . . or a class that shows us how to teach with limited books and materials, and a lack of art supplies?

As a teacher, I want to do everything I can, but on days like today, I feel like I am not doing enough. I am not doing enough to get materials into my classroom, or plan trips, or make the school a better place so my students might actually enjoy it more. But making the school better would only solve one tiny problem. We need better jobs so moms aren't working until 11 at night and students aren't making dinner for their siblings instead of doing homework. Then we need families that support their kids in their education.

Today, I feel like I am fighting a constant uphill battle. I am willing to fight, but I don't think I have enough weapons or knowledge to fight it effectively. I want dynamic lesson plans, but I also have to read for my college classes and do my own homework. Thankfully, we had a motivational speaker today, and while I found him, well, not really motivating at all, I did take away his last comment.

He told the story of the starfish. Rather, of the boy who was walking along the beach throwing the starfish back into the ocean. An old man chided the boy, telling him he would never be able to make a difference—that he couldn't reach all the starfish. The boy quietly picked up a starfish, threw it into the ocean, and replied, "I made a difference to that one." So, lesson of the day, I am making a difference in at least one classroom, hopefully for one student. Once I have my own classroom, I can build from there.

I look forward to seeing you tomorrow for our first observation! Our class starts at 7:52, but the kids are usually there by 7:40. See you then.

~ Anne Marie

From: Professor Z
To: Anne Marie Bettencourt
Subject: Week 3, Day 2—Low-Budget Learning

Dear Anne Marie,

Politics raises its ugly head again. As a result of not being better advocates for our children, some of America's youth face conditions found in no other industrialized country. Our children who come from poor households would do much better in almost any other industrialized country where they would be entitled to better food, better housing, better medical care, better schooling, and better social programs. The sad part is that we could have all this if we had the political will to help our children. Unfortunately, not enough people consider it a priority to take care of *all* of America's children.

It might not be smart politically (and in terms of getting a job) to help organize student sit-down strikes as a student teacher. However, I encourage you to set a good example by writing letters to elected officials and then showing the responses to your students. You might also get involved in or volunteer in other areas like community service. When you get a teaching job (hopefully in a school that supports your style of teaching), I encourage you to speak up and organize students, parents, teachers, and administrators to communicate with their representatives, who *can* do something about these issues on behalf of the students! Again, it is beneficial to all of us to have our children get the best possible schooling. We all gain from this! And yes, we can all make a difference one person at a time.

Prof Z

.... **MINI TIP** ....

Being a good teacher includes being good in and out of the classroom. In the classroom, a good teacher is effective in getting his/her students to learn. Outside the classroom, a good teacher advocates for his/her students so the educational system is set up to support the learning of *all* students. See *Advice from Urban Students About Teaching in an Urban School* in today's Tips, Strategies, and Relevant Data for some ideas on how to be successful in an urban classroom.

Tips, Strategies, and Relevant Data

Advice from Urban Students About Teaching in an Urban School

1. Do not judge your students. Give them as much respect as you can.
2. Teaching in an urban school is not easy. The teachers who are determined will make it and those who don't really care about the kids will not.

3. Good teachers are always well prepared and keep the students on task.
4. Good teachers either grew up in an urban community or can at least relate to an urban environment.
5. Good teachers stay after school and will work with us until we get it.
6. Good teachers are patient and don't lose their cool.
7. Good teachers are the ones who work with us and try to help us get into college.
8. Good teachers understand the stress that minorities have to live with.
9. Good teachers decorate their rooms with students' work, and posters representing all races and generations.
10. Good teachers can understand and connect with their students. If they don't, they can never be good urban teachers. It's all about relationship.
11. Good teachers know when to be serious and when to be funny.
12. Good teachers do not show fear. We smell fear easily.
13. Good teachers are open-minded.
14. Good teachers don't believe the hype about urban students, such as that they are all violent. They make their judgments after they get to know us.
15. One good teacher decorated the walls with her students' baby pictures and current photos. It helped us get to know each other better.
16. Good teachers have good control of the class.
17. Good teachers can put themselves in their students' shoes.
18. Good teachers give us a lot of hands-on work.
19. Good teachers make the students feel comfortable in the class.
20. Good teachers never underestimate the capabilities of their students. They treat them as if they can do anything, because in reality they can.
21. Good teachers never talk about race unless it is completely necessary.
22. Good teachers are hungry and really want you to learn. Teachers who are not hungry are not going to make it.
23. Good teachers motivate you to become something and push you to learn.
24. Good teachers are there for you when you need to talk to them.
25. Teachers should just be themselves.
26. Teachers who give respect will get respect.
27. Good teachers understand that urban schools are typically part of a system designed to have us fail. They try to give us a better opportunity to succeed.
28. Teachers should decorate their rooms with posters of people who have become successful in life.
29. Good teachers don't come into an urban school thinking they will change everyone's point of view in one day.
30. Teachers should believe in their students!

31. Teachers should not treat us as if we are ignorant. Many of us are very intelligent and many teachers treat us as if we were stupid.
32. Give us a chance. Who knows, we might be the best people you ever met in your life!

(Thanks to April Huckaby and her students in Hartford Public High School)

DAY 3

From: Anne Marie Bettencourt

To: Professor Z

Subject: Week 3, Day 3—My First Observation/ Da Bomb!

If I could have predicted how today's first observation by you could have gone, "TOTAL AND UTTER FAILURE" would NOT have been the first words out of my mouth. In my head, it was brilliantly planned and executed, and you left thinking, "Wow, that one is going to change the world someday." Instead, I can't help but think that after you left, you were thinking, "Wow. That one needs A LOT of work. . . ." I feel like the kid that gets up early on Mother's Day to surprise his mom and make her breakfast and instead of impressing her, he nearly sets the house on fire. Since hindsight is 20/20, I would have changed several things, starting with my outfit. Now if I COULD go back in time to give myself advice, here is what I would have said:

"Yeah Anne Marie, jeans are NOT a good idea this morning. No, no it doesn't matter that it's Dress Down Wednesday and all the teachers do it. This is your FIRST observation, and you want to look as professional as possible for your supervisor, not a few years older than your kids!" Mistake #1: Wearing clothes that are not professional. Lesson learned: Don't wear jeans when being observed.

"Hey, why don't you plan on getting to school at 7 AM tomorrow so you can get stuff set up before he arrives and make sure you have everything? At least you won't be rushing through the door with a stack of papers in your arms looking rushed for your FIRST CLASS OF THE DAY." Mistake #2: Getting to school right before period one begins. Lesson learned: Don't get to school right before the bell rings on your first observation day, or any day, for that matter.

"Hey did you really look over this lesson? It looks really complex for a 55-minute period. I know you want to dazzle Prof. Z and all, but let's look at this poetry workshop idea you have going on here. Why do you have three separate groups? Isn't that a lot of information to get across to your students? Are you sure they are going to be able to work in groups? How ARE you putting them in groups anyway? You know, I am feeling like you put this together to make it look good, and not really for your kids to learn anything. Prof. Z doesn't want to observe a puppet show. He wants to observe good teaching.

"Maybe stick with something simpler, like one concept, and have fun with it. You can still look creative with ONE concept instead of three. You know this—right? These workshops on rhyme scheme, internal rhyme, and rhythm and rhyming look really complex and don't flow correctly. Trash it. Start over and plan it this time." Mistake #3: Not planning the lesson well enough, and covering three concepts instead of one in a feeble attempt to impress the supervisor. Lesson learned: Put the time in to create a lesson that is well thought out and that you are confident about.

Yep, that smarter me with a functional brain and some common sense would have been so helpful to have around before I went to bed last night. I need to clone me, or *you*, actually, and keep one in my closet for such occasions. Especially those occasions when I am so nervous that my brain just shuts off and instead of thinking through these situations, I decide to crash and burn and worry about it later. I swear that I can teach better than that. If only you had watched E period!

I modified the lesson, the "disaster" lesson, and it was TEN times better in E period. I drove home that day going "stupid, stupid, stupid girl! What were you THINKING?" I beat myself up pretty bad. I think I made every mistake I could have except swearing out loud (yes I HAVE done that before, and then cringe to a chorus of "That's OK, Miss! We hear it ALL the time! We say it too!" Great role model. Yes, indeed.).

Now if one were to be positive about this, one could say, "Well that certainly leaves room for improvement!" And at least I can point out what I did wrong. They say you learn from your worst lessons rather than your best. If that is the case, then I supposedly learned a LOT today. And at least I have two more observations to find my self-esteem and my ego, wherever they might be at this time.

At the very least, I am determined to get this right. And I won't cry next time, I promise. OK, I flat out bawled, I admit. But it was my first time, and I BOMBED and you and Mr. B definitely noticed that. But I've got to say that after spending an hour with you going over everything I did WRONG, I really don't think those kids can do much more damage to my ego. Have you ever considered law? I think you could make criminals cry up there on the witness stand with your NO MERCY approach. And you seemed so NICE in your responses to my journals! ☺

Then again, I probably seemed like a great teacher in my journals, too. So much for first impressions! Yesterday I was in tears, and today I am trying not to grin and shake my head with a smile going, "What WAS I thinking? Well, whatever it was, I won't think it next time." Yep.

~ Anne Marie

PS: I am kidding, of course. I love that you are so honest, although I am sure the tears streaming down my face gave you a MUCH different impression. As much as it may stink to hear it at the time, I can't be a great teacher if I don't know what I need to work on.

From: Professor Z

To: Anne Marie Bettencourt

Subject: Week 3, Day 3—My First Observation/Da Bomb!

Dear Anne Marie,

Do you know what research shows is the biggest complaint by student teachers? I bet you will never guess. The biggest complaint is that they feel they are not getting reliable feedback from their cooperating teachers and supervisors.[2] When they know they have taught a lousy lesson and the supervisor tells them that the lesson was good, all credibility is lost. Student teachers are looking for honest feedback as well as help in problem-solving issues they are confronting in the classroom.

What you can count on from me is honest feedback. I truly believe that it works out best all around when supervisors are being honest and not trying to protect their students from critical feedback. For me, it comes down to judging how far I can push a student teacher. I see tremendous potential in you as a teacher, and I am not afraid you will fall apart upon hearing critical feedback. While I, too, *still* react with discomfort upon hearing critical feedback, I know it can be very

.... **MINI TIP** ....
Always convey to your cooperating teacher and college supervisor that you truly want to hear everything they have to say, whether it be positive or negative feedback. This may make them feel more comfortable in providing more honest feedback. See *How to Create a Good Working Relationship with Your College Supervisor* in today's Tips, Strategies, and Relevant Data section. Also see week 7, day 1 for tips on *How to Effectively Work with Your Cooperating Teacher.*

valuable data for the improvement of instruction. Ultimately, that is what I am committed to, not my ego.

I am confident that this will be a learning experience that you will use to grow as a teacher. OK! What's next? ☺

I did want to say something about looking professional. It is so important for student teachers to look professional. In many cases, you are only a few years older than your students! By dressing down, you are making yourself look more like your students. That might be fine if you are at a concert, but not so good if you want to be respected in the role of teacher. By dressing up, you are saying to the students that while you may only be a few years older, you *are* their teacher. Additionally, they can count on you to act like a teacher and know that you expect to be treated like one.

.... **MINI TIP** ....

Teaching is a profession. Act professionally at all times. See *How to Act Professionally* in today's Tips, Strategies, and Relevant Data section.

Also, I believe that the way you dress definitely affects your attitude. If you are dressed professionally, you tend to act more professionally. I was always amazed at how different our school was when the athletes dressed up on game day. Not only did they act more maturely, they were treated differently by other students and teachers.

Again, you are finding that the messages you send out to your students make a huge difference in how you act, how they respond to you, and how successful you will be as a teacher. Another lesson learned! That's what student teaching is all about!

Prof Z

Tips, Strategies, and Relevant Data

How to Create a Good Working Relationship with Your College Supervisor

1. Remember that they are there to help you. They want you to succeed!
2. Remember that their recommendation will be important in getting a job!
3. Be open with them about your successes and failures. Ask their advice on things you need help on.
4. Remember that the best way to learn is to try something and then reflect upon what worked and what didn't. By playing it safe (because you are afraid to fail), you hurt your students and your chances of growing into an extraordinary teacher. Take chances! Student teaching is a time to try new things.

5. Don't change your teaching style or lessons just for the supervisor. Show him/her your regular routine. This does not mean you shouldn't try new ideas for them. It just means to be yourself!
6. Hand in all of your college assignments on time and do them well. The work should represent who you are as a teacher.
7. Always call your college supervisor if you are sick and not going to school that day.
8. Always have a copy of the lesson you are teaching for the college supervisor.
9. If you are responsible for a daily journal, make sure you send them in on time and that it shows your ability to deeply reflect upon your teaching. It should not just be a diary of what you did that day but a reflection of what you learned.

How to Act Professionally

1. Always dress appropriately for your school. Because you are younger than most teachers (and sometimes only a few years older than some students), it is advised to dress professionally even if many teachers in your school wear jeans, etc.
2. Get to school early and leave late. Show that you are there to learn and that teaching is one of your highest priorities. By rushing out every day, it may appear that you are not willing to stay after school to work with students, stay for meetings, etc.
3. Watch your language. Speak professionally. Do not sound like one of your students. Do not curse or use words that are inappropriate for a teacher to say in a school.
4. Do not talk negatively about other teachers to students or other teachers. Do not ask students what they think about other teachers. Do not give agreement to students if they complain about a teacher.
5. Have a positive attitude.
6. Be respectful of everyone in the school—from the janitors to the secretarial staff to the principal.
7. Go out of your way for others. Be a good team player.
8. Get involved in school events. Participate in faculty meetings, if appropriate. Learn from the other teachers in the school.
9. Share educational materials you have found that others might be interested in.
10. Stay current with what is happening in the field of education. Read journals, attend conferences, and join educational organizations.

DAY 4

From: Anne Marie Bettencourt

To: Professor Z

Subject: Week 3, Day 4—Central High's Police State

Today was a great day for me but not so great for the principal. I had done all my lesson planning the night before, set up all my records, organized everything, and placed it in my backpack for school this morning. I got up at 5 AM, Tae Bo-ed myself into a tizzy, and got to school at 6:50 AM with my lunch packed. Those three things: exercise, lunch, and getting to school early, NEVER happen. I even beat Mr. B today! (I consider that a personal victory because he always says, "You have to get up pretty early to beat me here!"). I got my copies done early, and waltzed into my class relaxed and prepped.

My E period ROCKED THE HOUSE! We continued rhyme schemes using four poems from the Harlem Renaissance. They not only whizzed through it, and finished early, but we got an amazing game of Bust a Rhyme going. The way we play is this: I start out by saying a line, "I walked down the hall." Then I throw an eraser to a student who continues by saying, "then I took a fall" and throws the eraser to another student who continues, "but I walked to the mall." The goal is to see how many students we can get through without breaking the pattern or repeating a rhyme word. They loved it. My two students who are least likely to work, Izzy and Wil, even got into a one-on-one game where they started throwing the eraser back and forth shouting rhymes at each other. It was hysterical and lasted right up until the bell rang. I would say, definitely a successful day today.

Then in D period came the Search and Seizure. Liz's inclusion class got randomly selected for a wand search, which yielded several unregistered cell phones and a couple CD players that administrators confiscated from the students. Needless to say, the students were up in arms. Liz attempted to calm them down by joking, "Nothing like a search and seizure to put the students at ease!"

The principal was on a rampage today because an alarmingly high number of staff members were out. It was the school's own Orange Alert. Students were only allowed passes if it were an emergency (literally, the principal called it "An Emergency Pass Protocol"). I understand the point of it all, but I still found it amusing and pictured a mutiny taking place. Man, that would have been a fantastic time to boycott the MCAS. I found the juxtaposition of my two classrooms odd: in one—games, laughter, and learning. In the other: irritation, metal wands, and no learning due to disrupted class time. Liz said it best: "We are in a Police State." I tend to think that if you treat a school like a jail, then the students will be inclined to act like inmates. If, however, you command respect, instill discipline, and create an environment that does not include chipped paint, holes in the ceilings, and broken windows, then perhaps you get better attitudes. It might be a long shot on my part, as a naive, new teacher. Who knows?

So what if they have a CD player? If I took the bus for an hour, I would want music too. If they aren't using it in class, then why bother about it? We don't have a weapon problem or a drug-dealing problem as far as I can see, so why degrade our students by this search and seizure thing? I know it creates a safe school, but it also lets the students know that on some level, we don't really think they are "good kids" by adding this tagline, "just in case."

When was the last time we told the student body we were impressed with their behavior, with their attendance record, or with their respect for each other? Perhaps more of that would mean less policing. Or maybe I don't really know what it's like to work in "that kind of school" with (shhh, whisper here) "inner city kids." Then again maybe a few of us do, and the majority needs a few lessons. I am not sure. I think EVERYONE, students and teachers, should take a sick week. You can't search those who aren't there, test those who aren't there, or patronize those who aren't there. And the school would be peaceful, quiet, and perfect. I want to see them write up 2600 people for THAT!

~ Anne Marie

From: Professor Z

To: Anne Marie Bettencourt

Subject: Week 3, Day 4—Central High's Police State

Dear Anne Marie,

You bring up excellent points here. Congrats on "relaxing" and throwing a few erasers around. Nothing like some flying erasers to remind everyone that learning can be fun! But again, the key question you always need to ask yourself is not just whether the students had fun but whether they achieved your objectives. It sounds like they did.

I have seen many new student teachers who felt the lesson I observed was a success because the kids had fun. When I would ask the student teacher what the students learned, many times they were surprised to find that they couldn't really answer the question. This is why it is so important to write detailed lesson plans as a new teacher.

Writing detailed lesson plans forces the student teacher to think about all aspects of the lesson and how to easily assess student learning so it is obvious whether the objectives were accomplished. The thing I liked about the lessons you described was that you seemed to have hooked them into the content and could easily measure by your activity whether they were understanding how to create rhyme schemes. Good for you! This shows good planning.

.... **MINI TIP** ....
Do not get fooled into thinking that just because the students had fun in class that they learned anything. See *Advice from an Urban Teacher about Teaching in an Urban School* in today's Tips, Strategies, and Relevant Data section on how to be effective in an urban school.

Yes, the "search and seizure" does seem harsh and not conducive to having students feel that they are trusted or respected. It is a shame that the principal feels pressured to keep rules like these in place. I believe that students need to *be* respected before they will *give* respect. If they are treated like adults, there is a much better chance of them acting like adults. Here we are, as teachers, working hard each day to build positive relationships with students and then they have to deal with the humiliation of being "wanded."

.... **MINI TIP** ....
If you treat students like adults, they are more likely to act like adults.

Plus, your students know full well that they are not given the same respect as kids from wealthier schools are. It is not a situation that promotes high self-esteem or respect for the powers that be. It adds to the police state mentality you refer to. Frankly, I think that the school's policies on this are racist and classist. While I appreciate the concern for student safety, given the situation, I think this is more likely to ultimately cause problems than solve them.

Prof Z

Tips, Strategies, and Relevant Data

Advice from an Urban Teacher About Teaching in an Urban School

1. On your first day of school, get a writing sample from your students to get a sense of their capabilities. A good topic to have them write about is, "What do you think are the qualities of a good teacher?"

2. Put pictures of yourself, your family, your dog, places you have traveled on the walls.

3. Have students fill out an information sheet about themselves. Be sure to ask them to list sports teams and other extracurricular activities they participate in as well as professional teams they like. If you show an interest in seeing them play or if you show that you follow these sports, they will converse with you and help you to create a relationship with them.

4. Never miss a sporting event or something you are asked to attend. If a student asks if you will be at the game, he/she just asked you to go.

5. When you receive a gift from a student: 1. Always open it in front of the student. 2. Always thank them and tell them how you will use it or where you will put it. 3. Get ready to cry. While the gifts might be small and inexpensive, they might have tremendous meaning for the student.

6. Arrive early and stay late. During the winter, many students lack heat in their houses and will arrive at school early. They will appreciate having you there. This is a great opportunity to create relationships.

7. Keep snacks on hand. Many students come from food-insecure households where there is not always food around.

8. When you start the first week, have the kids work by themselves. Size them up and find out who needs help. Pair off your second week. The second month, go into threes. Do a great deal of group work.

9. Have a parent *and* a student of the month. When a parent receives a certificate in the mail, it can be emotional. Many of them have never won a thing.

10. Have at least three "cultural" lunches a year and invite families to join in.

11. Greet students at the door every day. Compliment them on what they are wearing, etc.

12. Give out nicknames.

13. Make the students laugh as often as possible. If you can't make a student smile, you can't make a student want to "buy what you are selling." Put funny things on the board in order to get them to do homework. (Frankenstein says read pp.101–110 of his book tonight and write summary. Frankenstein says you sure look funny. In ¼ page tell him why you look so funny. Frankenstein wants you to know the hot dogs served in school yesterday were from his dog.) The trick here is to have a homework assignment that contains a creative writing activity that students can connect to. (Discuss why people treated Frankenstein so poorly and how we make rush decisions about people.)

14. Keep your room clean and have the students help keep it clean.

15. Don't leave school on Friday until your room and your lessons are all set for Monday. Fill your weekend with positive things. Do not work

all weekend. You need a fun weekend so you will be more patient and relaxed when you go to school on Monday.

16. Learn how to write grants. This will make you a wonderful asset to your community. Write grants for books and other educational materials.

17. If a student dies, discuss it. Some teachers believe that school is only about the subject content. Students need to "get through it" before they will be able to give 100% to their work.

18. Sometimes your students will fail. Do not blame yourself. If you take everything personally, you will not make it. Give your best and know that is the most you can do. When you are not successful, go back, reflect, and refocus. Try something new.

19. If you are doing a lesson and it is not working, stop. Admit to the class that it is not working and ask them how they think it would be best to proceed. Maybe even have them do the reading or activity and have them teach it if you think their idea is a good one.

20. Hang out with teachers with positive attitudes. It will make you a better teacher.

(Thanks again to April Huckaby from Hartford Public High School)

DAY 5

From: Anne Marie Bettencourt

To: Professor Z

Subject: Week 3, Day 5—Tag Team's Back Again!

I was not mean in high school, and I was probably very naive, too. This explains why I have a difficult time understanding my angry, very street-savvy students. Somehow they figured out that "student-teacher" is code for "brand new, fresh meat—doesn't know the ropes and is easily fooled by false statements like needing a drink of water or forgetting a book in a locker."

I am going to kill Keisha and Tanissa. Well, actually if I could just blindfold them, I would be happy because I wouldn't get the "dagger eyes" all period. Keisha is tired of all the "black/white bull****" that we keep studying—the minstrel show, the Jack

Johnson video, etc. She says it makes her angry and then offered to go to Mr. S, the 9th grade assistant principal, rather than cause a ruckus during the video. I, thinking she was being honest and reasonable said, "OK, but I am sorry that you feel that way."

Little did I know Miss Keisha is currently angry at the world (another move back from the foster home to her grandmother's house) and definitely struggling with some issues. She is battling everyone she comes into contact with. Mr. B told me, "Yep, she's pushing her limits. Reel her in, and don't let her get away with dictating the curriculum." I didn't see her today, but next week, there is a "too bad, so sad" policy in effect. As in, if she doesn't like it, tough cookies. I understand she is going through tough stuff, but this is what we are learning. It is important and when she can ace a test on it, then she can tell me she doesn't need to be learning it.

I am sure I will get the dagger eyes for that. She keeps trying to move her seat back with Tanissa, too. That makes me so mad! When a teacher put me somewhere, I sat. I didn't mouth, I didn't complain, I didn't glare. I just did. Of course I was taught that when an adult tells you to do something (especially a teacher), you do it. No questions asked.

Now we are three weeks in and my students are still trying to buck my rules and push my boundaries. I anticipated this to last a week or so, but THREE? C'mon, isn't it obvious I am not budging? I know what it is. I was "nicer" in class the other day, and we had good educational noise so now they think that gives them license to talk again and do what they want. I want to pound my head against a wall. But truthfully, I've got to give them credit—these kids are good at what they do!

Secretly, I like the challenge of keeping cool. It is like a secret battle of who is going to break first. I will smile at her so much that my cheeks are going to hurt. But I will especially smile when I start giving her detention or not letting her get away with another stunt like the one she pulled. Especially because, once she gets involved, she is in for the whole lesson. I need to work on getting her negative energy switched into positive energy.

Also, the "let's watch a documentary and get excited about a black boxer" lesson didn't work. My C period is energetic. They won't sit passively through a video, and I don't know that I want them to anyway. Admittedly, even I was getting bored! I know that if I am bored, it's a bad sign. I didn't effectively use the video, or tie it into what we are currently learning. I mean, it is relevant, but not as a 55-minute activity. I should have posed some discussion questions, and asked them to correlate it to what we are learning in the minstrel show. So, note to self—use videos judiciously and make sure there is a clear connection with the lesson and a task for students to complete that ties the video to the lesson.

~ Anne Marie

From: Professor Z

To: Anne Marie Bettencourt

Subject: Week 3, Day 5—Tag Team's Back Again!

Dear Anne Marie,

Good points. You must give them something to do while watching a video or else it just becomes free time. I also love that you saw that without making the video relevant to them, they will not feel a connection to it and want to learn more about it. You didn't do this and in turn, they got bored. Live and learn!

> .... **MINI TIP** ....
>
> Students will keep testing you until you pass THEIR test! They want to know a few things before they will stop testing you. See *How to Get Students to Stop Testing You* in today's Tips, Strategies, and Relevant Data section.

Your attitude is a good one. Let them see how you appreciate their tests but that you are always going to come out on top (to be done with a smile and a knowing wink!). This might be a good time to "Fake it till you make it." Most importantly, it is important for you to do this while still indicating to them that you care for them and will continue to be there for them. I think it is also important for you to remember that both of these women seem to be hurting at the moment.

I don't know if we've ever discussed Maslow's hierarchy of needs and how they relate to this situation. Basically, Maslow says that lower-level needs, such as physical and safety needs, must be met before an individual will consider higher level needs (such as learning English and geometry).[3]

While I don't know Tanissa and Keisha personally, the fact that they are dealing with difficult life circumstances makes me believe that their physical and safety needs might not be being met. While you are not their mother (and are also responsible for teaching 25 other students besides them), there are things you could do to create a relationship with them (individually) that could help them meet some of their needs.

Remember, due to their actions, they have pushed many people away from them. This actually helps them justify their "hatred" of everyone ("See, they don't care about me anyway."). But if you are not so easily pushed away and you keep taking the small steps forward rather than the large steps back, you might see a change in their reactions to you. This will take a while and would have been better had you done it right from the beginning. But it is never too late.

They also need to know that you have a class to teach, that they cannot interfere with the learning of the other members of class, and that order must be maintained. It is a tricky road (and one that many teachers wouldn't bother with for these girls) but one that could make a big difference in their lives. It is not that I always had the

...... **MINI TIP** ......
Refuse to let an individual student interfere with the learning of the rest of the class. See *How to Get a Class Quiet—Stopping the Action* in week 5, day 5 Tips, Strategies, and Relevant Data section.

time or the disposition to do this for all of my students in need, but I certainly tried to do it as much as possible. My philosophy is that no child gets left behind, but I know that in 30 years of teaching I was not always able to walk my talk.

Prof Z

Tips, Strategies, and Relevant Data

How to Get Students to Stop Testing You

Before they will stop testing you, students need to know the following about you. They will test you on each of these until you "pass the test."

1. Do you show respect for them?
2. To what degree are you there for them or for yourself?
3. Do you like them? Are you happy to be with them?
4. Are you easily pushed away from them (so they could say, "I knew you really didn't care.")?
5. Do you want to know more about them?
6. Do you really want to help them?
7. Do you know your material?
8. Do you know how to teach?
9. Do you know the rules and the consequences of breaking them, and can you enforce them consistently?
10. Do you know how to control a class?

Discussion Starters for Week Three

1. Which of your high school teachers would best handle the discipline problems Miss B faced this week? What methods would they use? What methods would you use?

2. Make a list of things you should think about before being observed by your college supervisor.

3. What are your comments about the weapons check?

4. How do you feel about the comment that Miss B made, "We don't have a weapon or a drug problem in this school"?

5. How open are you to positive and critical feedback? To what degree do you really want your cooperating teacher and supervisor to be completely honest with you?

6. Think of the toughest students in your classes at your high school. How would you deal with them if they were students in your classes?

7. What rules will you have in your classroom when you get your first teaching job? How might they be similar or different from the ones your cooperating teacher goes by?

8. How do you feel about the idea of sending your "kicked out" students to another teacher's room (and vice versa) without sending them to the office?

9. Did you feel that your teachers listened to you when you had personal or academic problems? How did this affect you as a student?

10. Do you think students generally respond better to positive or negative reinforcement? Why?

11. Professor Z only had one rule in his classes—being respectful. Each student got one warning and was then asked to leave the room if they broke a rule after being warned. How do you feel about this system?

12. What are the consequences of not being consistent in enforcing the rules?

☑ Professor Z's Student Teaching Checklist

Classroom Management: Give some thought to each of these questions. If you need work on some, think about what you must do so that you will be prepared.

1. ___Attitude Adjustment—Are you clear that when you are teaching, the class is *your* class? You are in charge, not the students. It's all in the attitude. Once you get it, the students will sense that you truly are in charge. But *you* have to get it first!

2. ___Have you learned your cooperating teacher's classroom routines?

3. ___Have you learned what the general and specific rules of the classroom are (such as gum chewing, hats, bathroom passes, inappropriate language, students talking while others are talking, students not doing what they are told, and respecting others)?

4. ___Have you learned what the consequences are for breaking each of the rules? Be very specific about this as there are different penalties for infractions that could appear quite similar.

5. ___Are you sure the students know that you will uphold the cooperating teacher's rules? Make sure your students are clear about your expectations of them.

6. ___Are you clear as to what to do if a fight breaks out?

7. ___Are you clear about what to do in a fire drill?

8. ___Are you ready to consistently uphold your rules and consistently hand out appropriate consequences? Stop inappropriate behavior immediately.

9. ___Are you prepared to give no more than one warning before taking action?

10. ___Are you overly committed to being liked rather than being respected?

11. ___Do you have a method for learning students' names quickly, such as a seating chart or name plates?

12. ___Have you found out from the cooperating teacher if any students have special needs that you should be aware of?

13. ___Have you thought of ways of enhancing the learning environment to be more safe and inspiring than it already is?

14. ___Have you reviewed key notes/ideas from your methods courses that you feel might come in handy during your student teaching (classroom management techniques, teaching strategies, sources of materials, etc.)?

15. ___Have you thought about the best ways of getting the attention (stopping the action) of your students?

16. ___Are you ready to have fun? While survival and nervousness might be at the forefront of your thoughts at this time, don't forget to have fun. Remember that more learning will take place if you and the students are having fun.

Endnotes

1. Curwin, R., & Mendler, A. (1988). *Discipline with dignity*. Association for Supervision and Curriculum Development, Alexandria, VA.
2. Freiberg, H.J., & Waxman, H.C. (1990). Reflection and the acquisition of technical teaching skills. In Renee T. Clift, W. Robert Houston, & Marleen Pugach (Eds.). *Encouraging reflective practice in education*. New York: Teacher's College Press.
3. Maslow, A.H. (1943). A theory of human motivation. *Psychological Review, 50*, 370–396.

WEEK FOUR

"This is the true joy in life—the being used for a purpose. Recognized by yourself as a mighty one—the being a force of nature—instead of a feverish little clod of ailments and grievances complaining that the world will not devote itself to making you happy. I am of the opinion that my life belongs to the whole community and as long as I live it is my privilege to do forth whatever I can. I want to be thoroughly used up when I die. For the harder I work, the more I live. I rejoice in life for its own sake. Life is no brief candle to me. It is a sort of splendid torch which I've got a hold of for the moment and I want to make it burn as brightly as I can before handing it on to future generations."

GEORGE BERNARD SHAW

Day 1: Teaching Without Resources	Expecting the Unexpected, Teacher Issues (Anger and Stress), Politics of Education, School Resources, Classroom Management, Teaching Methods, Working with Parents
Day 2: I (Used to) Love Discussions	Starting Discussions, Lesson Planning, Best Practices
Day 3: Who Are You? Who Am I?	Developing Your Teacher Reputation, Student Behavior, Classroom Management
Day 4: To Group or Not to Group? That Is the Question!	Differentiating Instruction, Hetero and Homogeneous Grouping, Students with Special Needs, Best Practice, Teacher Expectations, Cooperative Learning
Day 5: Class Rebellion	Managing Rebellion, Classroom Management

Discussion Starters for Week Four
Professor Z's Student Teaching Checklist

Topics Discussed This Week

In this chapter, you will learn

1. How to work in schools that do not have enough working computers.
2. How to work with unruly students.
3. How to teach conceptually.
4. The role that cooperative learning can play in your classes.
5. How to most effectively start each lesson.
6. How to deal with a class rebellion.
7. How to deal with stress.
8. How to create your teaching reputation.
9. How to create lessons that will "hook" students.
10. How to successfully use group related activities.

DAY 1

From: Anne Marie Bettencourt

To: Professor Z

Subject: Week 4, Day 1—Teaching Without Resources

Murphy's Law of Teaching foiled me again today. I had the perfect lesson plan. My students were going to do Internet research on the Harlem Renaissance as part of a group project. I had lists of what they needed and gave them enough time to research it. It couldn't have been planned better.

Of course, all my students are psyched (as am I) to go to the computer lab, do some research, learn some STUFF! Then we get to the lab, or the two labs actually. Somehow, between two computer labs, I still couldn't get enough functional computers for my 21 students to use. Then the printer ran out of paper.

What was supposed to be a fun, enjoyable class turned stressful as I zipped around looking for computers for my students to use, assuring them that I would not penalize them for being unable to turn in research for that period. By the end of the period, I was thinking of the suggestion we got from our reading professor to integrate technology into our classroom to make it more exciting. My next thought was "OK, well what if the students don't have enough computers or the printer doesn't print?" We need a Methods class for Financially Challenged Districts.

Of course, the library has this funky, cool, new computer board that acts like a projector and computer all in one: it highlights, you can double click right on the wipe board, and you can erase and go forwards and backwards. Even one of my students wanted one. Man, those would be great in every classroom! Of course, the AP English teacher has one, but she bought it with her own money.

So how about having the students go home and do the research? Sure, but many of them don't have Internet access or even access to a computer. Clearly, we are doing a wonderful job of preparing them to work in the 21st century. And yet, at an East-hampton elementary school, the teacher e-mails all her students' assignments to their parents each day, so they can keep track of their child's work. This is what some would call a school located in the "boutique community."

Part of me gets very angry that our students don't get as much to work with or enjoy. We aren't taught how to work around these dilemmas. So, I scheduled the one day available in the library for a research session, and then had the books delivered to my class again today for a third research session. If I can't get to the research, I will bring the research to my classroom.

I know money doesn't solve all the problems, but it sure does help! I think we need a Guerilla Teaching 675 class, where we learn tactics to combat systems of inequality and come up with ways for our students to get the same benefits as their more affluent coun-terparts, without all the fancy gadgets and toys. Right now, I am thankful my classroom has a wipeboard.

I was also really tired today. I mean emotionally, physically, and mentally tired. And C period chose to test me on this day of all days. I didn't yell, but I pretty much gave over the class to my three rowdy students: Quan, Wil, and Keisha. We managed to get through reteaching rhyme schemes, where I used the students who aced it as "teachers" to help the other students learn it, but even that took ALL period.

Keisha was pissed off at life (what else is new in this poor girl's day), Wil refused to be quiet, do work, or cooperate in any way, shape, or form. I pulled out all my tricks. I moved his seat. I gave him and Keisha detention for repeatedly disrupting class, and they still went on, and on, and on . . . until the bell rang. I felt like I lost my reigns today. I was frustrated, and it showed, and I hate that, because that is a sign of an amateur teacher.

Rule #1: Never let your students see that you are angry, even if you want to kill them. Mr. D came to the rescue today. Mr. D is the most amazing history teacher I have seen at this school. He cracked me up the other day by answering a student's question about

Samurais in a deep, Mr. Miyagi from *Karate Kid* voice that rang down the hallway. Aside from that, he has a pantsuit in every color of the spectrum, and some in colors that I didn't know existed.

Today, he came up with a fantastic demonstration of how to take a kid outside, grit your teeth, glare, and get your point across, all without raising your voice above a murmur. I think I will try that after break.

I also think it's time to "Marshal the Forces," as Mr. B calls it, and make a few phone calls home to get the parents to give these three "a talking to." Quan's mother is a force to be reckoned with (she is on the teacher's side, THANK GOD) and he fears her more than life itself, so I know that will work with him. Wil's mom will also oblige, and hopefully Keisha's foster mom has a few tricks up her sleeve.

There WAS a plus to the day though. I decided to start implementing literacy strategies in my class since I have a few ESL students and thought "Hrmm, perhaps I can psych them into learning how to be active readers." So I modeled a "Think Aloud" to them— reading a poem and pausing frequently to ask various questions about it to myself. I had a student write the questions on the board, and by the end of it, two of the girls were asking almost as many questions about the poem as I was! I know it will take a few tries to get this off the ground, but for a first read, I had everyone's attention and they bought my "everyone can become a good reader, some just need to learn the tricks that good readers do almost naturally" speech.

~Anne Marie

From: Professor Z

To: Anne Marie Bettencourt

Subject: Week 4, Day 1—Teaching Without Resources

Dear Anne Marie,

One of the cons of working in a poor school is that you sometimes have to deal with inadequate resources. Again, not all poor schools have inadequate resources, but many do. One of the pros of working in a poor school is that you get to be creative in figuring out how to get around these issues! It is possible that kids can work in groups of two so there are enough computers. Or, you could divide the class in half and have some kids go to the computer lab on day one and others on day two. Or you can give each student 20 minutes at the computer. None of these are perfect solutions but they will allow you to move forward.

Again, you bring up the importance of becoming effective advocates for our poorer schools. I know I have said this many times before, but if every teacher called their elected officials, things would be very different. Look at Vermont, which completely changed the way schools are funded. Instead of schools being primarily financed by local property taxes, Vermont collected property taxes at the state level and distributed money to schools more evenly. It can be done. We just need to help educate people on how to stand up to fix the injustices in our society. We need a movement like the suffragette movement for our schools. We need people to see that what Gandhi said is true—"Without justice there is no peace."

Regarding your discipline issues, I wonder if Mr. B feels that the students who are disrupting the class shouldn't be sent out. I know we have discussed this before, but I don't see why he would want students in the room who obviously are not committed to learning. I would never let one student get in the way of another student's learning (or the rest of the class for that matter).

As I told you before, my rule was "one warning and then you are out." Simple as that! And I NEVER went back on that rule. After one warning, I would look at the student who broke the rule the second time and simply say, "See ya!" And then I'd go on with my lesson. After class, I would meet with the student to see what was up and to come up with an agreeable plan of action that would try to ensure that it would not happen again. Typically, that meeting actually improved our relationship. I would not yell. I would simply ask what was going on and work on a plan for the future.

If this didn't work, I would strike where it hurts. This would all depend on the student. If he/she was an athlete, I would speak to the coach. Coaches are typically wonderful when it comes to speaking to students about the necessity of behaving, doing the work, and being mature in class. Or, I would hold them for after-school detention so they would miss part of practice. This might prevent them from starting in the next game (something most athletes REALLY don't like).

Or, a call home for some kids could do the job (except when I know that the kid will get beaten up for my call, which is another story). It is most important to establish a relationship with the parents of your students right at the beginning of the year. While it might be too late to do this for a seven-week student

> **MINI TIP**
>
> If there are not enough computers available for your students, form small groups to work on one computer. See *How to Form Effective Groups* in today's Tips, Strategies and Relevant Data section.

> **MINI TIP**
>
> Sometimes it is necessary to tell a student to leave the room due to their misbehavior. In some cases, the student should be sent to the office. In other less serious situations, the issue might be resolved by simply taking the student out into the hall. See *How to Have a Meaningful Hall Conversation with a Student* in today's Tips, Strategies, and Relevant Data section.

teaching placement, I would suggest this for when you get your own classroom. Maybe send home a letter to parents in which you introduce yourself, tell them you are looking forward to working with them and their child, and tell them about some of the things the students will be learning about during the year, your expectations for homework, the supplies the students will need, discipline, etc. You might also give them your phone number or e-mail address, so they can contact you when they feel the need.

> .... **MINI TIP** ....
> It is very important to be able to work closely with parents whenever possible. See *How You and Your Cooperating Teacher Can Work Closely with Parents* in today's Tips, Strategies, and Relevant Data section.

Be in contact with parents as often as possible. Do not contact them only when something is wrong. Send them a note when their child does something well. After establishing a good relationship, they will tend to be more supportive if you seek their help when their child is not working well.

The bottom line is that students need to know that it is not worth it to mess around in your class. They need to know that you will be consistent in handing out punishment when the rules are broken. Once they know they cannot win, they will stop.

Lastly, you mentioned how tired and wiped out you are. Taking care of yourself as a teacher is extremely important. New

> .... **MINI TIP** ....
> Student teaching can create a lot of stress. Do things that will lessen your stress. Eat well. Get exercise. Talk with friends. Take time to listen to music. Do what works for you. Just like planning your lessons, you must organize your life in order to be most effective. See *How to Deal with the Stress of Student Teaching* in week 5, day 1 of the Tips, Strategies, and Relevant Data section.

teachers are typically sick more often, since their bodies have not become adjusted to the multitude of germs that are flying around the classroom. If your body is already exhausted, it is harder for it to fight off these germs. It is important for you to get an adequate amount of sleep, eat decently, and work out. You are worth nothing to anyone if you are sick or dead!

Prof Z

Tips, Strategies, and Relevant Data

How You and Your Cooperating Teacher Can Work Closely with Parents

1. Establish contact with parents at the beginning of your placement, even if it is only a note telling them how you look forward to working with their children and what they will be studying in your class. Tell

them a little about yourself, some of the work you will be doing in class, and what your homework requirements will be.

2. Send a note home to parents when their child has done something good that you feel he/she should be acknowledged for.

3. Contact the parents when you need suggestions as to how best to deal with a problem you are having with the student.

4. Invite the parents into your classroom or to participate in field trips, panel discussions, and so forth.

5. Create a Parent of the Month Award.

6. Publish a monthly newsletter telling parents what is going on in your class. Let the students write the articles. It will keep the parents informed and will also get the students excited about what they are doing.

How to Have a Meaningful Hall Conversation with a Student

1. Sometimes it is necessary to ask a student to step outside the room for a quick talk. This could help avoid sending the student to the office.

2. You can have a conversation with a student in the hall even if you are the only teacher in the room (it helps to have an aide, however). You just need to design the conversation carefully.

3. Make sure the class is working on something, either in groups or independently. This will help to avoid further embarrassment for the student, as the attention of the class will be on their work.

4. Place yourself in a position where you can see both the classroom and the student you are speaking to.

5. Before you make your point, ask the student what is going on with them to warrant their poor behavior. Ask if they are okay. Ask what they need so that the situation will not repeat itself. Listen closely so the student knows that you understand them. You should be gentle but firm when talking with the student.

6. Repeat the student's point to show that you understand what happened and then tell him/her what *you* need. State your point and state how their behavior was unacceptable and why.

7. Ask the student what you can count on from them in the future. If you are in agreement that these actions are acceptable, shake hands and offer an encouraging word before going back into the classroom.

8. If you are unable to come to an agreement, tell the student what will happen to him/her should they choose to misbehave again. Or, meet the student during lunch of after school to further discuss the issue.

How to Form Effective Groups

1. While every class is different, a good general rule is to put an even amount of boys and girls in each group.
2. Do not put more than four students in a group whenever possible. When sharing a computer, do not put more than two people on a computer at the same time. However, you might have a group of four that takes turns in pairs using the computer.
3. It is not always necessary to break up groups that are not working well together in the middle of a lesson. This could cause a domino effect and bring other groups down. Instead, work with the group in deciding what it needs to do to be productive.
4. Give each student tasks to do within a given time limit.
5. Break up cliques unless you know they will work well together.
6. To ensure success, assess students not only on the product they produce but also on the process (how well they worked together and demonstrated cooperative learning skills).
7. When breaking students into groups, have them understand that they will be evaluated both individually and as a group.
8. Make sure you give adequate directions before the group begins so you do not need to continually interrupt them once they start working.
9. When giving directions, always ask for an example of what the groups should be doing so they all can be clear as to what needs to get done.
10. Always tell the groups how much time they have for each activity. Make it a little less than you think it will take them. It is the teacher's job to create urgency so that students get right to work. If the class is working well and time has run out, you can always tell them they have another 3 minutes.

DAY 2

From: Anne Marie Bettencourt

To: Professor Z

Subject: Week 4, Day 2—I (Used to) Love Discussions

Regarding your comments on the computer issues: I DID put them in pairs and still struggled to find working computers. One of the other teachers told me there are lots of websites to check out that give a ton of ways to modify lessons with a lack of technology and still get the content the kids need. I'll have to search for some of these.

And the deal with the parents of my "difficult" students—I sent letters of expectations home the week I took over the classes, which also required a parent signature. I know this doesn't guarantee that the parent read the letter (or that they even care about what's in the letter). Quan's mom, however, is awesome. He told me today that she once took away his Christmas presents until Valentine's Day for something foolish he did. Way to go!

Mr. B has already told me that Wil's parents are not very helpful. They are the "shrug the shoulder" and "what can I do?" type of parent. And I know that none of Keisha's guardians have much say over what she does, so I am on my own here. Of course, it would be with the MOST difficult ones in that group, not the one student who only needs minor redirection.

Well . . . Happy Valentine's Day! I had the pleasure of a lesson bombing today. Well, no. I lie. It didn't bomb; it just didn't get off the ground the way I envisioned it, which, I think, is the problem with being a visionary. I get so caught up with the ideas that occasionally I forget to ask what potential pitfalls they could have.

My students and I were going to have a DISCUSSION today! I love discussions in English class. I pictured it right out of *Dead Poet's Society*. We would sit in a circle (what I call a "Round Table Discussion") happily commenting and debating Langston Hughes's "Let America Be America Again." Students would argue over his vision of America, contrast it with today, and walk away with giant smiles on their faces commenting on how brilliant today's class was and how much they love discussing poetry.

I don't have to tell you that was not the way it went at all. It was more like this:

Me: OK, so now that we have read the poem, who can tell me what group of people Hughes is writing about?

Class: (Silence, then one student timidly raises her hand. I cling to it like a life preserver.)

Me: Marissa! Yes?

Marissa: The working class?

Me: Excellent! Does anyone else have any other thoughts?

Class: (Silence)

So, instead of a fiery discussion, I was the teacher in front of the room going, "Bueller? Bueller? Bueller?" (*Ferris Bueller's Day Off*) to a roomful of intelligent-but-afraid-to-show-it (or they had no clue what I was asking and didn't want to look like the dummy saying that) students. What was a teacher to do? I did what any new teacher would do after class—I sought out Mr. D again.

By the end of fifteen minutes (in between his checking hall passes) I was enlightened! "Did you relate the lesson to something from their own experience?" he asked. (Silence.) "Did you let them discuss the question with a partner for a minute before answering?" (Silence.) "And finally" he concluded, "Don't ever call on the first person that answers. It is like your lifeline, and it will stifle conversation because other students who MIGHT have the answer don't get enough wait time."

Now it was my turn to be silent. But he definitely turned on the "EUREKA!" bulb in my head with ideas and suggestions for jump starting a conversation. Now I have a little kit in my brain titled "Jump starting a discussion for the self-conscious ninth grader" thanks to good old Mr. D. I don't expect the next class to be a firecracker, but I DO think it will be more informed and talkative.

~ Anne Marie

From: Professor Z

To: Anne Marie Bettencourt

Subject: Week 4, Day 2—I (Used to) Love Discussions

Dear Anne Marie,

Well, I'm glad to report that I would have given you two of the answers that Mr. D gave you—and I agree with the third. One, ask questions that relate to the student's lives first before going into the poem. Then relate the same questions to the poem. Two, use small group discussion on an interesting question (you might need to spend some time developing the "perfect" question) before asking for large group interaction.

I also like the suggestions he gave you about wait time. He is absolutely correct. Some students think more quickly than others or are at least quicker to raise hands than others. If you call on the first hands up all the time, the "slower" kids will not even bother raising their hands anymore. Not only that, they might not even pay attention anymore!

I must confess that I am still working on this myself. I am not good at waiting and will call on those first hands more often than I should. I once saw a student teacher do something fun regarding this subject. He would ask a question and then tell everyone in the class to raise

.... **MINI TIP** ....
Always give the class time to think about the answer to a question before you call on someone to answer it. Studies show that teachers typically wait less than one second to call on a student for an answer (or answer the question him/herself).[1]
....

their hands. Then he took his time calling on one of the raised hands. It was a good idea for two reasons. One, the class thought it was funny. Two, it reminded him to slow down and carefully select the student he wanted to answer the question.

Mr. D told you to do exactly what I teach my methods course students to do—to teach conceptually, using the big ideas as the main part of the lesson and incorporating facts as a way of reinforcing those concepts/big ideas. The beauty of teaching conceptually is that it will create a better understanding of the topic for the students.

Every concept can be used in hundreds of applications that can easily be related to students' lives. For example, if you were going to teach a lesson on the causes of the Revolutionary War, you could come in and just start talking about the names, dates, and places associated with the Revolutionary War period. However, these are all facts and cannot apply to many other situations. I teach my students to concentrate on teaching the key concepts and the big ideas they would like their students to come away from the lesson with. These are big ideas that students will remember years from now, not facts that they will forget two days after memorizing them for a test.

There is too much factual information for anyone to learn. Furthermore, facts have little power to create useful or meaningful knowledge by themselves.[2]

.... **MINI TIP** ....

Make sure that for every lesson you plan, you are very clear about the big idea (concept, theme, generalization) that you are trying to teach—not just the facts. See *How to Teach Big Ideas* in today's Tips, Strategies, and Relevant Data section.

Relying too much on teaching facts and on memorization takes away from teaching concepts, which are critical to a child's understanding of his/her world.

Another wonderful thing about using concepts is that they can all be related to the students' lives. Thus, you can start any class by using these concepts/big ideas as part of the opening motivator or hook for the lesson.

My methods class came up with the following idea for teaching the causes of the Revolutionary War in a conceptual manner. They decided that the key concept for this lesson would be "revolution." For their opening hook, they decided that the teacher would walk into the classroom and state, "Bill, isn't the pizza in the cafeteria a ripoff?" The student would most likely agree. "Do you know that on top of the $1.25 you are paying for the pizza, you are also paying 25 cents in tax? Isn't that a ripoff? What do you think we should do about it? Oh, you want to complain to the person who runs the cafeteria? What if he/she doesn't respond favorably? Oh, you want to talk with the principal? What if he/she doesn't respond favorably? Oh, you'd go to the superintendent? Maybe boycott the pizza, have a sit-down strike, or even dump the pizza out the window! Great ideas! Well, Sam Adams and company, back in the 1770s were having the same problem with taxes on tea, sugar, and other items and they ended up doing many of the same things you would do about the pizza. . . ." And then they would go right into the meat of the lesson.

The key was that they related the concept to the student's lives. That is the beauty of teaching conceptually. I cannot think of ANY concept that cannot be applied to a student's life and can't be used to open up any lesson.

Good job, Mr. D!

Prof Z

Tips, Strategies, and Relevant Data

How to Teach Big Ideas

Instead of concentrating on giving your students many names, dates, and places to memorize, spend much of your class time teaching big ideas. For example, in a health lesson on the topic of alcohol and tobacco, one student teacher did an excellent job of identifying the big ideas she wanted to teach.

Concepts
1. Addiction
2. Peer pressure
3. Decision making
4. Responsibility

Understandings
1. The students will understand that there are internal and external factors that influence one's decision to use or not use alcohol and tobacco.
2. The students will understand that an addiction is very powerful and cannot usually be easily broken.
3. The students will understand that the media plays a large role in terms of adolescent consumption of alcohol and tobacco.
4. The students will understand that peer pressure plays a large role in why students begin using alcohol and tobacco.
5. The students will understand that they are responsible for their actions and decisions.

Generalizations

1. The younger a student starts to use alcohol and tobacco, the more likely it is that he/she will develop an addiction to that substance.
2. The more peer pressure put on a child to use alcohol and tobacco, the more likely he/she is to try it.
3. Good decisions are often informed decisions.
4. Risky behaviors can have negative outcomes in the short and long term.

DAY 3

From: Anne Marie Bettencourt

To: Professor Z

Subject: Week 4, Day 3—Who Are You? Who Am I?

The light bulb went on today. It really, truly did. I am so excited right now I can hardly sit still to write this. Mr. B told me today, "I feel that you will be able to achieve the control you want in the classroom with what you have been doing the past few days. Class has gone really well and they were very productive." I was beaming.

Today was a review of "Policies and Procedures." We had a chat about the fact that (1) They do not run the classroom, I do. (2) They don't speak when I am speaking or vice versa. (3) The "I forgot," "I couldn't do it," "I didn't know what to do" excuses weren't going to fly anymore (penalty—reduced grade and THREE pages on the topic). I don't want to hear any of those phrases out of their mouths again.

I think it worked well. Quan spent some time in the hallway for breaking the "three strikes" rule on talking, and he hated it. He begged to come back in, and today when I looked at him twice, he said to Wil, "Man don't talk to me, I'm going to end up in the hall again. Be quiet!" Granted, it has only been two days, but so far, when I want quiet, I get it, and when I don't get it, the class understands that there will be consequences. I just have to be consistent and not slip back into "nice" mode again, because that is exactly when they will get me. They are just as sneaky as I am—we both have our tricks, so it is a war right now. Actually I prefer to think of it as a game, and I am REALLY competitive, so I don't plan on letting my students beat me for control of my own class!

But after lunch, classes are brutal. In my C period, I know I'm in trouble when the word "Miss . . ." comes out of their mouths. If you are familiar with 50 Cent's "I'll Ask 21 Questions" song, then you understand what I am talking about. The skills they have to derail a teacher are amazing. It starts off as an innocent question like, "Miss, are you gonna read our poems today?" and somehow, two minutes later, the class is off discussing how "wack" Quan's rhymes are, or humming a song and saying, "but Miss, I am practicing my rhyme schemes!" And I am sitting there wondering, "HOW did they do this?" I am almost tempted to wag my finger at them, smile, and say, "You guys are good!" but I know that is completely unacceptable. That is a normal C period after lunch.

Somehow, today, I did not get a normal C period after lunch. They came in, made a few comments, and sat down expectantly waiting for work. I almost had to look twice to make sure I had the same class. "What are we doing today, Miss?" Tony asked. That was it. No tangents. Hrmmm, I thought, surely they are playing a trick on me. After all, it's after lunch! Either that or Mr. B's suggestion to have higher expectations paid off, along with my fake "mean" attitude of getting down to business.

They turned out great stuff today—amazingly talented interpretations of Langston Hughes's "Salvation" (via pictures), and great questions on their "Think Aloud" questions. And to top it off, I was able to hold individual writing conferences to help students with weak spots on their Open Responses. Mr. B helped me watch over the class, and at first, I assumed he was going to rail me for something. But to my surprise, he said he felt the class was ready to work today, and the class now had a totally different feel than it did last week regarding classroom management. I am improving—and he didn't feel it was because he was in the room. WOW!

The funny thing is, I am starting to feel it, too. I am starting to understand what an "in control, good noise" classroom looks and feels like and what an "off track, bring it back down" class feels like. The whole difference is whether or not I feel like I can bring the class back down, or up, or whatever I need to do. On days when I don't feel like that, I know it was a bad day. On days when I feel in complete control, I know I had a good day. Now I just need to work on being consistent with it.

The next battle is Keisha. Mr. B is awesome about giving me hidden clues to a student who is asking to be "anchored" as he calls it. Keisha came in with her hood up today. Mr. B told me that meant she was already in a bad state and looking for a confrontation. He modeled what to do by staying hard on her, demanding her hood be put down, and telling her not to respond, and when she didn't get on task immediately, he kicked her out in the hallway.

The result? She eventually asked to come back into the class, did ALL her work, settled down, and told Mr. B she did better work on her own, which got her praise for being intelligent about her decisions. I see now why this stuff takes YEARS to nail down—you have to figure out "whole class" skills, and at the same time, work on what it takes to get to individual students. And of course I am taking classroom management this summer. Excellent. Right after my student teaching is done.

Trial by fire indeed!

~ Anne Marie

From: Professor Z

To: Anne Marie Bettencourt

Subject: Week 4, Day 3—Who Are You? Who Am I?

Dear Anne Marie,

WOW! The light bulb *is* going on! It certainly sounds like your classroom management skills are improving. Many of the things that you understood intellectually before are now being put into practice. It is no longer just an idea or a long-term goal. You are actually starting to achieve the results. Your class is becoming YOUR class. Good for you!

.... **MINI TIP** ....
Classroom management is essential if you are to be a good teacher. See *How to Effectively Manage Your Classroom* in today's Tips, Strategies, and Relevant Data section.

Classroom management looks so simple on paper, doesn't it? However, it took me years to get to a place where I had complete confidence in my ability to control a class. Of course, by that time, I also knew how to create meaningful and fun lessons. This, by itself, helped to avoid discipline problems in the first place. I developed a reputation as a fun teacher who was a real nice guy until a student would "cross the line." Once a student crossed the line, I ceased to be a nice teacher and could be a very mean guy who was NOT a lot of fun. They did not want to go there, as it was not in their best interest.

The problem for me was always where to draw the line and how to be consistent. As a result of having a "fun" class and doing lots of group work, my classes were noisier than most in the school. Most of the other teachers were more traditional and did the "sage on the stage" deal. But, since I was brought up with the Cone of Retention chart that I included in Week One (students retain most when they are actively involved in the material and retain least when they are simply lectured to), I thought of lecture as a teaching strategy I would use only if I couldn't find any other way to teach the material.

During my first year of teaching, my assistant principal told me that my classes were too noisy and that I should teach more like the other teachers and keep the noise down in my room. I did that for three years. Then I got tenure and everything changed. No longer could I get fired for choosing my constructivist methods of teaching. So, from then on, I taught the way I felt my kids would learn best. While my assistant principal wasn't happy about my decision at first, there was little he could do. Luckily, I was starting to get a reputation as a good teacher. And, it turned out that my students did fine during the year and on the Regents Exam. It eventually became a nonissue for him.

Regarding where to draw the line was tough because I did not want to stop the fun when it was getting loud. But I also didn't want the class to be too loud. The problem with working with seventh graders is that they sometimes can't control themselves when they are excited. They ARE loud. I would love how excited they were about the lesson but I also needed them to keep it down. So, I would say (in a nice way), "Keep it down, folks!" or "Raise your hand" probably more times than I should have. But I usually found a happy medium. It just takes time.

It is great to see the teacher in you emerging! Now, you need to sustain it. You will be up and down on this. You will have good days and bad ones. It is simply easier at first to let things go sometimes. And, unfortunately, you will. And it will get you into trouble. You must be diligent and consistent. It takes work. But it is worth it in the long run.

I really enjoy watching your transformation as a teacher. I look forward to seeing your progress when I observe you again next week.

Prof Z

Tips, Strategies, and Relevant Data

How to Effectively Manage Your Classroom

1. Establish fair classroom rules and consequences and enforce them consistently. State these rules in a positive manner (e.g., "Work quietly" instead of "No talking").
2. Create lessons that students find useful and relevant so that they are deeply involved in their work.
3. Make your expectations of the students very clear.

4. Make sure your lesson plan has been well thought out so you can anticipate what will actually be taking place during the lesson before you even teach it. When planning your lesson, see how you can eliminate any unnecessary transitions that will take the class off task. Also, make sure you will be engaging students throughout the entire class period. Overplan!

5. Establish a routine.

6. Make sure you "stop the action" immediately whenever the class is not doing what you want. Do not compromise in terms of getting exactly what you want. Your students will learn better if class is run according to your expectations rather than theirs.

7. Good management includes ways to keep students on task. Work on ways to encourage and motivate the students to give 100% on their work.

8. Use a friendly voice when asking students to do something.

9. Make sure your students know you care about them and respect them.

10. Most importantly—Convey in your attitude that it is YOUR class and that it will be run according to YOUR rules.

DAY 4

From: Anne Marie Bettencourt

To: Professor Z

Subject: Week 4, Day 4—To Group or Not to Group? That Is the Question!

My insight today was in my after-school help session with my students. I asked how this class was going for them and, to my surprise, they replied that sometimes, it was GASP, easy. I cringe when I hear that word. Easy?! My class is EASY?! Yet I knew what they meant. Half of my class gets things at the speed of light, and the other half needs an extra week to pick it up.

The dilemma is this: How to challenge my quicker picker uppers, while maintaining a comfortable pace for my students who need more time, which is the majority of the class. I may sound conservative here, but I think we need to go back to ability-level classes. It is a serious mistake to put kids of all different abilities in the same class and say, "Teach." The fast ones get bored and the slower ones struggle if you move quicker. And while I think having students teach other students is a good idea, they get sick of it fast, realize what is going on, and become even more disenchanted. Besides, it does nothing to challenge them, which is the goal of education, to make them think critically. Tutoring is great to help review material, but they are not getting paid to teach, so let's not use them as teachers all the time.

I really think students need to be in classes grouped by their abilities. I don't believe in tracking, where the slower students get "dumbed down" work. No, you can teach the same material and have the same expectations. It is just the pace that is different. Instead, now I have to provide alternate assignments for my students who get it faster, to prevent them from being bored while I catch everyone else up. So, really, they aren't all doing the same work anyway in my class. I am still varying assignments to make them more difficult for some, and slowing down on others to make them more understandable.

Students deserve an equal opportunity for education. But human brains are not all built the same and don't all learn the same, so why on earth is there shame in differentiating people by ability in order to benefit them? Mr. B agreed, and noted that we are doing the students a huge disservice by placing them all in the same classroom. "You end up tracking anyway," he said, "because then you have to come up with different assignments for the brighter students." I learned today that ALL of our students have special needs. And really, the system is not just failing one, but failing them all.

~Anne Marie

From: Professor Z

To: Anne Marie Bettencourt

Subject: Week 4, Day 4—To Group or Not to Group? That Is the Question!

Hi, Anne Marie,

When I was getting my doctorate, there were a few things that I didn't think I could say out loud because I thought they would be seen as SO politically incorrect that my degree could be on the line. Tracking was one. I believe that while there are certainly good reasons to have multiple ability levels in a classroom, I think that it is usually better to put kids together who have similar ability levels AS LONG AS we train teachers to have appropriately high expectations for ALL students. In other words, teachers who teach the "slower" students need to have appropriately high expectations for them.

Now that is easier said than done. We have all experienced teachers who are biased for or against certain groups of kids. We've all had teachers who seemed to favor the boys over the girls (or vice versa), the "jocks" over the "nerds" (or vice versa), or the whites over the non-whites (or vice versa). Do we really think that teachers don't have biases against students of different ability levels?

I have heard so many teachers say that our poorer students need more "structure." To me, this is code for "worksheet them to death." Worksheets provide the "structure" these kids need, according to these teachers. In fact, worksheets are typically boring and do not get students excited about the subject matter, nor do they usually challenge them to use higher-level critical thinking, which is usually fun for most students.

I would favor the tracking of students as long as we give special training to teachers who are not teaching the more gifted classes. They would need to examine their stereotypes/biases of students in these "lower" groups to see that they are capable of teaching these students so that they not only succeed, but also achieve their highest expectations.

Another way to work effectively with different ability groups is to use more cooperative learning in your lessons. Cooperative learning has been shown to be an effective teaching strategy for students of all ability levels. Studies have also shown that students of high ability have much to gain by working with students of less ability.[3] And, given how you describe your students, it could be a good strategy to use for bettering your student's social skills, individual accountability skills, leadership skills, and critical thinking skills, and for getting more students involved in the learning process!

The best advice I can give you regarding the use of cooperative learning is to make sure that every student has a job in the group. In a typical group, one student can be the reporter, one might be responsible for time, another might be

.... **MINI TIP** ....
Use cooperative groups to address the needs of students with different ability levels working together. See *What You Need to Know About Cooperative Learning* and *Why You Should Use Cooperative Learning in Your Classroom* in today's Tips, Strategies, and Relevant Data section.

responsible for making sure all members are participating, and one can record the data and take notes. Furthermore, students must be aware that they are being graded on the process as well as the product. Cooperative learning is not just throwing kids in groups and hoping they will keep themselves busy (which is what many student teachers call cooperative learning). It is a strategy in which kids learn the social skills necessary to function well in group situations, an important skill when one lives in a democracy!

I know you have been doing group work with your students. Have you been emphasizing the cooperative learning process as well as being interested in the final product? Let me know if you need more work on this and we will talk about it.

Prof Z

Tips, Strategies, and Relevant Data

What You Need to Know About Cooperative Learning

1. Cooperative learning is not the same thing as group work. When students are working in groups, many times one student does all the work while the others sit around and essentially cause problems. Is this really cooperative learning? Many student teachers will call all group work cooperative learning. Don't do this!

2. Cooperative learning is a teaching strategy in which students at different levels of ability work together to gain content knowledge and skills in working with others. Students learn and practice skills in personal interdependence (because everyone in the group has a specific role to play), in cooperation (listening, trust, discussing, leadership, supporting others, reaching consensus, and reflecting) and are assessed not only by the product they produce but by the process they take in getting there.

3. There are many forms of cooperative learning, but each form has students working together in groups with each student being responsible for achieving one aspect of the assignment, and requires students to realize that everyone must contribute to achieve success.

Why You Should Use Cooperative Learning in Your Classroom

1. It is an excellent way to promote learning. Research has shown that mastery of new content is facilitated when learners are actively engaged in organizing new information and connecting it to what they know.[4]

2. It allows individuals to work closely with others who have different learning styles.[5] This allows students to realize that they can learn information in different ways, and it helps them develop their problem-solving skills.

3. Students develop good problem-solving, communication, and conflict-resolution skills that transfer to settings beyond the school.[6]

4. It promotes warm relationships between teachers and learners because it allows teachers to work more closely with students in small groups.[7]

DAY 5

From: Anne Marie Bettencourt

To: Professor Z

Subject: Week 4, Day 5—Class Rebellion!

I DO need help with groups. We didn't do a ton of cooperative learning in my methods class, so any hints you have on how I should group kids together (what to look for in personalities, putting academically strong kids with weaker ones, and so forth) would be super helpful. And I haven't been doing the whole "process and product" thing, since Mr. B is pushing for me to stay on schedule. I am trying to just get it done at this point. I hate teaching on a timetable.

However, I now have a new experience to put in my teaching portfolio. I had a whole class rebel on me today. Just when I thought I was getting the hang of this discipline thing. They didn't rebel outwardly. And I wasn't THAT surprised. As I might have predicted, my C period just didn't do their punishment essay for homework. So, next week, it's going to be a detention party with all my students. I think they were surprised that I was actually serious about keeping all of them for detention. I definitely got raised eyebrows, surprised stutters, and glares, but hey, the wall is the wall, and I got pushed through it.

Tanissa decided to push even more today. She put a folder up in front of her face to mouth something to another student about .5 seconds after I told her to quiet down (with a smile, too!) so I booted her to Mr. S's office. Mr. B backed me when she mouthed off, and this was followed by the door slamming and a loud F bomb that echoed in my classroom. Now THAT I hadn't gotten before. But rather than being stunned, I merely shrugged my shoulders and continued with my lesson.

Minutes later, Wil was also taking a trip to Mr. S. "Dang, Miss B is not playing around," Keisha noticed. Oddly enough, I got the best work from the rest of them that day both on our reading, and in discussion. So, I must say, the structure feels nice, and having them buck it in little ways was not so much a problem. But the door slam and the swearing, I was not prepared for. That's the "rebelling against structure" part that Mr. B mentioned, but that I had not yet encountered.

Mr. B and I have noticed that it is indeed six students who seem to be recurring problems. He suggested that I keep sending them to Mr. S's office, after I chat with him about the fact that these six will be sent down there if they blow it in class. Mr. B also said to keep the detentions coming and eventually they won't show and will have in-house suspension for it.

"You've got to worry about the class as a whole first, get the distracting individuals out. Then, once that is established, worry about getting to the root of the problem with the individuals." Sounds like good advice so I am sticking to it.

I did catch Mr. S in his office and he was more than happy to speak to my class as a whole, and he recognized most of the names I mentioned. His advice? "You've got to go in with all guns blazing. None of this, "Please sit down" stuff. It's either your way or the highway. That's it. Maybe halfway through the year or three quarters through you can let up, but especially as a new teacher, you've got to go in tough." OK, coach!

But I agree to a point. I am struggling more now because I was too lenient in the beginning. I know that for class safety reasons and to create an environment that is conducive to learning, I have to create structure for my students. Now I don't have to be a drill sergeant about it, but I have to be firm and consistent. I am still working on it, but the idea gets clearer each class, and I am getting better at knowing when I let something go too far.

I totally thought Mr. B was mean when I first watched him crack down on the class. Now I realize that he wasn't being mean at all. He was merely setting up an environment that our kids need desperately, and want, although they won't come out and say it. I am totally looking forward to my detention party next week as an open forum where we can discuss student behavior, consequences, etc. OK! I am done writing about classroom management for a while as I am sure you are sick of it. Besides, there are more interesting topics going on that I can rant about! I just wanted to let you know that conceptually I am getting it, and emotionally, it is improving, or at least Mr. B says so. And I'm starting to see it. I just need to get a holster for my "blazing" guns.

I hope you will be able to see the difference during our second observation on Monday!

~ Anne Marie

PROFESSOR

From: Professor Z

To: Anne Marie Bettencourt

Subject: Week 4, Day 5—Class Rebellion

Hi, Anne Marie,

It is incredible to watch your steady transformation on the issue of discipline. Instead of your light switch being flicked on, yours seems to be one of those on a dimmer switch that keeps turning the light on slowly but surely. You are certainly making progress! It does seem like you are getting it.

Plus, you seem to be getting the same advice from almost everyone you ask. Mr. S is saying the same thing that Mr. B and others (including myself) have said. You need to be in control. It is not about being nice. Your job is to teach. Without order, nobody can teach or learn. Therefore, order comes first. Remember that being firm is not the same thing as being mean. You do not have to be mean to keep order. You have to be fair and consistent. (Have I said these two words enough?)

You also have to give students opportunities to experience success. When you give students appropriately difficult tasks in which they can succeed, they will work harder and will refrain from negative behavior. Most students love the feeling of doing well on something that is challenging. That is why it is so important to plan effectively. All lessons should include performance tasks in which students can be successful.

Plus, kids expect a teacher to keep order in a classroom. That is one of the jobs of the teacher, in their eyes. When teachers are not able to do this, kids lose respect. This is not what you want.

.... **MINI TIP** ....
Teachers need to provide students with opportunities to experience success. See *How to Provide Students with Opportunities to Experience Success* in today's Tips, Strategies, and Relevant Data section.

.... **MINI TIP** ....
Being fair and consistent can only happen when you have your rules, consequences, procedures, and routines in place. Without these, you and your students will not be clear about what is acceptable and what is not. Without these, any time you discipline a student, it might seem arbitrary because these are not clearly defined.

I liked how you handled the Tanissa situation. You are learning some valuable lessons about discipline:

1. Never argue with students. Do not go down to their level. Take the high road.
2. When you say you will do something, do it!
3. Be consistent in enforcing the rules.

One more thing to remember (which is hard to do when you are being tested) is to retain your sense of humor.

Again, discipline can be a roller coaster ride. Just when you think you've got it nailed, something will happen to set your kids off and rolling again. It takes time, patience, and practice! You are certainly doing the right things, and in time, you will have the class doing what you want them to do.

Prof Z

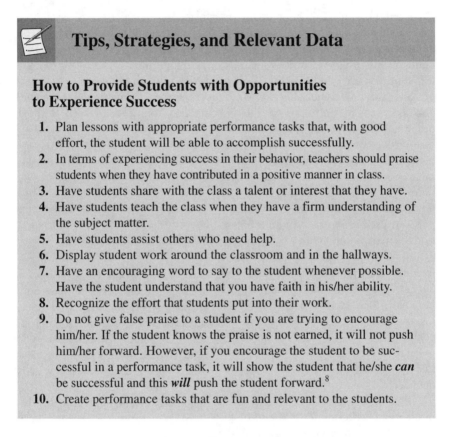

Tips, Strategies, and Relevant Data

How to Provide Students with Opportunities to Experience Success

1. Plan lessons with appropriate performance tasks that, with good effort, the student will be able to accomplish successfully.
2. In terms of experiencing success in their behavior, teachers should praise students when they have contributed in a positive manner in class.
3. Have students share with the class a talent or interest that they have.
4. Have students teach the class when they have a firm understanding of the subject matter.
5. Have students assist others who need help.
6. Display student work around the classroom and in the hallways.
7. Have an encouraging word to say to the student whenever possible. Have the student understand that you have faith in his/her ability.
8. Recognize the effort that students put into their work.
9. Do not give false praise to a student if you are trying to encourage him/her. If the student knows the praise is not earned, it will not push him/her forward. However, if you encourage the student to be successful in a performance task, it will show the student that he/she *can* be successful and this *will* push the student forward.[8]
10. Create performance tasks that are fun and relevant to the students.

Discussion Starters for Week Four

1. What are some of the judgments you hold about people who are poor? How might these judgments affect your teaching of students who fit into this category?

2. How will you earn the respect of your students?

3. Do you respect your students? How will they know?

4. What will you do to create excellent relationships with your students?

5. How good are you at waiting for many hands to be raised before calling on someone (wait time)? How can you improve/extend your wait time?

6. What are some teaching practices that you admire among "seasoned" teachers in your school?

7. What are ways you can modify your lessons to incorporate technology in a "one-computer" classroom?

8. How do you deal with students who anger, annoy, or irritate you?

9. What do you think about Professor Z's "One warning and you are out rule"?

10. Should teachers penalize student athletes who misbehave in class by keeping them after school and making them late for games or practices?

11. When you teach, do you typically call on the first or second person who raises his/her hand? What are the pros and cons of doing this?

12. List a concept that you will be teaching in one of your classes at some point. Create an activity like Professor Z's that will make the concept relevant to student's lives before you transition it to the major objectives of the lesson.

13. How do you feel about grouping students? Would you feel the same if you were a parent of a child with a disability? Would you feel the same if you were a parent of a child with no disabilities? Would you feel the same if you were an administrator?

14. Would you have reacted the same as Miss B when the student cursed at her while she was leaving the room? Explain.

15. What are your thoughts about using cooperative learning in your class? What do you see as the difference between cooperative learning and group work?

☑ Professor Z's Student Teaching Checklist

Effective Teaching Methods: Give some thought to each of these questions. If you need work on some, think about what you must do so that you will be prepared.

1. ___ Are your lessons well planned? Planning is the secret to success. If you plan lessons in which students are having fun and working on activities they see as relevant to their lives, there will be more learning and fewer discipline problems.

2. ___ Do you incorporate the cone of learning in your lessons? Students retain 10% of what they read, 20% of what is lectured to them, 30% of what they see, 50% of what they hear and see, 70% of what they say or write, and 80% of what they teach others.

3. ___ Do your lessons demonstrate that you can teach in a constructivist fashion? Don't always be a "Sage on the Stage." Be a "Guide on the Side." Create a laboratory of learning in which you design activities (experiments) for students to work on that forces them to learn the material themselves.

4. ___ Do you know how to hook each student at the beginning of each lesson? Are your lessons relevant to students' lives? Teaching conceptually is a great way to do this. Concepts can be related to hundreds of different circumstances. Find the key concepts in your lesson and begin the class with an activity that connects or relates the concept to students' lives.

5. ___ Are your lessons fun?

6. ___ Are your directions clear in your verbal commands as well as on your handouts, activity sheets, etc.? Giving clear directions is key to maximizing learning time.

7. ___ Do you have ideas as to how to get parents involved in your classes?

8. ___ Are your lesson plans done in great detail? The more detail in your lessons, the more you are able to visualize how each part of the lesson will play out. By the time you teach the lesson, you will have already "taught" it several times in your mind.

9. ___ Do you use different teaching methods to meet the learning needs of different students?

10. ___ Do you use many visual cues in your lessons to meet the needs of visual learners?

Endnotes

1. Stahl, R., DeMasi, K., Gehrke, R., Guy, C., & Scown, J. (2005, April). *Perceptions, conceptions and misconceptions of wait time and wait time behaviors among pre-service and in-service teachers.* Paper presented at the annual meeting of the American Educational Research Association, Montreal.

2. Sunal, C., & Haas, M. E. (2005). Social studies for the elementary and middle grades. New York: Pearson, Allyn & Bacon.

3. Johnson, D.W. & Johnson, R.T. (1994). *Learning together and alone: Cooperative, competitive and individualistic learning.* Englewood Cliffs, NJ: Prentice Hall.

4. Winitzky, N. (1991). Classroom organization for social studies. In J. Shaver (Ed.), *Handbook of research on social studies teaching and learning* (pp. 530–539). Upper Saddle River, NJ: Merrill/Prentice Hall.

5. Jarolimek, J., & Foster, C. (1993). *Teaching and learning in the elementary school* (5th ed.). Upper Saddle River, NJ: Merill/Prentice Hall.

6. Marr, MB. (1997). Cooperative Learning: A brief review. *Reading and Writing Quarterly:* Overcoming Learning Difficulties, 13 (1), 7–20.

7. Olmstead, J.A. (1974). *Small–group instruction: Theory and practice.* Alexandria, VA: Human Resource Research Organization.

8. Dreikurs, R., Grunwald, B., & Pepper, F. (1998). *Maintaining sanity in the classroom* (2nd ed.). Philadelphia: Taylor and Francis.

WEEK FIVE

"I have come to a frightening conclusion that I am the decisive element in the classroom. It is my personal approach that creates the climate. It is my daily mood that makes the weather. As a teacher, I possess tremendous power to make a child's life miserable or joyous. I can be a tool of torture or an instrument of inspiration. I can humiliate or humor, hurt or heal. In all situations, it is my response that decides whether a crisis will be escalated or de-escalated, and a child humanized or dehumanized."

DR. HAIM GINOTT, *Between Teacher and World*

Day 1: My Second Observation/Still Da Bomb! — Being Observed for the Second Time, Teacher Issues (Confidence and Stress), Classroom Management

Day 2: Stickers?!!! — Using Positive Reinforcement and Building Relationships with Parents, Motivating Students, Working with Parents, Injustices in Our School Systems, Best Practices

Day 3: We Are Just Like Our Students — Relating to Your Students, Motivating Students, Lesson Planning, Teacher Issues (Not Taking Things Personally), Time Management, Teacher Responsibility

Day 4: Go Ahead and Make My Day — Failing to Give Up, Classroom Management, Teacher-Student Relationships, Teacher Expectations, Teacher Issues (Attitude)

Day 5: I (Used to) Love Fridays — Making "Deals" with Students, Classroom Management, Working with Administrators

---

Discussion Starters for Week Five
Professor Z's Student Teaching Checklist

Topics Discussed This Week

In this chapter, you will learn

1. The dos and don'ts of being observed.
2. Techniques for not taking things personally.
3. The three most important areas to immediately work on as a student teacher.
4. The importance of being clear as to why your subject is a relevant one to students and being able to explain how it will help them in their lives.
5. The appropriate use of positive reinforcement in the classroom.
6. The art of "making deals" with students.
7. How to work effectively with parents.
8. Appropriate uses of intrinsic and extrinsic motivators.
9. New classroom management strategies.
10. Ways to deal effectively with administrators.

DAY 1

From: Anne Marie Bettencourt

To: Professor Z

Subject: Week 5, Day 1—My Second Observation/Still Da Bomb!

All my life, I have been able to pick things up pretty fast. In fact, my younger brothers spent most of their time grumbling about how unfair it was that I never studied as hard as they did, and that I never had to practice as much to become proficient in things like sports and music as they did. I prided myself on my ability to write "A" papers the night before they were due. I would even be successful in professor's classes who "didn't give A's." It has never taken me long to "get" something.

That is, until now. And NOW I understand why I pissed my brothers off so much. Watching other teachers who seem to flawlessly control their class and deliver the perfect lesson, with perfect pacing and perfect skills, I have become my brothers. I walk by grumbling, "Well sure, they have the AP kids. Of course they are going to behave." Or, "Well he's a 6'1" guy with a voice that reaches to Madagascar. Of course they are going to listen to him." You have no idea how frustrated I was to hear today that, yet again, my classroom skills are not up to par.

I thought I HAD it! During our post-conference, I babbled away about how well I thought the lesson went and was expecting to hear, "Yeah, you were amazing." Not only did I NOT hear that, but I also heard (again) why it may take YEARS for me to get these skills. As I was talking, you may as well have written, "Are you kidding me?" in the air above your head. I could feel my smile oozing into the floor, where I wished the rest of me could have followed. Years? I am not the sort of person who takes years to become a great teacher, losing tons of students in the meantime. I am irritated with myself that it has taken WEEKS!

Then again, I noticed that the lesson didn't flow as well as I had imagined it would in my head. And I know if I really want to be honest with myself, that I didn't feel like I truly "had it" either. Thanks for noticing that I was trying out different methods, but it is hard to hear when those methods crash and burn, especially when I have been working so hard on them the past month or so. Oh, and don't tell me to ask Mr. B for help. I already tried that. He shrugs his shoulders and says, "I don't know, classroom management was never much of a problem for me." That makes me feel so much better. Does anyone else struggle with this as much as I do? Are there other new teachers who go home pulling their hair out and then pep talk themselves into class the next day, struggling to figure out the lines between strict, jerk, and doormat? Why is this so difficult?

Regardless, I am still determined. It will not take me years to get this down. I swear I will have this by the end of my practicum if it kills me, which I think right now it has the potential to do. Ever the optimist, I am choosing to look on the bright side of things (after I grumble that is). I have two weeks left to master this, and hey, I didn't cry this time, or wear jeans. ☺

~ Anne Marie

From: Professor Z

To: Anne Marie Bettencourt

Subject: Week 5, Day 1—My Second Observation/Still Da Bomb!

Dear Anne Marie,

I told you last week that discipline is an up and down thing. You will have good days and bad days. This was not one of the good ones. So, you reflect on what worked and what didn't and move on from there. That is what learning how to teach is all about. And because you are a deep reflector, I am confident that you will have many more breakthroughs before your practicum ends.

Today, what didn't work was that unintentionally you became a "Dr. Jeckyl and Mr. Hyde" teacher. The lesson involved a fun activity—one that would create a fair amount of noise in the classroom. So, the kids were doing exactly what you asked them to do (and having fun doing it), but then you yelled at them for being noisy. You were sending conflicting messages: "Have fun and participate, but not too much so that you are noisy." If you want them to be quiet, don't pick an activity that will obviously create a fair amount of noise!

I am sure the students were confused by your anger at them, especially since they probably thought they were doing what you wanted them to do. I have a suspicion that part of your anxiety may have had to do with the fact that you were being observed. Being observed can be quite stressful! I think you might have been afraid that I would judge the higher noise level negatively, and you wanted to show me that you were in control of the class. I have found this to be a problem with observing student teachers at times. Being observed is just one of the many things that cause teachers stress.

> **................ MINI TIP ....**
>
> Don't confuse your students with conflicting messages. For example, don't put them in groups for an exciting activity and then yell at them when they get excited. Additionally, only tell them to be quiet if you *really* want them to be quiet.

As a supervisor, I can easily differentiate between educational and noneducational noise. There are limits that teachers must place on each. Typically, I don't have much, if any, threshold for noneducational noise. This is noise that hinders the educational process. But if the kids are having fun and working, I will be much more tolerant, as it is furthering the learning process. However, there are limits as to how loud a classroom can be even when it is educational noise. There are ways of letting students know when they are getting too loud. For example, you can state in an encouraging voice without anger, "SHHHH — Keep it down." In time, students will learn what your thresholds for noise are.

> **................ MINI TIP ....**
>
> Being observed can be quite stressful. See *How to Deal with the Stress of Student Teaching* in today's Tips, Strategies, and Relevant Data section.

Given that I think this is what happened, I would not worry that this is a huge setback for you. Just take it in stride, learn from it, and don't worry. You are on the right path, and this will be a learning experience for you. For our last observation, pretend I am not there. Do the lesson you want to do and do not change anything simply because you are being observed.

Being observed and evaluated is stressful! I still hate being observed and I've been teaching over thirty years! And, yes, I admit that I sometimes act differently when I am observed than when I am not. So, I can appreciate what you are going through. My advice still remains: Try to pretend that I am not there for your final observation!

Prof Z

Tips, Strategies, and Relevant Data

How to Deal with the Stress of Student Teaching

1. Set realistic goals for each class and each day. Don't set goals that will be impossible to meet. You can only do so much in one day.

2. Establish priorities. There are many things to do each day. Decide which ones are most important and do them first.

3. Do as much work as you can at school so you don't have to take it home with you. If it is possible to do your lesson plans for the next day at school before you leave, it will allow you to enjoy more personal time at home. Similarly, if it is possible to stay late on Friday to do your planning for the next week, this will allow you more time to relax and recharge your batteries and not have schoolwork hanging over your head all weekend. Of course, as a student teacher, this may not be possible at times. But it is something to strive for whenever it is possible.

4. Give yourself a break. As a student teacher, you are not supposed to know how to do everything well. You are just learning. When you make a mistake, look at it as a lesson learned. Do not get down on yourself.

5. Don't be afraid to ask for help when you need it. You have many resources available to help you when you are "stuck." Call your cooperating teacher and other teachers in the school, your supervisor, college professors, teachers you had in your old public schools, other student teachers, parents of friends who are teachers, school administrators, your roommates, your parents, and relatives. All of these people most likely will appreciate how hard it is to become a teacher and will gladly talk to you about different ways of proceeding.

6. Be organized. Keep your work space clear by filing papers in an organized fashion. If you typically are not an organized person, ask for help from people who are. A trip to a local stationery store could give you ideas about how best to organize yourself.

7. Eat well. Eat foods that will help you stay healthy and vital. Avoid foods that make you sleepy. Bring a lunch to school so you are not forced to eat at the cafeteria when they may not have anything that will support your well-being.

8. Get plenty of sleep. You may not be able to hang out with your old gang of friends as much during your student teaching. Remember, the goal is to learn as much as possible and then get a teaching job. The recommendations you get from your cooperating teacher and supervisor will be key factors in determining whether you get a job or not.

If you look tired and worn out from partying, it will send a message to them that teaching is not a high priority in your life. Getting an appropriate amount of sleep will help you have plenty of energy for teaching.

9. Reward yourself. Teaching is a tough job. It is important to reward yourself for your accomplishments. Go out for dinner, get some ice cream on the way home from school, hang out with friends, go shopping, watch some TV, go to a sporting event or play, call an old friend, or do something else you enjoy.

10. Learn how to manage your time. Again, a trip to a stationery store might give you ideas on using date books and calendars to better manage your time.

11. Make sure exercise is part of your daily ritual. The right exercise will give you more energy in the long run and alleviate stress.

12. Ask students for feedback on how you can make your classes more beneficial to them. Rather than wondering what is working for your students, just ask them. This will take away the stress of not knowing how the students feel about what is working and what can be improved.

DAY 2

From: Anne Marie Bettencourt

To: Professor Z

Subject: Week 5, Day 2—Stickers?!!!

Here's an interesting little tidbit. My students totally like stickers! Like the ones we would get when we were little kids. God bless the focus group I went to on Monday that gave me this idea. Apparently Prof. McD uses stickers to promote class participation. She allows her college students (that's right, college students) to earn stickers towards participation points in her class. At first I laughed and thought, "Don't be ridiculous. Stickers are so third grade. My ninth graders would scoff at that idea." Then I noticed how many stickers were on Prof. McD's students' nametags. "We're super competitive" one of her students was saying, "We fight for those stickers like you wouldn't believe." Hrmmm. Really. . . .

So one trip to Staples and 600 stickers later, I entered the classroom a skeptic. My students were slowly finishing their open responses and looking idle, so I called the idle ones to the front of the room, asked them to pull up some rug (aka "sit down") and play a game with me. We did rebus puzzles and word pictures. In other words, in a box on the board, I wrote the words "History History History" and asked them to tell me what phrase it was (history repeats itself).

At first, I thought it was going to be a chore to get them involved but after about five minutes, I had a rug full of students vying to put stickers on their journals! Any teacher walking by would have seen half of my students working intently on their essays and the other half on the floor like first graders at story time. It was great. They stayed excited right up until the bell rang. I never thought it would come down to stickers. It was eye opening!

Why do we get rid of things that work for elementary students altogether, just because we think our high schoolers are too cool for them? Apparently, if you modify the use of stickers, they're still cool. I would not have believed it if I hadn't seen them fighting over the sticker book today and happily decorating journals, with other students asking, "Hey, how come they have stickers . . . what game are you playing there?" I even had one student ask me for an extra sticker "for my mom."

I almost lost it. I think sometimes we are so intent on having our students grow up that we forget that they like to be kids, too. They are half and half—half adults, half kids, and hey, I guess we all like to be kid-ish sometimes. I even got excited about the stickers. So what else will work? I don't know but positive reinforcement and prize motivation seems to be doing the trick in my class thus far. I think I may start visiting more elementary and PE classes to get more ideas for my own classroom!

I also went to what we refer to as the Parent Conference "Fair" in the afternoon. The process is as follows: The teacher walks into the library shuffling papers and holding notices for conferences on four different students, all scheduled between 2:30 and 3:30. The library is full of parents and teachers sitting at tables with placards on them with students' names. The teacher awkwardly goes from table to table smiling and trying to read placards without looking like she has no idea which parents are sitting where.

After 5 minutes of wandering, the teacher figures out that the parents are not there yet and sits down at a computer to wait. When a parent that she recognizes finally does walk in, the teacher greets them with a wave and a smile of relief. The teacher goes over grades with the parent, sympathizes about dealing with teenagers, shakes hands hurriedly, smiles, then rushes off to the next table to greet the next set of parents. What an utterly useless waste of time.

I am pretty sure that each one of those parents had similar questions: What can I do to keep my kid from failing? What advice would you give? What are the common problems you are noting in class? WHY ARE THEY ACTING THIS WAY? I am pretty sure most of the parents, if not all, want their child to succeed. They just (a) forget what it was like to be in high school surrounded by their peers, (b) remember too well and prefer not to revisit that time with their child, or (c) have no idea what it means to "help your child succeed."

My suggestion would be to have a monthly seminar for parents held at a church, a community center, or a central meeting place, either on the weekend or in the evening, for one hour, on what you can do (specifically) to help your child succeed. Topics might include how to help a child with homework, people at the school to contact for different services, free tutors and study services available in the area, one-on-one teacher meetings to discuss home culture vs. school culture and expectations, and resources for ESL parents and students.

Most of the parents I talk to have no idea what their children are learning, why they are learning it, what the discipline procedure is, or how to help. I am not saying that we should take over and be parents, but I think parents need some input on our school culture other than the obligatory open house once a year. We want our kids to be educated and be good citizens but we don't model what that means—getting involved in our community, working together to solve problems, and trying to bridge gaps in understanding and communication.

I know teachers are tired after school, but who said teachers had to run all the workshops? We could get people like community leaders or ministers to work with teachers to pull these kids and their parents in. We don't have to feel so isolated and pitted against one another. Yeah, it requires us to go into their communities, eat at their restaurants, and take an interest in what they do, but isn't that what we ask of them when they are in our class? We want them to be engaged, to ask questions. If we truly want these kids to succeed, then we need to go beyond the walls of the classroom and the school to get it done.

The education problem does not begin or end with our students, especially those who are failing or unmotivated. If we say the problem is the "parents" then why not try to find some solutions to the problem? Will every parent show? Of course not, but some may—the ones who realize teachers are trying to understand and create a community of diversity and different perspectives. Instead of repeating these useless conferences that aren't working, why not try something NEW (oh no, naive teacher idea again, doesn't she know that NEW is bad?) and see what happens?

~ Anne Marie

From: Professor Z

To: Anne Marie Bettencourt

Subject: Week 5, Day 2—Stickers?!!!

Hi, Anne Marie,

I'm with you. It takes a village to raise a child. One of the important differences that I have noticed between poorer urban schools and wealthy suburban schools is that kids in the wealthier schools are expected to go to college. Parents, teachers, friends, family, and television constantly reinforce these expectations. Kids who go to poorer urban schools do not always have these expectations pounded into them. In fact, many times they are being sent the message that college is *not* a place for them, they are *not* capable of getting accepted and they would *not* do well even if they somehow got in!

Many of these students do not have family members who have gone to college and can guide them through this experience or give them reasons why a college education is so important. In many cases, teachers hold biases and stereotypes and truly do not expect these urban kids to go to college. Many do not think they could make it in college, which creates a self-fulfilling prophecy for the students who might conclude that based on their teacher's attitudes and the grades and attention they receive from that teacher that it must be true that they truly are not college material. Many times, there is little extended-family support, and the media perpetuates the idea that urban kids typically don't go to college (but can succeed as athletes).

> .... **MINI TIP** ....
> Treat all students equally. See *How Teachers Communicate Appropriately Positive and High Expectations for Every Student* in today's Tips, Strategies, and Relevant Data section.

In fact, there is much we, as teachers, can do to rectify this situation. For example, research by Kerman (1979)[1] demonstrated that teachers who treat students equally help student achievement go up and keep the number of discipline problems and absentees down. Teachers in the study called on all students equally, gave equivalent feedback, and maintained positive verbal and nonverbal behavior. Again, it is important to look at your personal biases and the judgments you have made about your students. They might be getting in the way of your being a good teacher to some of your students.

My wife works in a school for Latina women who have dropped out of high school to have babies. In speaking with them, it became clear that NONE of them had ever been "prepped" for college in any way by the high school—the same high school that my daughter attended. While my daughter was put in SAT classes, had guidance counselors talk about college, had teachers refer to college, and was given guidance by sports coaches on getting into college, none of the Latina women had ever been told about college by anyone. Is this an example of racism and classism or what? Do the counselors really think that Latinos are not capable of going to college?

What is remarkable about the school my wife works in is that it not only helps the women complete their high school education, but it expects them to go to college. A tremendous percentage of them do! And many of them succeed. Imagine how different their lives would have been had they been encouraged in high school!

Yes, it takes a village to raise a child. And it takes teachers who are willing to encourage ALL children to be all they can be!

Regarding the stickers, who would've known? However, you should know that the jury is still out on using rewards like stickers and candy. Some research on intrinsic motivation (motivation arising from internal sources such as curiosity, enjoyment, and innate strivings for growth) and extrinsic motivation (motivation arising from the desire to get a reward, earn a high grade, please someone else) should be considered. Some research shows that when extrinsic motivation is used, learning becomes a means towards an end. The student believes his or her behavior is controlled by external rather than internal causes, which can reduce feelings of competence and self-determination.[2]

Early studies suggested that individuals are either intrinsically or extrinsically motivated to learn. However, current research suggests that for any given activity, one or both orientations may be at work.[3] I think it is important to consider that while stickers have some excellent qualities, they may harm a child's desire to learn for the sake of learning.

I have also been intrigued by the question of how much positive feedback to give students. I don't know if you are familiar with the work of Alfie Kohn (alfiekohn.org), but he has some very interesting points to make about the number of times a teacher says, "Good job," to his/her students. Some of his ideas are found in an excellent article in Young Children Journal titled, 5 *Reasons to Stop Saying "Good Job!"*[4]

His main points are that even though it is important to support, encourage, love, and/students hug and help them feel good about themselves, we should watch how often we praise them. I have even noticed that in my students' lesson plans, many will actually write, after an activity, to "praise the students for doing a great job." This is written in their lesson plan even though they have no idea how well the students will actually do on that activity! What if the students had done a terrible job? We know that one of the worst things we can do for a child's self-esteem is to tell him/her that they have done a good job when even the student knows that he/she didn't.

.... **MINI TIP** ....
Never praise a student when he/she doesn't deserve it.

The same is true in research on student teachers. As I mentioned before, one of the biggest complaints student teachers have is that they think their cooperating teacher (and sometimes the college supervisor) is trying to either protect them or not hurt their feelings by telling them that they did a good job on something when they know they did not. The result of trying to protect them is often the loss of trust and credibility. So, while I have spent much of my teaching career going by the theory that one can never give too much positive reinforcement, I now think we need to look more closely at how much we give and the repercussions of what we do.

Kohn brings up some other reasons why we should be careful about how much praise we give our students. He believes that it can be used to manipulate our students to get them to comply with our wishes. Since students are often longing for our approval, he believes that they will do what we praise them for simply to get that approval, which actually increases their dependence on the teacher. He argues that by saying "good job" all the time, teachers are telling students how to feel and, in fact, reminding them that they are constantly being judged (and many people don't like to be judged). He would rather hear his students tell him that they felt they did a good job than have them wait to hear from him whether it was or wasn't good.

He brings up a study done by Joan Grusec,[5] which showed that praise does, in fact, motivate kids. But it motivates them to get more praise at the expense of their commitment to do whatever it was they were doing that got the praise! Kohn seems to agree with Grusec and believes that maybe we should say nothing or just say what we saw ("You just got the highest mark in the class") to show the student that we noticed—or simply ask the student questions ("What was the hardest part about writing the paper and how did you figure out how to organize like you did?").

He ultimately points out that continually praising is a hard habit for many teachers to break because the teacher may feel that he/she is withholding something that would make the student feel good. He believes that many teachers say it because THEY need to say it rather than because the student really needs to hear it. He asks whether our reactions are helping the student to feel a sense of control over his/her life or to constantly look to us for approval.

While I don't always agree with Alfie Kohn, he is one of my favorite authors on the subject of education and he provokes us all to reconsider the ways we educate our children.

Prof Z

Tips, Strategies, and Relevant Data

How Teachers Communicate Appropriately Positive and High Expectations for Every Student

1. When you ask a question, call on all students equally to answer. Don't just call on the first students to raise their hands. Be aware of whether you are calling on boys more than girls, nonminorities more than minority students, high rather than low achievers, or high socioeconomic status over low socioeconomic status. Calling on all students shows that you believe that all students can learn and that you expect all students to learn.

2. When students cannot answer a question in front of the class, make sure you leave them with a "win." Ask follow-up questions until they are able to correctly answer at least one of the follow-up questions and then the original question. This shows that you expect all students to be able to answer questions.

3. When girls, minority students, or low achievers give incorrect answers, provide as much information about why their answers are incorrect as you would for boys, non-minority students, and high achievers. All students deserve a detailed explanation.

4. Make eye contact with all students and have your body facing individual students as you speak to them.

5. Periodically change seating arrangements in your classes so everyone gets a chance to be in the front at some point during the year. Move around the classroom as you teach so you are physically near your students as much as possible.

6. Take time to get to know each student. Ask them about their lives, their family, their special interests, or a recent accomplishment. Students will appreciate the individual attention they receive from you.[6]

DAY 3

From: Anne Marie Bettencourt

To: Professor Z

Subject: Week 5, Day 3—We Are Just Like Our Students

Regarding the stickers, I agree and disagree with you here. It has been my observation that many inner-city students have lower academic self-esteem than their more fortunate suburban peers. Most of my students have gotten 15-years' worth of explicit and implicit messages telling them they are failures both in and out of the classroom. This leads to tremendous feelings of doubt and resistance when they come across a teacher who pushes them and has higher expectations than all their previous teachers, as is the case with Mr. B and myself. Therefore, I think they need *more* praise, and stickers and rewards to get the ball rolling and get their confidence up initially. Once the students realize they can, in fact, perform at high levels, I would do away with stickers and work towards more intrinsic rewards.

I see it as a poker game. Many urban students come to the table with fewer chips to play with (in terms of resources, skills, and home lives) than their suburban counterparts. Therefore, our urban kids are going to take fewer risks and hold on to those chips more fiercely, since they have more at stake than their more affluent peers, who have a ton of chips (so a few risks won't result in a loss of all their chips at the table). By giving urban students praise and rewarding small accomplishments, we are adding to their poker pile. Eventually they will take those bigger risks, realizing that they've gained some chips and can afford to take more chances. Does that make sense?

I had an interesting realization today. As I was sitting and twirling on the "whirly" chair of my C and E classes, I realized that learning for adults really isn't that different from learning for kids. I was SO bored. My kids were writing their final drafts for a long composition, so I had to "spectate" and I was beside myself with boredom. I leaped from my chair when a student had a question or when a group of them asked to play the "word picture game thingy" that we did yesterday (rebuses). But it really hit home during my two college classes tonight. First off, I was sick, and therefore a most unwilling participant, and second, I was dead tired and bored.

It started in Professor A's class. He had this awesome game we played with poker chips—trading chips for points, and then organizing us into "you suck at life," "medium businessmen," and "apprentice material" groups based on the chips we acquired. It was a really interesting way to get us to think about how groups are arranged in society by unfair advantages. However, despite the awesome game, I did NOT want to play. I did anyway, but put minimal effort into my "trades" and thought, "OK great, I get the point of this, can we move on now, or can I just go to sleep?"

I was appalled at myself. If my students had done that, I would have killed them. "But I am SICK, and I am tiiiiiiired" I whined to myself in a futile attempt to rationalize my lack of participation. Usually I am the excited one who jumps at these things. Then

I thought, "Hrmmm, well my students could also be sick, or tired." I hope Professor A didn't take it personally. Light bulb! Why would I then take it personally if a student is just having an "off" day when I know I have planned a fun and exciting lesson (this is one student, not the whole class mind you, because then it's the lesson, totally)?

Then came last night's college class. I was contemplating skipping it altogether for the warm, snuggly bed I was napping in. But I went to class and we were reading obituaries and working on the writing process. Kara and I got there, looked at each other, and mouthed, "Why are we doing this?" to each other. One student wanted to read them all. Kara and I looked at him like he had three heads. Read them all? Whatever. I wasn't reading mine. I tried really hard not to doodle and to listen to what Professor A was saying about expanding our writing (I know it already. I teach it to my own students. Tell me something I DON'T know that I can use please.).

Then, we had to brainstorm. OH MY GOD. I wanted to shoot myself in the head. I HATE brainstorming. And we had no fun markers, or pencils, or graphic organizers to play with. Why brainstorm? I know what to do, just let me write. I stifled a groan and made feeble attempts to do my work. This was NOT fun.

I stopped and looked at Kara and said, "We are so our students today." We both burst out laughing once we realized what we were doing—complaining, zoning out, being bored. I was so not focused it wasn't funny. If you could have juxtaposed the way we, mature adults interested in education as a serious profession, were acting next to my class of ninth grade immature goofballs, you would have seen ZERO difference in the behavior. I was so quick to get frustrated with the behavior of "immature" students until I realized that I was doing the exact same thing they were. I was trying so hard not to laugh at my own actions after this realization.

That was until Laura, another student in the class, spoke to me about her brainstorming and what she wanted to be known for in her obituary. "So can I say I am great in bed? I want to be known for that." And with that, I was out of my bored slump and off writing my eulogy and trying not to fall off my chair laughing. Note to self: Humor goes a long way in the classroom and behavioral issues are not always the result of the students' ages.

This made me think I should let the students talk. It may give them some ideas and get them out of their slump. Now, I realize I am an adult and can tell when I get off track and can get back on track. But I thought it was interesting that we are so quick to judge our students and shake our heads and call them "irresponsible," "immature," and "lazy" and yet, given a similar scenario, I and other graduate students sometimes do the EXACT same thing. And it wasn't the class, and it wasn't the teacher. I was just tired that day.

Our students get tired too, and sick, and bored. So, I learned that activities need to be changed up at least once or twice during an hour period, that talking definitely helps (occasionally), and that despite my "off" day, I needed to realize that the work had to get done. Thank GOD my professors walked around or kept conversation going to make sure we stayed on task.

Since it was so interesting to play "student" for the day (and quite a humorous eye opener—I was tempted to make paper footballs), I suggest we have our students play "teacher" occasionally and then have them reflect on what they learned. And when they "teach," I will talk loudly, interrupt, apologize, talk again, and be as unmerciful as they are to me. We can all learn something once we are on the other side of the fence.

On another note, I am learning that teaching is like dieting, or (to use a more p.c. term—adopting a healthier lifestyle). You have to go slow, and learn one new thing at a time. If you try too many new things at once, you burn out and say screw it to the treadmill, and hello to the ice cream. Student teaching, however, is like putting someone who just started Weight Watchers in a buffet style restaurant. It is IMPOSSIBLE to focus on that one goal when there are so many things to try! Let me explain how this relates to teaching (I swear, it does).

Rafe Esquith is an amazing elementary school teacher in the LA Unified School District at Hobart Elementary School. He wrote a book on urban teaching, and he got George Bush's medal for the arts for his work with his students, including having them stage a yearly Shakespearian play. I was lucky enough to meet him several years ago. When I mentioned to him how amazed I was to see this well-orchestrated class in action, he gave me one pointer: "Do one thing at a time."

First, he told me, he worked on getting his reading instruction down to a science. Then, he focused on getting better science lessons. He said that if he had tried to perfect everything his first year of teaching, he would have gone nuts.

Awesome, I thought, it's the Flex Points system for new teachers. During your first year, you get so many points for classroom management. During your third year, you get points for nailing writing paragraphs. I think that makes sense. You can be a teacher forever and always have something to finesse. But tackling one issue at a time will keep you sane. Then you don't overload yourself or set unrealistic goals by trying to have a perfect everything. THEN I was introduced to student teaching, the buffet of education.

As student teachers, we are expected to try new things DAILY. We have graphic organizers, cooperative learning, stickers, posters, group work, solo work, direct instruction, and progressive teaching. Case in point—Mr. B handed me a book (I can't remember the name of it) on standards-based teaching that was the length of an atlas and the width of a phonebook. I was excited and hopped on my bed at home to pore through it. A half hour later, I was dizzy from all the suggestions, comments, facts, and ideas on assessment, planning, products, quizzes, and questions contained in the book. Like the buffet, they all looked so good, I didn't know which one to try first, and then of course, I wanted to try them all.

In my head, my day looked like this: While I am sending kids to Mr. S, the assistant principal, I will do direct instruction based on what I just read in that book. OK, but before I do that I have to build my lesson according to these 20 questions, and then I can incorporate multiple intelligences, and then worry about putting some higher order thinking in there, and I mustn't forget to check for gum chewing and watch interactions with behaviorally challenged students. That includes checking for understanding, modeling, and assessing all at once, too.

Student teachers get all kinds of advice on what to do and what not to do, but I think the one thing we don't hear enough is to SLOOOOOOOOOW down and focus on one thing at a time. Week one, work on nailing classroom management. Week two, work on getting that vocabulary lesson up to par. Week three, try out some cooperative learning activities. Otherwise, like the dieters, we get burnt out, fizzled, and ready to give up, convinced we just can't do it. I think we need a nutritional education program for new teachers where we encourage them to really think about the things that are important to them, and work on them, one at a time.

~ Anne Marie

From: Professor Z

To: Anne Marie Bettencourt

Subject: Week 5, Day 3—We Are Just Like Our Students

Hi, Anne Marie,

What a great realization—that you were being your students! You could relate to being sick and tired and not wanting to do work. Yet, you realized that the teacher was doing all the right things to keep you on task (getting you talking, walking around and checking your work, and coming up with interesting activities).

What a great lesson. Now you know not to take it personally if some lessons don't go over with some kids. There are many reasons why your lesson might or might not work that have nothing to do with you or the lesson. However, by preparing well and using good teaching skills, you have the best chance of getting your students motivated regardless of their situation.

With that said, I want you to know that I believe it is still your responsibility to get students motivated no matter what. While you could hold the philosophy that "you can lead a horse to water, but you can't make it drink," I prefer to hold myself accountable for getting students motivated and participating in the work. If I acted out of the horse and water philosophy, it would be just too easy to blame the kids and take away my responsibility in the matter. My job is to teach the kids—not just the "easy" kids but also the "tough" kids. It is my job to figure out how to do that for all children. So, if I see a student not working or not motivated (like you and Kara), I would take actions to get you going and hopefully not stop until you are working.

Point well taken that new teachers are inundated with so many things to try, books to read, etc. that it is good self-advice to say, "Slow down." I like your idea that new teachers should try to work new things in at an appropriate pace and not try to do it all at the same time. But what method/practice should they work on first?

Once my students are in the classroom I always recommend that they work on three main areas first: (1) Learning rules for the classroom, and consequences for not following them, (2) Establishing positive relationships with the students, and (3) creating effective lesson plans.

I know this is a tall order and that you will most likely have to learn a lot of this in a short amount of time. However, I think my order of priorities might help in organizing how much of an emphasis you put into each area during this particularly tough part of the learning curve!

The bottom line is that in order to become an extraordinary teacher, you not only have to work hard but you also have to work smart. Good teaching takes a lot of work. But I agree that it is important to not try to do TOO much at once.

I also like your poker game analogy of why you feel it is fine to give stickers and rewards to your students. I think you are doing the right thing in this situation. It seems to be working and is needed at the moment. Go for it!

Prof Z

Tips, Strategies, and Relevant Data

How to Organize Your Priorities as a New Student Teacher

1. *Learn the Rules of the Classroom and the Consequences of Breaking Them, and be Consistent in Enforcing Them:* Without a good system of classroom management, very little learning will go on. The learning environment must be a safe and supportive for kids to learn. No

matter how good a teacher you are, you cannot teach in chaos. Work on classroom management skills as one of your first priorities.

2. *Establish Positive Relationships with the Students:* Find out as much as you can about them. This is important for several reasons. They want to know that you care about them and are interested in them. You need to know about them so that you can relate the material to their needs and experiences.

3. *Create Powerful Lesson Plans:* Good lesson planning is the key to good teaching. Be creative in coming up with lessons that are student-centered and relevant to the lives of the students, and that involve good content and critical thinking. Know where you can find help in creating good lessons (the web, teacher's guides, etc.) so that you don't have to re-create the wheel each time. Besides, if the lesson is a good one, students will want to participate and will not be tempted to cause discipline problems.

DAY 4

From: Anne Marie Bettencourt

To: Professor Z

Subject: Week 5, Day 4—Go Ahead and Make My Day

I have two kids in my E period class who I am absolutely fed up with—Chefon and Wilson. Wilson is Mr. Mouth. He won't do any work, but he can come up with ten thousand lines, excuses, jokes, or comments to get me off track. Then, when I discipline him, he refuses to do any work whatsoever. Either way it's a losing battle for me. He talks to all my other students, and no matter what, he is bent on not working. Chefon, is a sassy ninth-grade repeater with self-esteem on the floor. She'll roll her eyes, get cocky, and say, "I don't care," and has informed me more than once that she is perfectly content working at McDonald's and getting that paycheck. Little does she know how expensive rent and groceries are. So, she is content to scrape by, not do the work, and talk in class. And, if I discipline her, same thing, no work either way.

Lately, I've noticed that I have started waiting for them to screw up so I can pounce on them. I am not sure if it is a combination of the stresses I've been having in my personal life (let's not go there) or my consistent efforts to get them on track and failing to do so. But in the past three days or so I have snapped at them or shrugged my shoulders and muttered things under my breath about not caring if they fail or not. I can't seem to control them no matter what I do. And it is pissing me off. Wilson is a doofus, a clown, a goofball. I've tried making him class helper and giving him positive attention, but he blew that the first day by making comments to students and writing on the board. I tried putting him in the hallway and he walked off. He gets in-house detention and now he is failing because he is missing four assignments, which I can BET he won't come to me to make up.

What has happened? I'm that teacher who has pegged two of my students as "problems!" I hate those teachers! And I certainly do not want them to fail, and I really wish Chefon would pull her grades back up to the A− she had first term, which slipped to a D− second term, and now a D−/F with me. Wilson's mom is no help, and that goes double for Chefon's. So, I am on my own with these two. I am ready to give up—another thing I swore I would never do.

But honestly, I am sick of fighting them. I fight outside of school with my own stuff and now I am fighting daily with them. I am ready to say to them, "Listen, do you want to fail? Fine with me. Get out and don't come back until you are ready to chill out and work and get your head in the game. I want you in this class, but obviously you don't want to be here. So fail. It isn't my life. I HAVE a degree." Now, I am sure that is *not* a good attitude for a new student teacher to have, so I need to figure out how to become positive about this, fast. I need some new strategies.

When I say, "I think Wilson and Chefon are going to fail and they're OK with that," even Mr. B just shrugs his shoulders now and nods. "Yeah, well, sometimes that happens," he said to me. How much chasing do you do as a teacher before you throw up your hands and say, "I give up?" When *do* you give up on a student?

I hate the way that sounds, but I am trying to meet them halfway, and getting garbage out of them. What do I do? How do I solve this problem? Is it solvable or are they going to get big fat F's now? I am tired of hearing, "I'm not doing work in this class. No, I don't feel like being here today, this class is boring." (On a day when my whole class is cutting out life-size portraits of each other, painting, laughing, and listening to music.) "Whatever Miss, I am not doing this work." Short of putting pens in their hands and writing for them, I am not sure what my options are.

~ Anne Marie

From: Professor Z

To: Anne Marie Bettencourt

Subject: Week 5, Day 4—Go Ahead and Make My Day

Dear Anne Marie,

While you tell me bits and pieces about the students, I am not sure whether you have met with them one on one and asked them what they need. Teaching is about relationship, and relationship is built upon good communication. You need to take the time to talk with students individually to find out what they need and to tell them what you need.

I have no problem with making deals with kids so we both get what we want. If they want to be left alone, you can leave them alone as long as they do their work and are quiet so others are not disturbed. If they want to be called on more in class, that can be done as long as they raise their hands and do it appropriately so they do not disrupt your class.

Would it be easier to just keep kicking them out than to spend more time working on the problem? Possibly. But I do not believe in ever giving up on a student. Sometimes students are testing you to see if you will finally give up on them

.... **MINI TIP** ....
Meet with students individually to ask what they need to be successful.

and then they can say, "Hah, I knew you'd give up on me, just like everyone else." I basically tell them I will never give up on them, but they've got to meet me part of the way. Granted, I don't have your students, but I still feel that our job involves never giving up.

I do know that every student has "keys" that will open them up for learning, and that it is the teacher's job to find the right ones. It seems clear that these students don't see that what you are teaching them is going to help them in their lives.

Keep trying! Find those keys. You might be the one who makes the difference in their lives!

Prof Z

.... **MINI TIP** ....
You need to help students create a vision of what their lives are all about and show them how the content or the skills learned in your course will help them achieve their goals. See *Professor Z's Ideas on How to Sell Students on the Importance of Your Course* in today's Tips, Strategies, and Relevant Data section.

Tips, Strategies, and Relevant Data

Professor Z's Ideas on How to Sell Students on the Importance of Your Course

A common complaint of student teachers (and teachers) is that the students don't care about school or about the course they are teaching. Students complain of boredom and want to know why they have to learn the subject being taught. Here is how to address the issue.

1. *Students will not work hard if they do not see the point of learning the material.* It is up to you to "sell" your course to the students. They have to see how they need the content/skills/attitudes learned in the class in order to get something they want, like a good job, good grades, to get into a good college, or to obtain a skill.

   For example, I start off my Multicultural Teacher Education course using activities that bring out the various stereotypes and biases my students each hold about people of other socioeconomic classes, races, genders, sexual orientations, and so forth. Generally, my students are unaware that they actually hold these biases. I ask them to describe different teachers they have had who exhibited biases towards a particular group of students. Then I ask them to describe their reactions to these teachers. Generally, they hated these teachers because they did not think they were fair to all students and they lost respect for them.

   I ask them how they would be able to give each of their students an equal education if they hold biases of which they aren't even aware. They realize that they do not want to be a teacher who is seen as unfair and that this course will help them become the type of teacher they want to be. Once they are sold on what they will learn in the class, they are more likely to work hard in it.

2. *Do activities with your students in which they can "design their future" and see how doing well in your course and in school in general will help them achieve their goals in life.* I once observed a middle school teacher who had his students design the type of life they wanted by using classified ads. He asked students where they wanted to live when they got older. Students then used the classified ads to see how much houses cost in the area they wanted to live in and what their monthly payments would be. He asked what kind of car they wanted to drive and then had them look at the cost of cars and how much their monthly payments would be. He asked if they wanted

cable TV, air conditioning, and a pool, and if they were going to have children, pay for their college, and eat out a lot.

For each of these needs or wants, students would determine how much money they would need to earn to live the lifestyle of their choice. Then, they would look at the salaries of the jobs they wanted to get. For the sake of the assignment, they were not allowed to choose to be a professional athlete or rock star, given the statistics on how few people ever get to live this lifestyle.

The teacher would ask the students what they thought they would have to do to get the job they wanted. Most answered that college was necessary. The teacher would then ask what they need to do to get into college. Students would respond that they would need good grades. He would then have them examine their report cards to see if they would be eligible for different colleges. Many would see that they needed to do better and work harder on their studies if they wanted to get into a college that would allow them to get the job they wanted.

3. *Make sure you make your course relevant to your student's lives.* English teachers need to sell students on the importance of learning how to read and write. They must demonstrate how these skills are needed to do well in whatever profession they choose. They should also be shown how their failure to learn the skills and material will present serious roadblocks to their future.

Social studies teachers need to help their students understand the importance of becoming active democratic citizens. This needs to be done differently at different ages. For some, it might be how to avoid making the mistakes of the past by being good and active citizens (you must give specific examples that students can relate to here). For others, it might be how our democracy might be taken over by special interest groups if citizens do not get involved.

Math teachers need to show their students how math is used in numerous ways throughout every day. They need to see that they will use math to calculate how much money they need to make and how to save and borrow money wisely, how to finance houses and cars, how not to be taken advantage of by others, and how it is used in numerous fields such as engineering and medicine.

Science, health, and physical education teachers need to help their students understand the importance of knowing how their bodies work, so that they can live healthier and happier lives. They must also help students understand the importance of having a sustainable planet and of preserving nature.

Teachers of art and music must help their students understand the importance of music and art in our lives as a means of expression, enjoyment, and mental and motor skills.

4. *Every teacher must be able to answer the common student question, "Why do we have to learn this stuff?"* It seems like this would be an easy question to answer, but it is not. In fact, if you are unable to answer this question when a student asks you (and they will!), you will dig yourself into a hole that might be very difficult to get out of. Why should the students learn the material when even the teacher doesn't know why it is important to learn?

You need to form strong and compelling answers to this question. Students will not buy into a stock answer like "The reason we need to learn Social Studies is to prevent making the same mistakes we made in the past." The teacher must give relevant examples to make the point. A teacher might say, "How many of you have a friend or relative who is fighting in Iraq? How could a better knowledge of history have told us more of the serious problems we might face by getting involved like we did in Iraq?"

Answering this question strongly fortifies your own convictions on the subject. When I first started teaching, I was not driven by the importance of creating active democratic citizens. To me, social studies was simply learning many names, dates, and places because that is what was supposed to be taught in social studies. There was no higher purpose in learning the material.

Now, I am quite clear to my students that if we are to continue to thrive as a democracy, we need teachers who can help create good citizens. By itself, this gives me all the reason I need to keep teaching and to excel in it. It is something I am passionate about. Every teacher needs to find the purpose of teaching his or her subject matter that makes him/her passionate about the subject. I cannot emphasize this enough.

DAY 5

From: Anne Marie Bettencourt

To: Professor Z

Subject: Week 5, Day 5—I (Used to) Love Fridays

Ugh. It is Friday and my red light went ON. And so did I. I took it all out on my C period class. And I was all excited for C period too! I had a game planned, and it tied in nicely with the open responses we had been working on. And it was Friday. Who doesn't love

Fridays? Then the class actually started. It took FOREVER to get to the actual game.

I had side commentary going on while I was trying to talk, so I stopped, and waited, and waited. And I did this several times (mistake numero uno). I warned, and warned, and warned (mistake numero dos) because I desperately wanted Friday to end on a good note, with a fun game and a happy class. But it just wasn't happening.

My repeated requests of "Stop talking," "Keisha, knock it off," and "Quan, enough" went ignored. So at 2:15 I had had ENOUGH. Of course now I was pissed at myself for having let it get that bad and at them for ignoring me. So I had Quan write on the board an assignment for the class: a "two-page essay on why talking keeps teachers from teaching and students from learning." This, of course, led to more talking and buzz. So I waited. I tore into them. Quietly, and calmly of course, but I let them have it. I gave them a two-minute spiel on being respectful and I apologized to the other students for having to take a hit because of their peers. And wouldn't you know in the middle of my spiel, of my saucy six (Quan, Christina, Tanissa, Tony, Keisha, and Wil) at least THREE continued to smirk, or laugh, or mutter!

Of all the things that piss me off, having a student smirk or laugh at me gets under my skin the most. I upped the assignment to three pages. I told them that if it wasn't done, they would have a detention with me. Tanissa glared, Christina smirked. "I don't care if you love me or you hate me all semester long," I said calmly, "but you will NOT interfere with other students' learning in this class, and you WILL succeed in here if I have to call your mom every single day in order for it to happen. You think it's a joke? We will see who is laughing when parent conferences come up next week."

I was ripped. But I still ended class with "have a good weekend!" Then I went upstairs to the teacher's room and let out a growl of frustration. I asked the wise and all-knowing Mr. G what to do. He is an absolute knight in shining armor. "Have you tried having Mr. S come in and talk to them yet? Or sending them right to his office? He would be more than happy to talk to the class, and he won't want to see them after that, so he won't be lenient if they get to his office."

AHA! Next week, I am going to ask him to speak to my class. Mr. S is the assistant principal for our grade, and he is a force to be reckoned with. When he walks into a hallway or room, talking ceases immediately. While he has come in to pull out individual students for discipline issues in other classes, I have never asked him to come and speak with my entire class before. I was running out of my own ammunition and needed to call in the big guns here.

Since Mr. B told me I couldn't have multiple kids in the hall (I had three last week at once), the new plan of attack is to send students off to Mr. S's office after one warning. But what about, "That's not fair, everyone else is doing it, why are you punishing me?" comments? "You've got to start somewhere," Mr. G argued, "and tell them to worry about themselves, or tell them that may be the case, but you are starting with that individual."

I am really tired of trying to be nice. Nice has gotten me nowhere. They want structure? They'll get it. They want rules? They'll get them. And so help me, the first person to dare attempt to tread on me next week in that class is in for a very RUDE awakening. Even better, I am determined to do it smiling or laughing, which only makes them angrier. Get under my skin? I don't THINK so! You might know how I am feeling, but I will never let THEM know! ☺

On the good side, I think I struck a chord with Akeem. He is my talk talk, talk, talk, comment, respond, etc. student in E period. He's got to put on a show and likes to be the center of attention. I love him to pieces, but he knows it and he gets away with murder in my class. So, I thought positively, "Now how can I turn his need for attention into a good thing for ME?"

I read your opinions on making deals with students and wondered what I could do with Akeem. Lo and behold, he and I came up with an idea. I am going to let him be class helper for the week—take attendance, write on the board, give out stickers, etc. in exchange for his silence when I request it. His eyes lit up when I mentioned this little deal to him. I don't think Edison could have come up with brighter bulbs. "You mean it? Miss, I want this in writing" (even better, because now I can nail his signature on it). I thought he would have scoffed at the idea and acted like "this is SO lame, whatever" but he was actually interested.

Again, it's experimental and it may very well backfire, but it is worth a shot. On the plus side, Mr. G did remind us that we student teachers were in a tough spot with the students, coming in the middle of someone's class and redoing the rules and methods. He said that if we could do this successfully, we really could teach anywhere and that some of the problems would disappear when we had our own classrooms next year. Cross your fingers on that one!

~ Anne Marie

From: Professor Z

To: Anne Marie Bettencourt

Subject: Week 5, Day 5—I (Used to) Love Fridays

Hi, Anne Marie,

I agree with Mr. G. You have several things working against you as a student teacher. First, you are a new teacher, and you are bound to make new teacher mistakes. These mistakes tend to put you in a hole that you need to dig out of. Second, you are taking over a class from another teacher who possibly has different values, rules, and consequences. Plus, kids don't always respond well to change. I agree that when you have your own class, you will be creating the rules and consequences that YOU want and will consistently uphold.

Additionally, you will have learned lessons from experiences like the ones you are now going through. As we've discussed, it takes a while to find your groove. Once you find it, you will be home free. Keep trying out different techniques. Some will work and others won't.

This is what student teaching is for—to try things out, and make lots of mistakes and learn from them before you get your own class.

.... **MINI TIP** ....
Don't be afraid to make mistakes while student teaching. If you don't take risks, you won't grow as a teacher.

One of the techniques for getting students quiet is called "Stopping the Action." We may have discussed this before but I wanted to remind you that it can be a very effective way to keep your class in control.

You know what to do. It is just a matter of doing it. You know that constant warnings get you nowhere. You need to have fair rules and uphold them consistently, such as one warning and you suffer the stated consequences the next time I speak to you. Once students know that you will be fair and consistent (you WILL kick them out after their first warning with no "second, third or fourth chances"), they

.... **MINI TIP** ....
Use the strategy of "Stopping the Action" to keep your class in control. See *How to Get a Class Quiet— Stopping the Action* in today's Tips, Strategies, and Relevant Data section.

will stop testing you. Also, with the right student, deals can be made that work. We shall see if Akeem is one of those kids. Try it out and see how it goes with him.

Best wishes,

Prof Z

Tips, Strategies, and Relevant Data

How to Get a Class Quiet—Stopping the Action

Situation: The class is busy on a group assignment and you need to stop them to move on to the next part of the lesson. How do you get their attention? Stop the Action!

1. Announce—In a nice, loud, and enthusiastic voice say, "Okay everybody. You have 30 seconds to finish up! Thirty seconds!
2. Second Announcement—In a nice, loud, and enthusiastic voice say, "You have 10 seconds. Let's go! Come on, group number two and group number three!"
3. Cheerlead—In a nice, loud, and enthusiastic voice say, "Time is up. Let's move on. Please sit down, get out your responses."
4. Cheerlead with Names—Lower your voice and tone a little and say, "Let's go, Bill. Susan, please sit down. Sharon, please take out your notes."
5. (If still not completely quiet) Time to Get Serious—In a low, more stern voice, say, "Bill, let's go. Susan, I will not ask you again. Sharon, come on."
6. Once it is completely quiet, look around the room, count to 5 (to yourself) and slowly and in a low voice begin the next part of the activity. The key is to wait 5 seconds. It might seem like a long time but it will assure you that student conversations will be over. By speaking in a low voice, it will be easy to hear if a student begins to talk again. This whole process should take less than one minute.

Discussion Starters for Week Five

1. How realistic is it for Miss B to say she will "have classroom management down" by the end off her placement?

2. Do you agree with Professor Z's advice to Miss B that for her final observation she should pretend he is not there? To what degree do you think you should teach for the supervisor?

3. How do you think the teacher-parent meeting could have been more productive? What would you do?

4. Given the research on intrinsic and extrinsic motivation, to what degree will you use rewards (like stickers or candy) in your classroom?

5. Do you agree with the statement, "We can never give our students enough praise"?

6. To what degree is it the responsibility of the teacher to have students learn? Is it enough for the teacher to "lead the horse to water" or is the teacher also responsible for making the "horse" drink?

7. When do you feel it is appropriate to give up on a child if he/she seems to not want to learn?

8. To what degree would you be willing to "make deals" with students? Give some examples of deals you would make and ones that you would not.

9. How did your best teachers deal with discipline problems? Give specific examples.

10. Did any of your teachers give out candy or stickers? Do you think it is an effective way to motivate students? What are the drawbacks to using this method?

☑ Professor Z's Student Teaching Checklist

Things to Remember to Do During Your Placement: Give some thought to each of these questions. If you need work on some, think about what you must do so that you will be prepared.

1. ___Are you collecting artifacts for your portfolio?

2. ___After you teach a lesson, are you reflecting on it and writing suggestions for how you could improve upon it the next time it is taught?

3. ___Are you writing letters home to parents telling them about special projects and activities that you will be doing? Invite them in to participate. Also, let them know when their children are doing well and when they are struggling.

4. ___Have you videotaped yourself teaching? Watch the video. Reflect on what you like and what needs improvement. Remember, you might need to get permission to videotape in certain schools.

5. ___Have you asked your students for written feedback on your teaching?

6. ___Have you been keeping track of your hours in the classroom?

7. ___Have you thought about who might be willing to give you a recommendation at the end of the placement?

8. ___Have you invited the principal of the school into your class to observe you?

9. ___Have you tried many of the teaching strategies learned in your methods course?

10. ___Have you collaborated with any other teachers (besides your cooperating teacher) on a lesson?

11. ___Have you become proficient in taking attendance, computing grades for report cards, etc.?

12. ___Have you attended student extra-curricular activities like games and plays?

13. ___Have you communicated with parents?

14. ___Have you attended community events?

15. ___Have you sat in on a team meeting dealing with a student's IEP?

Endnotes

1. Kerman, S. (1979). Teacher expectations and student achievement. *Phi Delta Kappan, 60,* 70–72.

2. Meece, J. L. (1997). *Child and adolescent development for educators.* New York: McGraw-Hill.

3. Harter, S., Whitesell, N.R., & Kowalski, P. (1992). Individual differences in the effects of educational transitions on young adolescents' perceptions of competence and motivational orientation. *American Educational Research Journal, 29,* 777–807.

4. Kohn, A. (2001, September). 5 reasons to stop saying "good job!" *Young Children Journal.*

5. Grusec, J.E. (1991). Socializing concern for others in home. *Developmental Psychology, 227,* 338–342.

6. Kauchak, D. P., & Eggen, P. D. (2007). *Learning and teaching: Research-based methods* (p. 131). Boston: Pearson/Allyn & Bacon.

WEEK SIX

"Any genuine teaching will result, if successful, in someone's knowing how to bring about a better condition of things than existed earlier."

JOHN DEWEY

Day 1: Ninth-Grade Goofballs
Acting Like a Real Teacher, Teacher Issues (Taking Things Personally, Wanting to Be Liked, Confidence, and Feeling Overwhelmed), Being a Reflective Practitioner, Teacher Expectations

Day 2: This Is MY Class!
Connecting with Students, Classroom Management, Teacher-Student Relationships, Teacher Issues (Attitude), Using Student Feedback

Day 3: The Way It Is and the Way It Ought to Be
Politics of Education, School Resources, Teacher Issues (Goal Setting, and Attitude), Curriculum

Day 4: Helping Students Create Life Goals
Advising Students, Teacher-Student Relationships

Day 5: Success Is 80% Attitude
Developing a Positive Attitude, Teacher Issues (Attitude and Philosophy)

Discussion Starters for Week Six
Professor Z's Student Teaching Checklist

Topics Discussed This Week

In this chapter, you will learn

1. The difference between being liked and being respected (and how you can be both).
2. How to deal with confidence issues by not taking everything personally.
3. How to turn the "negative conversations" in your head into positive ones.
4. How to create good relationships with students.
5. The importance of soliciting student feedback.
6. How to incorporate your philosophy of teaching into your curriculum.
7. How to prepare students for standardized tests.
8. How to teach "outside the box."
9. How to deal with students who threaten suicide.
10. How to keep a positive attitude in a sea of negativity.

DAY 1

From: Anne Marie Bettencourt

To: Professor Z

Subject: Week 6, Day 1—Ninth-Grade Goofballs

Thank GOD it's a snow day! I just need some time to reflect on all that is happening. I need a break! For the past week, someone has sent the Angel of Hell on Earth to visit me in my classroom, my seminar, and my life. Even though there were some good things that happened in the classroom, it ended up as a most frustrating, disappointing, and disheartening week. I put up the white flag all weekend. I hid under the covers, turned on the TV, cried myself to sleep miserably, and let my brain go on "standby" for a couple of days.

And here I am writing a journal on a day when there is no school! But I do find these journals a great way to get things off my chest. I am just sitting here thinking about my life as a teacher. I know I am committed to it and I know I have the skills to become a good teacher, but it is HARD!

I keep thinking about my troubles with discipline. I think about how my kids have been acting for the past few days. My first thoughts were, "I am going to kill my students. How DARE they not behave well! I can't wait to yell and be mean, since they are mean to me." I pictured myself going on a tirade: "You know at Cathedral High (a local

Catholic school) they don't act like this. They have *respect*. They actually *try* at their work. They aren't *rude*. They don't blatantly misbehave. And if they misbehave, they are sneaky about it! Here, let me teach you how you can be sneaky . . . " and then, in spite of myself, I started to laugh. Teach them how to be sneaky? I should be so thankful that they are honest enough to do it in front of my face! And in reality, that is what makes them so cute and adorable, because they are so open, even on the days they drive me up a wall.

The guys really aren't too bad. They gripe, and then they leave. The girls—well now, they are another story. I *hate* the ones that talk back to me. And when they throw in that "Miss Thang" attitude, I am two seconds away from pinning them to a wall, smiling ever so sweetly, and in a whisper saying, "DO. NOT. MESS. WITH. ME. I know this game. I have played it and can play it better than you. I will kill you and no one will ever find your body. Do you understand? Excellent, now get in there and get some work done."

And why do I let them upset me so? Because I take it all personally. In my mind I am thinking, "Hey wait a minute. I am fun. I am trying to mix up class a bit. I am understanding. And you are *walking on me* for it! I don't yell. I don't glare. And I don't kick you out before you can talk. So why do you treat me this way?" And then I realized the problem . . . I AM TAKING IT PERSONALLY.

Clearly, it isn't a personal affront directed at me. They are, as Mr. B puts it, "Ninth-grade goofballs." Of *course* they are going to talk, and tease each other, and groan about writing essays. I turned to myself and said (to myself) "You are an idiot. Are you teaching college literature? No. Most of these kids have been told from day one that they can't write and they stink at school. On top of this, they have had many horrible teachers who have kept pushing these negative stereotypes on them. You think that your coming in here for seven weeks is miraculously going to give them stunning confidence and that they will start to beg for harder essays to write and love coming to school? Sister, YOU are the one being ridiculous, not your students."

And even more clear to me is that my insecurity with my own ability to teach and with understanding why the material is important is coming across to my students. Why should they feel like the material is important when even I am not sure why we are teaching this stuff to them at times? I also wonder why I am so afraid to piss my students off when THEY are the ones who are not following MY rules and who are disrupting MY classroom?

Well, I guess I want them to like me! I want to have that class full of laughing students joking about literature and puns, and then posing challenging questions to each other about the things they read. I want students who are self-directed, and who do things without being asked, because Miss B asked for it, and since she rocks, it's going to get done. Simply put, it is supreme lack of confidence in myself as a person and my abilities as a teacher.

OK, so I have the answers, but no solutions. I know what it is that is causing me to let my students run over me occasionally (or every other C period), but I have no ideas (yet) as to how I can overcome this. It was good, though, to talk to the other student teachers having similar problems at the school. It seems we all feel the same way: We don't fully see ourselves as teachers yet. We know we are still learning and we aren't confident in our field, so we make more concessions to our students because we are not so secure. We also feel frustrated by the curriculum, and aren't entirely excited about what we are teaching sometimes. So, of course, we understand kids who are bored or acting out because we would be, too!

I wonder how the male teachers feel. Maybe our problem is that we women have way too much empathy for our students. Maybe we are more insecure in the classrooms, because men are used to being in charge. As a result, maybe we are letting kids get away with murder. I feel like I am borrowing somebody's classroom, and I think that the kids know it, too. So it sounds like this, "OK, we both know I am in training. You students are the guinea pigs and you obviously know that I don't REALLY know what I am doing, so just cut me some slack and I will do the same for you."

That is it. That is why I am afraid to piss the kids off. I am afraid of them turning around and saying "Well, it isn't like you KNOW what you are doing anyway. You aren't a real teacher. You are just practicing and clearly you don't have it together yet, so why are you on MY case?" Now, if you have a solution to that, I would be highly interested in hearing it. But can you solve insecurity or do you just have to outgrow it? If it is the latter, then it may take some time before I really get the class I want. I know what I want, I just don't think I have earned that class yet and perhaps that is why I don't have it.

~ Anne Marie

From: Professor Z

To: Anne Marie Bettencourt

Subject: Week 6, Day 1—Ninth-Grade Goofballs

Dear Anne Marie,

First, I am honored that you write these journal entries to me. Yes, I know you *have* to write journal entries, but you certainly do not have to go to the length that you do. And I have *never* had anyone write a journal on a day off from school! I also feel privileged that you share your feelings with me, and I am delighted that the journal process is a good one for you. Thanks for your trust.

Bottom line: I totally understand where you are coming from. I could have written much of this myself a few decades ago! I have a few suggestions for you. Some of these I have mentioned before but this might be a good time to say them quickly again:

1. Fake it till you make it! Even though you *are* a student teacher, try to act the way an experienced teacher would act. Pick a teacher who represents someone you would like to emulate. Be your version of them. Do what they would do. Say what they would say but in your own words. Put yourself into that mindset. Try to feel as secure and confident as they seem to be. So, you think the kids can see right through you? Show them a woman who is in charge and is confident, yet someone who is willing to learn from failure and success.

2. So you are unsure of your ability to maintain discipline? Remember my "red light theory." Whenever something is happening in your class that you don't like, stop it! I'm sure you've got a little red light that goes on in your head and a voice that says, "This should not be happening." New teachers will *think about* taking an action for a long time, contemplating all the reasons for and against taking an action. My red light theory says that you must train yourself to recognize the red light the minute it goes on and then take immediate action ("No talking over there while I am talking! Please sit down!"). Create a classroom atmosphere that is exactly the way *you* want it—not just the way you think the *students* want it. And do it with the "look" in your eyes that asks them if they really want to mess with you (because they would have to be *crazy* to do that).

3. Continue to talk to other teachers about what classroom management strategies work for them. It would be particularly helpful for you to shadow some of the students you are having problems with for the day to see how other teachers deal with them.

4. Not to get too "new agey" on you, but remember that your interpretations of classroom interactions are just that—*your* interpretations. They are not real! They can be changed to empower you if you want them to. When I was a younger teacher, I can remember going into classes and looking at the students and thinking, "They don't want to be here. They hate me. They hate my class. They are bored. Blah, blah, blah." But that was just my personal interpretations of them. If I had acted out of this interpretation, I can assure you that the students would have seen a suppressed, paranoid teacher who was *not* having a lot of fun. How to stop this negative cycle? I had to remind myself that the

.... **MINI TIP** ....

Ask other teachers about the methods of classroom management that they use successfully. See *How to Develop Successful Classroom Management Strategies* in today's Tips, Strategies, and Relevant Data section.

interpretation I had created was simply a negative interpretation and that it really didn't work for me to be acting out of that interpretation, particularly because I didn't even know if it was true. Don't listen to the negative conversations. Create positive ones like, "Wow. These kids look tired and bored. They need ME to wake them up! I'm going to go change their day! And this lesson is just what they need!" You'll bring the positive energy needed and have a much better shot at having a great class.

5. Ah, the need to be liked! It took years for me to get over this one and it is a problem that I occasionally still deal with. Yes, like you, I like to be liked. And I must admit that it still bothers me sometimes when I sense that someone does not like me. However, I think I have finally realized that (a) as a teacher it doesn't really matter if students like me as long as I give them a good education, and (b) I'm never really sure if a student likes

> .... **MINI TIP** ....
> Don't worry about your students liking you. What matters is that they respect you. Spend your time thinking about how to give them a good education.

me or not, so why take it personally? Most of us are inherently likable. Most kids will like you as long as they know that you care about them, that you are committed to them, that you will not be easily pushed away from them (as others have been), that you know your material, that you try to make it fun and relevant, and that you are fair and consistent. Practice these traits and you will be fine. You, Anne Marie, have demonstrated that you are capable of all of these. The real trick is to be respected. If you do your job well, kids will respect AND like you.

In my third year of teaching (yes, it took THAT long), I realized that I *really* needed the kids to respect me more than I needed them to like me. I realized at that time I was more interested in the kids liking me than I was in being an outstanding teacher who pushed his students forward. I realized that I might have to be tough on students to get them to work—not just be a nice guy who lets them off the hook. Once I realized this, I started to become the teacher I always wanted to be. The students respected me, and because I really *am* a nice guy ☺, they still liked me. It was gaining their respect that made me a better teacher.

All this takes is practice controlling negative conversations in your head and creating better ones. Thank the negative ones for sharing. Create more empowering conversations and live out of those. I think that is one secret for a happy life (not only a happy teaching career). While I, too, have a pretty thin skin, I have profited simply by turning the negative conversations into positive ones.

You surely will feel more confident and secure as you achieve success in this arena, Anne Marie. I am absolutely confident that you will do so and will thrive as a teacher.

Prof Z

Tips, Strategies, and Relevant Data

How to Develop Successful Classroom Management Strategies

Kauchak and Eggen (2007)[1] recommend interviewing and observing other classes, teachers, and students in your school and other schools about the following topics. Following are some possible questions to ask.

1. *Classroom Management*: Ask teachers
   a. What are your goals for classroom management?
   b. How have these changed over the years?
   c. How does the class that you teach right now influence either your management goals or how you implement your management plans?
   d. How do your management strategies change over the school year?
   e. What is the most difficult or challenging aspect of classroom management?
2. *Classroom Rules and Procedures*: Ask teachers
   a. What are your classroom rules and procedures?
   b. How are they communicated to the students?
   c. What are the biggest problem areas?
   d. How have they changed over the years?
   e. What management advice do you have for the beginning teacher?
3. *School Rules*: Observe students as they move and interact in the halls.
   a. Infer what the rules are regarding dress, appropriate hall behavior, tardiness, and the bell.
   b. Discuss your inferences about the rules with a teacher.
   c. What role will you play in enforcing school rules?
4. *Classroom Rules*: Ask several low-ability and several high-ability students the following questions and then compare the responses of the two groups of students.
   a. What rules do you have in your class?
   b. Which ones are most important?
   c. Why do you have them?
   d. What happens if they are not followed?
5. *Classroom Procedures*: Observe a class for several sessions and try to identify the procedural rules that are functioning for the following activities:
   a. Entering the class.
   b. Handing in papers.

    c. Sharpening pencils and accessing materials.

    d. Volunteering to answer a question.

    e. Exiting class.

6. *Interactive Management*: Tape and observe a classroom lesson. Identify places in the lesson where the teacher either verbally or nonverbally exhibited the following behaviors/characteristics:

    a. Withitness (the teacher is aware of the total classroom environment and communicates this awareness to students).

    b. Overlapping (the ability of teachers to do several things at the same time).

    c. Accountability.

    d. Momentum (teaches the lesson at a brisk pace, fast enough to keep learners involved but not so fast that they get lost).

    e. Smoothness (teaches well-planned lessons that run according to plan with a well-established system of rules and procedures that maintain order).

DAY 2

From: Anne Marie Bettencourt

To: Professor Z

Subject: Week 6, Day 2—This Is MY Class!

I have been practicing the "fake it till you make it" spiel. For instance, I practice giving "teacher looks" in the bathroom mirror. I play out student behavior scenarios and then work on responding to them in a firm tone that says, "Miss B don't play!" Since I do this while driving and when my roommates are home, I have definitely gotten looks and smiles from passing drivers and from the girls as they pass my door and see me glaring at my pillow and saying, "First warning: Don't make me say it again or I will be seeing you after school."

On that positive self-talk stuff though, I go fifty-fifty on the "new agey" stuff. Some days it works great. Other days the negative talk refuses to simmer down and I end up thinking, "Oh, who am I kidding? This absolutely stinks right now." I guess I will have to keep working on that, along with the 50 billion other suggestions you've given me. You have given me so much advice (most of it good, thankfully) that I am running out of Post-its and space on my desk! ☺

Well, I was all set to lay down the law today. I was ready for that first student to test me. Maybe they saw it in my eyes. Maybe they read my thoughts, because nobody messed with me at all! In a way it was too bad because I was SO ready for them! I am just so ready for this to be MY class, doing things the way I want them to be done and when I want them to be done. The class needs to be run on MY schedule, not theirs! And it was!

However, two things really stood out in my mind today: (1) Girls can be incredibly cruel and mean spirited (I know this might sound sexist), and (2) You get to know students best when they hang out after school with you. Let's start with the first so we can end on a happy note.

Keisha is normally a fragile girl. On any given day she can be irritable and is set off by the littlest thing, which sends her on a tangent. She is in foster care. But she is also looked after by her grandmother, so there is not much stability in her life. That being said, she is incredibly smart. Then we have Ms. Thang, the Diva herself, Tanissa. She is thin, in the latest fashion, always has a huge smile on her face, and enters class doing a dance move or humming a song. Her favorite adjective to use is "sexy." She uses it to describe just about anything actually.

Today, Keisha came in the classroom looking red-hot mad. She took her desk to the hall and remained there for most of the period. The red-hot mad turned into tears, and eventually she went to the bathroom for a good cry. What caused this? Tanissa had drawn up a horrible, cruel note about Keisha's sex life, with pictures to boot, and the most derogatory names you can think of.

I was enraged when I found out what she had done, but I ran into a problem. I didn't directly see or hear Tanissa do this. I heard from a few other students via my "Ms. B Cares" grapevine what had taken place. I did see the note. I just didn't see Tanissa give it to her because all of it took place that morning before class.

How can I address a problem I didn't witness but most probably occurred? Just in case Tanissa didn't do it, I didn't want to get angry at her and then find out that my sources were mistaken (as is often the case with teenagers). But I knew I couldn't let disrespect and cruelty go unaddressed in my classroom either.

I did ask Keisha how she was doing, and what she wanted me to do about the issue. She did ask me to address it. However, Tanissa cut me off at the pass today, and we were able to work it out, thankfully. But I don't totally believe that Tanissa didn't do it. I think she is lying to me, but I have no evidence.

Secondly, on a happier note, Alicia came after school for some questions on her essay and we ended up taking a half hour to talk about the military ball, drill team, and why our class talks back. Alicia actually gave me some amazingly mature insights into the family structure of some of my students—how they are raised to talk back, defend themselves, and talk over people. I immediately got a sense of her maturity and perceptive nature.

I wish all my students would stay after school so I could get to know them better. I didn't see Alicia as just a student today. I saw a person who is a whole other being outside of the classroom. I don't get to see her when 22 other people are there because she is normally shy and quiet. Today though, she talked for a whole 30 minutes and laughed and joked and really, really ended my day on a happy note. We gained (I think) a better understanding of each other through our conversation and for a minute, I wasn't a teacher. I was an ear and an observer. I think we all need to take time out as teachers and become better acquainted with our students via other routes, whether it is picnics, field trips, or after-school get-togethers. Perhaps that is one key to better classroom management. The more connected you are, the fewer disruptions you have because your respect level goes up (in theory anyway).

~ Anne Marie

From: Professor Z

To: Anne Marie Bettencourt

Subject: Week 6, Day 2—This Is My Class!

Hi, Anne Marie,

As I have stated repeatedly, teaching is all about relationships. Students will want to learn more from you when they know that you care about them. Students would ask me at the end of every year to sign their yearbooks. Every year, I would buy a yearbook. I would only sign their yearbook if they signed mine. So now I have 12 years of yearbooks that are some of my favorite memorabilia!

If I ever feel low, or if I ever need to be reminded why I am a teacher, all I have to do is read those yearbooks. Interestingly enough, not one student ever thanked me for teaching them social studies! They thanked me for listening to them, for talking to them about things that others wouldn't, for being their friend, for teaching them things about life, for being their basketball coach, for playing music at their senior prom, for teaching them how to play guitar, and for being a fun teacher. I am certain that I got more out of my students because we had created a good relationship with each other, and they knew I cared about them. In some cases, that is all it takes to motivate students to do well in your class.

I, too, have learned much from students on how I can be a better teacher. I remember that when I was a student teacher, Priscilla, one of my students, would sometimes hang out in my room after school. I will never forget the day I yelled at a student for the first time. While I was yelling at this kid, I started to laugh at the absurdity of the situation. Why was I, an adult, screaming my head off at a 12-year-old kid? Priscilla, always trying to be helpful, told me that while it was good that I yelled at the kid for what he did, she believed I would be a bit more effective if I didn't start to laugh while I was doing it. Thank you, Priscilla!

She also told me a lot of background information about the other students in her class and her opinions about each of them. Granted, these were all *her* perceptions of the other students, but a lot of these were very helpful to me and gave me a new perspective on many of them. She also gave me good ideas on how best to handle certain students. She was the one who told me that I could get any athlete to behave by simply keeping them for detention after school so they would miss practice or a game. That came in handy, for sure.

My dissertation was about the effects of student feedback on student teachers. I studied 13 student teachers who were soliciting feedback from their students. The student teachers were at first afraid that the kids would give them horrible feedback. In fact, the kids gave honest feedback that was full of good ideas. The student teachers reported feeling closer to the students. The students felt honored that the student teacher was asking them for input. Plus, the students gave the student teachers excellent ideas on how to improve their teaching.

> .... **MINI TIP** ....
> Solicit feedback from students on a regular basis. See *Why You Should Use Student Feedback: The Positive Effects of Soliciting Feedback from Your Students* in today's Tips, Strategies, and Relevant Data section.

At the end of the week, try giving your students the last 3–5 minutes of class to write some comments on what they like about your teaching and what could be better. Ask them to include specific ideas for improvement. Make sure that the students do not give their names. I think you will be surprised at how helpful this is!

Prof Z

Tips, Strategies, and Relevant Data

Why You Should Use Student Feedback: The Positive Effects of Soliciting Feedback from Your Students[2]

1. Student feedback is typically useful in determining what teaching methods and teaching styles work best for students in a particular class.
2. Student feedback is usually honest and accurate.
3. Student feedback is, in many cases, perceived by student teachers to be more accurate, more useful, and of better quality than feedback from the cooperating teacher and college supervisor.
4. Student feedback can be helpful in learning about student perceptions of the student teacher's teaching methods.
5. Student feedback is usually perceived as a "confidence builder" that encourages student teachers to take action in problematic teaching areas, particularly discipline.
6. Student feedback usually opens up and improves channels of communication between the student teachers and the students. Students are typically honored and pleased that a teacher would seek their input on this matter.
7. Student feedback usually leads to improved instruction.

DAY 3

From: Anne Marie Bettencourt

To: Professor Z

Subject: Week 6 Day 3—The Way It Is and The Way It Ought to Be

It's amazing what happens to students when you give them limited options. Aside from giving them time to critique the day's lesson, last week I started to give them choices on assignments, such as what topics they would like to write on. I also asked if they wanted time in class or at home, and whether they wanted to work in pairs or groups of three, and you would not BELIEVE what a difference it makes. Students that normally make me cringe when they raise their hands have given great ideas and feedback! Way to go for choices.

Today was another day off from teaching. Mr. B gave me permission to go to an educational social justice conference in Boston. I was so excited when I woke up this morning. But now that it is over, all I can say is, "Man, what a waste of a day!"

Gladys and Kate (two other student teachers) and I climbed into the little blue Honda full of ideas on how to change the world. Our ride down to Boston was full of gripes about No Child Left Behind, the democratic process, and our frustrations with the curriculum. We were all hoping for something amazing at this conference. Someone, we hoped, was going to shine some light on this social justice "thing" and show me how to do it in my classroom. I had the "why," I had the "what," and now, finally, I was going to get the "how."

But it didn't happen. In fact, nothing happened. There we were in Harvard Square at Harvard Divinity School, smack in the middle of brilliance, or so they tell everyone, and what do we get out of this conference? Nada. Shameless plugs for social justice organizations around Boston; workshops that are all about singing, crying, and saying, "We changed the world!"; the power of language; and not one useful tip or idea for how to bring social justice to students who understand the word *oppression* because they live it every single day of their lives. We had smarty arties from the Boston Charter School say how successful they were in getting kids on board for the MCAS. Hrmm, that couldn't have a thing to do with their classes having only 15 kids in them and having schools with books, computers, etc? It couldn't have anything to do with their school being located in field-trip Disneyland and grant city, could it? Nah, must not be related at all.

I know I sound like a grumpy teacher. But honestly, come on! Show me a school, a district, or a TEACHER that has no funds, no resources, limited books, hardly any computers that work, no tutors, and 35 kids in a classroom that has managed to miraculously beat the system, or work within it successfully. I DARE you. You know what I heard today? "Let the kids know they have a sense of self-efficacy, of agency, that they can change the world."

Oh, gee, that's brilliant. Well, Ms. Harvard Masters student, first you need to explain those words to my kids, then wait for the laughter to subside. Explain to my student who deals drugs and is rolling in cash how they can effect positive change. Scrap my curriculum and build it around the negativity of drugs, you say? Good idea, now go tell that to my department head and tell me what she says. By the way, let me remind you, I am a student teacher. Not only do I not have a job yet, if I say "Screw this, I am doing my own thing," I won't get one either.

Clearly, after yesterday, I decided that I didn't find the "how" because very few people actually know. It looks like it is up to me to figure it out on my own. My ideal classroom would not read Dickens. They would not read Jane Austen or Emerson. I would not sit at home making sure my lessons focused around standard 8 or 9 and that I could assess each standard individually every single time.

My class would read "Speak" about a girl who gets raped and remains silent (she is in ninth grade), and Malcolm X, and Anne Frank, and we would focus on *ideas*. They would learn to write letters to the paper, essays on protests and arguments for change. We would have debates and create mobiles, put on plays and pick an issue in our school to work on and spend the year studying it and working to change it. Through that, my students would learn to read, to write, to analyze literature, and to identify voice and speaker. They would also learn that they have a say in their own lives.

They wouldn't do arcane writing for MCAS where they are given a topic, no time to research it, and no background, and told "write." When does that ever happen that your degree depends on it? When was the last time you were given a piece of poetry and told to write about the irony without going over the poem first? Perhaps they can't do it because the stories stink and the material bores them. I don't even want to look at open response anymore, and all I do is grade them! I can imagine what my kids are thinking.

Yet, if you ask them to tell you whether or not Pluto is an actual dog, the class erupts in arguments citing Pluto's lack of clothing and inability to talk (so no) or the fact that he has long ears and a tail, and looks like a dog (so yes). If you ask them if Jay-Z and Fifty should have gotten in that shootout, they can relate events that happened years ago between the rivals that led to the brawl. They can cite lyrics that contain hidden messages. They can make an argument and defend it eloquently. Oh, but it doesn't count because it wasn't on Shakespeare or Julio Polanco.

Is their writing perfect? No. Are their arguments perfect? No. But they get a lot better once they are engaged and interested in what you are talking about. Does everything you teach have to revolve around hip hop, rap, and BET? No, but it *does* have to connect to their lives in some way, shape, or form. And that is *not* what our curriculum is doing for them. It is *not* what MCAS is doing for them. And I definitely didn't get any ideas from the stupid conference today on how to get that process going or what it even looks like. I learned how eloquently people can espouse authors, cite literature, and hear themselves talk without even knowing what they are saying.

When I get my own classroom next year, I am doing what all the high school teachers tell me to do—putting construction paper up on my door, shutting it, and doing things my own way. I'm tired of hearing my students ask, "Why are we doing this?" and not really knowing what answer to give them except, "Because you need to know it for MCAS." Honestly, that answer isn't good enough for me. And I hardly expect it is good enough for them either.

Next year, I am revamping my class's entire reading curriculum so that I can have engaged, literate, thoughtful students who like to read, and want to read, and want to be in my class because we discuss meaningful literature, real issues, and relevant topics. My kids will improve their skills not with tests, but with lots of writing, and a portfolio where they can actually see their own improvement and set their own goals. Ten bucks says I get fired within the first six months because they are actually DOING something. THAT would be rebellious.

~ Anne Marie

From: Professor Z

To: Anne Marie Bettencourt

Subject: Week 6, Day 3—The Way It Is and the Way It Ought to Be

Dear Anne Marie,

Getting fired might indeed be rebellious but it is also a pretty foolish thing to do, both for yourself and for your kids! It might be better for all concerned to get a job in a school that will support you and your ideas. Being fired will hurt both you and the kids. It will be a red flag for future employers. And, your kids will no longer have you as a teacher. Besides being hired in a school that will support you, you could also try to change the school you are in. But I must warn you, school change is typically slow! I encourage you to learn how to work effectively towards school improvement, no matter where you teach.

I spent 12 years teaching grades 7–9 in the public schools. Until I got tenure, I was your typical teacher—teaching the stuff I was supposed to teach, teaching it in a typical way. I did lots of lectures since my assistant principal complained that my class was too noisy because of all the group work I did. The students were bored and wondered why they had to learn this stuff that seemed to have little relevance to their world. As a new teacher, I was just trying to figure out how to do the job the way it was "supposed" to be done and not get fired doing it!

Obviously, I didn't quite understand at that time many of the things you already understand—that teaching must be relevant, that it needs to connect the student's lives with the content, and that you need to use teaching techniques that have a high level of success (lecture *not* being one of these techniques). You understand that it is okay to go "outside the box" if necessary to get students to learn. You understand that we should use materials that will create active citizens who have content knowledge and critical thinking skills that they can use to make the world (including *their* world) a better place for themselves, their families, and others. I still thought my job was to give my students the typical content that they were supposed to know and leave it at that. I had no bigger understanding of why this stuff really *was* important to the student and to the world.

I guess I was pretty naïve. Much of this changed after I got tenure and attended a meeting at a local church that changed my life. I went to a meeting on world hunger (a subject I knew little about) because a prominent citizen in town had told me I *should* go—after all, I was a social studies teacher. At the meeting, I learned that 40,000 children died every day because of hunger and hunger-related diseases, but that these deaths could be prevented. There was more than enough food in the world but feeding children just wasn't a priority for most governments, including our own.

I was appalled and moved to action. Thirty years later, I am still deeply involved in working to find ways to get our elected officials to recognize the problem of child hunger and poverty and take concrete action. But in the process of trying to figure out how to end world hunger, I saw that my social studies class could be about something more than just teaching the stuff we were supposed to teach (for little apparent reason other than to pass the Regents Exam, the state standardized test). I saw that my class could be about making the world a better place. I saw that social studies could be used to teach the content, tools, skills, and attitudes of active democratic citizenship at the local, state, national, and global levels. I saw that the content could be used to effect real change and that if I could get my students to think critically, they would be armed with the tools that could help them be more effective citizens. Ah! Now I had a goal that made teaching much more than just a job. It was about preparing my students to make a difference in the world!

That said, I still had to prepare my kids for the Regents Exam. But I found ways to "do my thing" 90% of the time and do the "Regents thing" the rest of the time. I must caution you. You must learn to play the game before you do anything too crazy. By "playing the game," I mean that you must do the things that are expected of you if you want to remain in your position. Having your students do well on the state exam is one of those things. Just remember that you do your kids no good if you get fired. Learn how to play the game.

For me, I found little parts of the NY State Social Studies Curriculum that I could use to back up my "real teaching." I found that current events, world hunger and poverty, and citizenship were required content areas. If a parent got upset that I wasn't just giving little Jimmy 50 pages of notes on names, dates, and places related to each war the United States had fought in, I could point to the curriculum and assure them that I was fulfilling the state requirements. We did some great things and I got into lots of trouble.

I was called before the school board several times. On one occasion, I was told to stop a pen pal activity with children from a small island country called

Tuvalu through the organization Save the Children. Our school board was concerned about a "communist connection" with the Save the Children organization (which is another long story).

On the other hand, my students would sometimes be recognized for their involvement in social justice issues. For example, my students coordinated an upstate New York version of "Hands Across America." We called it "Hands Around Gilbert Lake," and we raised thousands of dollars for local poverty organizations. We had over a thousand participants, and my students learned facts pertaining to hunger and poverty. It also taught them about such things as working with local officials, marketing, and math. School administrators gladly took the credit, even though they had tried their best to stop me at the beginning. Yet, participating in learning experiences of this type are the things students remember and learn most from.

It got scary at times and required a lot of energy to keep fighting for doing what I knew was right. If I had a relatively rough year fighting the powers that be, I would take the next year off in order to get up from the ground, clean myself off and go at it again the next year. But you've got to learn how to play the game. I repeat—*you are not helping your students if you get fired!*

Regarding your fear that the curriculum is not relevant to the kids—I say that it is the job of the teacher to *make* the curriculum relevant. By teaching conceptually, you can make a lesson on *any* topic relevant to the students. That is the beauty of having the goal of each lesson be the learning of concepts and big ideas (both of which contain facts) instead of just a bunch of facts. Students will remember concepts and big ideas. And by learning these, they will more easily remember the facts related to them.

I recently worked with the librarians at our college to help create an effective "library skills workshop." They were disappointed when they had led previous workshops because their students seemed bored, were rude to them, and did not seem to be paying attention to them. They wanted to create a presentation that would work. I volunteered to help them.

.... **MINI TIP** ....
Have the goal of each lesson be to teach a big idea rather than just a bunch of facts. At the beginning of the school year, explain to students that while facts are important, what you are looking for is a true understanding of the big ideas. Make sure that your assessments reflect this philosophy. See *How to Teach Your Students the Importance of Learning Big Ideas* in today's Tips, Strategies, and Relevant Data section.

Essentially, all I did was to help them create a powerful lesson plan. We came up with a *general purpose* (to teach their students shortcuts in gathering data), *objectives* (the students will be able to use shortcuts to gather relevant data sources), *a great hook*, and *an assessment tool/performance task*.

But what would hook the students into a lesson on library skills? Library skills are boring! So, I asked them to give me a situation that students could relate to that would show them the benefits of using shortcuts in life (shortcuts being the key concept in the lesson). One of the librarians came up with the idea of asking the class how many of them used cell phones. He would then ask whether they had ever used text messaging. Then he would ask if their text messaging had gotten any faster since they started doing it and why. He assumed that students would say they got faster because they learned shortcuts on how to write text messages by not spelling out all the words but using symbols ("lol" for example).

He would then ask how students would go about researching a term paper for a class they were now taking. He assumed they would probably respond that they would just Google the topic and get hundreds of sources. He would then ask, "Which source would you use?" He predicted that they would say they would choose among the first to come up. He would then point out the absurdity of using just the first five out of several hundred, assuming these would be the best.

OK. Now he has their attention. And now, the *real* hook! He would tell them that in the next 45 minutes, they would learn research shortcuts that would save them time and effort on every single paper they write for the rest of their lives. He would say that as a result of learning these "tricks," they would get better grades and not waste time trying to decide which sources to use.

Bingo! He's got them! And then he would move into the lesson, which contained facts as well as a good amount of time for students to experience the shortcuts on their computers.

How was that for turning a dull lesson into a lesson that students couldn't wait to learn? The librarians were teaching the same material as before, but they were teaching it in a way in which the concepts (shortcut) and big ideas (by using research shortcuts, it will save you time and effort and will likely get you better grades) were clear. Students would also be very clear that this material was relevant to them and was important to learn.

This can be done for every lesson, no matter what you are teaching. Again, the key is to emphasize big ideas and concepts for the lesson instead of just teaching the facts. You must hook the students by making those concepts/big ideas relevant to their lives.

See what you can do by thinking out your future lessons in a conceptual manner. I will be glad to help with this.

Prof Z

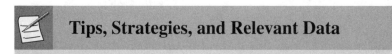

Tips, Strategies, and Relevant Data

How to Teach Your Students the Importance of Learning Big Ideas

I do a lesson for my methods classes in which I pretend to be Pablo Picasso (I sometimes even come in wearing a beret and cape and speak with a terrible French accent). I tell the class that besides being their teacher, I am also a world class artist and that they are lucky to be in my presence while I draw for them a "masterpiece." I would then draw on the board what looks like a random set of circles, lines, curves, etc. and then have the class study it closely. It would look something like this:

Piccaso 1

Figure 6.1 Piccaso 1

I would then erase it (after taking a bow, of course) and ask the students to take out a piece of paper and replicate my "masterpiece" as closely as they could. When finished, I would have them compare their drawing with their neighbors to see how similar or different they were. They would conclude that many of the lines and circles were in different places in the drawing, had different shapes and numbers of items, and were generally not that similar.

I would then have them put their pens down and tell them that I would draw for them another "masterpiece" using the same number of lines, circles, and curves as the first drawing. However, I would put them in a different formation this time. The drawing would look like this:

Figure 6.2 Piccaso 2

I would ask the students to study it carefully, and then I would erase it. I would ask them to replicate my latest "masterpiece" as best they can. When finished, I would ask them to compare their drawings with each other. This time, they would conclude that they looked similar. We would then discuss why the second drawing was easier to replicate. We would conclude that the second drawing (Picasso Two) was structured in a pattern that had a recognizable label (a stick figure), whereas the first drawing

(Picasso One) appeared to be a random smattering of shapes that did not mean anything to them.

I would then ask my students what a typical week of social studies class was like in high school. Many students would tell me that their teachers would put lots of notes containing names, dates, and places on the board that they would have to memorize for the test on Friday. They also pointed out that they would typically have forgotten much of what they had memorized by Monday, when they would go over the test. They would conclude that they did not really understand or learn much when being taught in this manner.

I would then discuss the difference between teaching conceptually and teaching factually. Teaching a random group of facts to be memorized for the test on Friday (and forgotten by Monday) serves little purpose. I would label this as a "Picasso One lesson." When you teach in a Picasso One manner, little learning is actually taking place.

Teaching conceptually enables students to truly understand the big idea and to remember key facts related to the big idea. The best part about using concepts and big ideas is that you can relate *any* concept or big idea to *any* student at *any* time! You can turn what might be boring content into something that kids can relate to and find important.

Give your students plenty of examples to help them understand the difference between a fact and a big idea. Remind them that a fact can only be used in so many ways whereas a big idea can be used in many different ways.

"Thomas Jefferson was the third president of the United States." That is a fact. It can only be used in so many ways. A big idea like, "A change in one aspect of a culture affects other aspects of that culture" can be used to analyze any culture at any time period. Students will remember this big idea and will use facts to give examples to support or refute the statement. Congratulations! You are teaching critical thinking skills instead of having

DAY 4

From: Anne Marie Bettencourt

To: Professor Z

Subject: Week 6, Day 4—Helping Students Create Life Goals

Thanks for your ideas about teaching conceptually. I will try them out. It makes a lot of sense. I'm sorry I did not have you for methods class!

Today was an awesome day. Mr. B said he was really liking my work lately in class. He said I am addressing standards clearly and letting the kids know what objectives they are reaching for, and he can see it all coming together. I agree with him. I can feel it, too. Yay!

I also had Keisha after school today. She wrote in her journal a week ago that she was going to kill herself. I read this Friday, and ASAP went to the adjustment counselor with it. After dealing with her after my fiasco with Josh, I knew she was the best resource I had for dealing with troubled kids. I handed her a photocopy of the journal entry (always photocopy things for your own records!) and proceeded to tell her about the issues I was getting from this student in class, like glaring, refusing to do work, showing up with her hood up, and making loud comments. The counselor didn't look surprised and, it turned out, she actually had Keisha on her file but hadn't seen her in a while as Keisha kept skipping their appointments.

Keisha found me today and was astonished that I told someone. Not in a negative way, however. I gave her a hug and told her I cared about her and that legally, I had to say something! She showed up after school for a detention, which then turned into a heart to heart on getting her head straight because, honestly, this child is brilliant and could do honors work, no problem, if she just *did* the work.

It turns out, that even though she is having problems at home, she eventually wants to go to college and then to graduate school for law. Well, I couldn't sit on this excitement so we started talking about courses and lo and behold I introduced her to Peterson's College Quest, where we spent 15 minutes looking at Bradley University in Florida. "I think I found my college!" she exclaimed. Well, at least she has a focus now.

Since I know that people rarely say the word *college* to some of my students (as your wife found out from her students at the CARE CENTER), I hopped on that bandwagon as soon as I got the chance. I think junior year is a tad late to start the college talk with students, after their grades and self-esteem are in the gutter. Why not start in elementary school, or middle school? I don't think the "talk" is enough either. They need to be out on internships, seeing what they like and don't like, and exploring! Plus, the community could use some extra help anyway, so it would be a symbiotic relationship.

Our kids see negative every day. So why not show them the positive immediately, instead of telling them to wait it out for three years and *then* we can show them where they can go? What sense does that make? Sheesh, the HAAAAAARVARD babies get that talk when they are like, five, so I don't see it as a big deal to start talking about it now. If anything, I believe we fall short on the issue of getting our students to recognize what else is out there, and what school can do for them beyond the classroom.

But I was super-duper happy to see that Keisha has goals and big ideas, and I am all about backing her up on those. I want to plan a field trip to Springfield College in May for them, but Mr. B said I couldn't justify that with the English Frameworks (um, perhaps we disagree here, but I think some things in education don't *always* have to align with the frameworks to be important). I just wanted them to get a feel for some options they have, what a campus looks like, what dorms are, what they could study, and things they may not have even *thought* were majors (athletic counseling for example) to get the wheels turning.

Keisha, for example, before we did this college quest thing, was hell-bent on Harvard, Yale, or Springfield Technical Community College. It took a search for her to realize that there are many other options than that! And the more educated students we have, the more I can shut down "the man" and his machine. I am all about covert attacks on the system. I am going Greek and preparing a Trojan Horse of smart, skilled students to get inside the fort and then tear it all down. At least, that is the legacy that I want to leave behind.

~ Anne Marie

 From: Professor Z

To: Anne Marie Bettencourt

Subject: Week 6, Day 4—Helping Students Create Life Goals

Hi, Anne Marie,

Way to go, Keisha. Way to go, Anne Marie. You might have had the most important talk with Keisha that she has ever had. As a teacher, you almost never know when you've had *the* talk that makes a difference. I remember watching an *Oprah* show where she reunited a middle-aged woman and her junior high school social studies teacher who had supported her when she was going through rough years as a teenager. She told how he gave her all she needed simply by listening to her and giving some adult advice when other adults weren't listening to her.

She then told the story of how she was so poor, she could only give him a pretty rock she found as a Christmas present. On the stage, she asked the teacher if he remembered that Christmas present. He reached into his pocket, pulled out the rock, and told her that it was one of the most meaningful gifts he had ever gotten. Talk about tears! You never know for sure how deeply you can impact student lives.

But there is one thing I know: We all need a vision to which we can aspire. We all need goals. We need to have a life purpose that excites us and pushes us forward. Children of wealth typically have these goals because there are confirmed expectations (from parents, relatives, teachers, etc.) for them to do well in school, go to college, and choose a career that fulfills them. As I pointed out previously, many children, from urban schools in particular, don't have these expectations.

Remember Maslow's thesis: If you are so busy simply trying to meet your survival needs, there is no space for creating or achieving your highest ambitions. If one is hungry, doing well on a math test is not a high priority. If one does not have a safe place to go for the night, doing homework is not a high priority. If one feels threatened and unsafe in school, paying attention during a lecture is not a high priority.

I strongly believe that we need to include topics in our classrooms such as creating a life purpose, goals and aspirations, and looking at the ways our students can achieve these goals. If they begin this process by middle school, they will see how school can be useful in them getting what they want out of life. For example, if they want to join a profession that requires a college education, they will see that they need to do well in school in order to get into a college that will train them for that profession.

I have thought about writing a book on this subject. I think it is THAT important!

> .... **MINI TIP** ....
> Have students be in touch with a vision for their future so they can see that what they are doing in school will help them achieve that future. One of the ways to do this is to use service learning as a teaching strategy. See *How to Use Service Learning in Your Classroom* in today's Tips, Strategies and Relevant Data section.
> ....

You are doing a great job, Anne Marie. You are full of possibility! Your future students will be lucky to have you!

Best wishes,

Prof Z

Tips, Strategies, and Relevant Data

How to Use Service Learning in Your Classroom:
What Is Service Learning?

Service learning is a teaching strategy in which students learn the curriculum while participating in carefully organized experiences that meet community needs. It is a useful vehicle for establishing a connection between your students and the world beyond the school. It allows students to use what they have learned in a real-world situation. Additionally, it allows them to learn about things they would never be able to learn in a classroom.

What Are the Different Types of Service Learning?

Savage & Armstrong (2004)[3] identify three types of service learning:

1. *Indirect*: This type of service learning engages students in activities within the school or in groups involving fellow students that connect to larger community needs or projects—for example, a car wash or a bake sale to raise money for the local soup kitchen. To get hooked on the project, students have to learn about specific community problems (the content) and how they might solve the problem. In other words, the project is connected to the content and provides a service to the community.
2. *Direct*: This type of service learning takes students out of the school and into the community to provide—for example, cleaning up a riverbank, assisting people who are old or sick. Students typically enjoy contributing to the outside world while learning the curriculum.
3. *Advocacy Activities*: This type of service learning involves students in work on behalf of a cause. For example, they might raise community awareness about problems with bullying, poverty, and other injustices. To do any advocacy, students must know the arguments and facts supporting their case. This strategy also demonstrates to students that citizenship is more than just talking about rights and responsibilities.

How to Plan Service Learning Experiences—Savage and Armstrong also provide excellent tips on the steps to take when undertaking a service learning project:

1. *Preparation*: The first step is to find a project relating to the curriculum that also meets the needs of the community. The project will depend on the age and skill of the class and the teacher. Try to have

the students pick the project. They will have more of a stake in it and will work harder on it. In this stage, a clear purpose and specific objectives are necessary. It should be very clear what the students will be doing, when they will be doing it, how they will be supervised, and how it will be funded. Your planning must establish a clear tie between the intended community service work and the academic content of your course.

2. *Orientation*: In this stage, students need to be provided with a good overview that describes the purpose of the project and tells what each person is expected to do. Again, it is crucial that students are motivated and engaged in the project if it is to be successful. The more the project is created by the students, the more ownership they have in the project, and the more likely it is to be successful.

3. *Curriculum Integration*: Tie in the project to as many content areas as possible. A good project could involve social studies skills and facts along with math, language arts, science, art, or music.

4. *Collaboration*: Service learning provides an excellent opportunity for students to learn how to work together with classmates as well as members of the community.

5. *Reflection*: This is an essential component of a successful service learning project. Participation in the project does not ensure that learning will take place. Reflection should be done throughout the project, so students are continually asking themselves questions about the project and the content being studied.

6. *Celebration*: Celebrations give you an opportunity to reinforce the big ideas learned and to reward members of the class and community for their efforts.

DAY 5

From: Anne Marie Bettencourt

To: Professor Z

Subject: Week 6, Day 5—Success Is 80% Attitude

Mr. B gave me the "Success is 80% attitude" speech today and I must say, I deserved it. It was my fault for lingering in the teacher's room this morning before school listening to the teachers rant and rave about sinking health insurance and retirement and talking up getting jobs in Connecticut, New Jersey, and anywhere but here. What a positive way to start my day!

I mentioned it to Mr. B and he gave me the "Oh come on—are you serious?" look. "But," I spluttered, "what happens if all the good teachers leave and all us newbies are stuck with no one to learn from?"

"Are you serious? Get real. There are always people to get advice from." He then informed me that he has known teachers to complain even in the best of times. "Isn't attitude half the battle right there?" he countered. He explained that while this is not a business, we might do well to think positively, like businesspeople. Say the glass is half full, believe it will get better, and don't whine, complain, and be victimized.

Negative thinking never really did anything for anybody and it rubs off a lot easier than positivity does. I needed some positive in my life. So I went to Wal-Mart, bought myself a Nerf Basketball Hoop and some candy, and went to town on E period. We reviewed material on the unit test by shooting hoops, answering questions in teams, and snacking on Snickers second period. Nothing like watching my students shooting baskets for an instant pick me up: "Hey Wil, you gonna build a house with all those bricks?" (as another ball bounces off the rim). "C' mon, India, she has nothing on you, nothin!" "Isreal, aim for the rim, aim for the rim, sweeeeeeet!" I want to remind you that this was my "dragging horses through the mud" class at the beginning of the semester, and in the past few weeks they have grooved, shouted out answers, and started to perk up a little.

Another plus, I have yet another student who went and bought *The Color of Water* by James McBride, after my shameless plug for "One Book, One Springfield" event. I have about six students reading it right now, and another ten that want the book. While I suspect part of that is because I offered to buy them dinner and accompany them to his talk and jazz concert at the end of May, I don't care. I just want them to read. I am not above bribery to achieve literacy, which is why I remain committed to my urban kids. When I hear these teachers talk of leaving, I walk down the halls and I see Ashley, Marissa, Maria, Ariel, Israel, Wil, Kirk, and Jaime, and I wonder what will happen to these kids. Who is going to teach them? Who is going to inspire them? We tell them to struggle through tough projects, not to give up, and what do we do? We leave when the going gets tough.

Now, that does not mean I want to live in Springfield forever. I love the woods. But, I figure there are enough woodsy areas near urban cities to accommodate my preferences. Then I can take the kids camping, hiking. . . . Ok, I am getting ahead of myself.

A quote from Mary Kay Ash comes to mind when I think of the dire situation here: "Aerodynamically, the bumblebee should not be able to fly. But the bumblebee does not know that, so it just keeps on flying anyway." I feel like we new teachers are the bumblebees, and the teacher's room is the person saying "No, that won't work! What makes you think you can fly? Don't even bother." Hrmm, well I think I might just keep on flying anyway. I won't make excuses. I will look at the problems and find solutions. And I *won't* hang out in the teacher's room!

No seriously, if Rafe, that amazing teacher I met from California did it, I can too. His class is packed with fifth through eighth graders on a Saturday in May ready to do SAT Prep work and math work from 9 to 1 every weekend. If he can get his fifth graders to read *Catcher in the Rye* and perform *Hamlet* complete with a student band, then I can create a totally awesome class of high school students that defy all logic of the urban school. And I promise, I will.

~ Anne Marie

From: Professor Z

To: Anne Marie Bettencourt

Subject: Week 6, Day 5—Success Is 80% Attitude

Dear Anne Marie,

Okay. I confess. You drew tears on this one! I am so inspired by your passion and commitment to your "kids!" Be the bumblebee! Don't ever stop! Life is all about having a vision and goals. Don't let anything get in your way.

I agree with you. Attitude is everything! We could talk for hours on this one. How we deal with the negativity is how we end up experiencing life. And the nice thing is that we are the ones who choose which conversations to honor and which not to, and we decide what we are truly committed to in this life.

I love that you are creating a very powerful vision of how you want to teach, what your kids will get out of your classes, and how you will work with parents and deal with issues. Fantastic!

.... **MINI TIP** ....
Create a teaching philosophy that provides a vision for where you want to go as a teacher. A vision provides you with an idea of what the classroom of your dreams would look like. Creating this classroom would be your goal. As we know, once you have a goal, it is much easier to get to where you want to go. It is hard to achieve anything when you don't have a goal. See *How to Create the Vision for Your Future Classroom* in today's Tips, Strategies, and Relevant Data section.

Stay away from that teacher's room and hang out with the teachers who inspire you.

Best wishes,

Prof Z

Tips, Strategies, and Relevant Data

How to Create the Vision for Your Future Classroom

To create the future classroom of your dreams, consider the following:

1. Becoming the Teacher You Always Wanted to Be—Describe the teacher you always wanted to be. What personal characteristics would that teacher have? What would you want the students to say about that teacher after the year is over?
2. Creating the Classroom of your Dreams—What will your room look like? How will the room be arranged? What furniture will it have in it? Will there be computer stations? How will the desks be arranged? What will be on the walls? What will the lighting be? What role will art, music, and literature play in the learning environment?
3. Creating the Students You Always Wanted—Describe the behaviors of the students in your classroom. Describe how they would behave, work together, and learn together.
4. Creating the School You Always Wanted—Describe what the school of your dreams would look like. What features would it have—for example, a swimming pool, athletic fields, good natural light?
5. Creating the Administration of Your Dreams—Describe the administration in the school. What philosophy would the principal have? How would he/she deal with discipline problems? How would he/she mentor new teachers? What would his/her attitude be about supervision and assessment of instruction?
6. Obviously, you will probably *not* teach in a school that has every aspect of your dream. Wherever you teach there will be things that make it special in both positive and negative ways. The question is, how will you make the most of whatever you have? How will you impact not only your own students but be part of making the entire school environment a better place to teach and learn? And finally, how will you go about making the educational system work to ensure a quality education for all children—rural, urban, or suburban?
7. Creating a vision helps you to set a scenario of what you want that you can then "step into." Think outside the box. Go towards your

vision even if the reality of your situation looks nothing like it. Keep the vision alive by doing what it takes to create it step by step! Don't simply accept that you will never have your vision. Read *Schools that Work* by George Wood to get ideas of how teachers have not settled for what they were handed, but used their visions to create the educational environment they thought was best for their students.

8. Create the classroom of your dreams even if you do not have all the materials you would have hoped to have. Be creative. How will you acquire those books or computers you are missing? What outside resources are there that could help?

9. Create the school of your dreams even if it doesn't look anything like your original vision. What part could you play in moving your school forward? Who else could contribute towards your vision?

10. Create the students of your dreams even if they don't look anything like those in your vision. See the good in all students. Find out what makes each one of them special. Grab hold of their strengths and bring them forward. All kids are special in so many ways!

11. Finally, do what it takes to be the teacher you always wanted to be. Do what it takes to be the teacher that your students will always remember as their *best* teacher. There is no better job than being an extraordinary teacher. What could be better than helping a child learn and grow? The key is to be extraordinary. We already have enough ordinary teachers and don't need any more! It may take years for you to get there, but once you do, you will wake up each morning just dying to get to your kids!

12. It all starts with your vision!

Discussion Starters for Week Six

1. To what degree do you agree/disagree with Professor Z's five suggestions in Day 1? Explain.

2. Which of Miss B's ideas for her future classroom that she discussed in Day 3 would you consider including in your future classroom?

3. Does reading this book make you more or less likely to want to teach in an urban school? List the pros and cons of urban teaching.

4. What methods do you use when you are surrounded with many negative people?

5. Would you ever ask students for feedback on your teaching? Why? Why not?

6. In terms of your teaching, to what degree does fear run your actions? Are you afraid to confront students? Are you afraid to give them difficult homework assignments or projects?

7. Compare the reactions of men and women in your class to similar or differing insecurities they have about teaching. If there are differences, what do you think accounts for them?

8. Make a list of things that your future students might do to test you in the beginning of the year. How might you handle each of these situations?

9. What will you do in your classroom to encourage good citizenship? In what way will you be a good role model in this endeavor?

10. How will you go about preparing students for standardized tests? What do you think of Prof Z's method found in Day 3?

☑ Professor Z's Student Teaching Checklist

Teaching in Urban Schools: Think about each of these questions. Take appropriate actions when necessary.

1. ____ Are you aware of the effects of poverty on student learning (hunger, homelessness, lack of health insurance, etc.)?

2. ____ Do you know how best to teach students who have English as a second language?

3. ____ Have you developed a positive climate in your classroom?

4. ____ Is your classroom emotionally and physically safe for each of your students?

5. ____ Is your classroom orderly and focused on learning?

Advocating for our kids: Give some thought to each of these questions. If you need work on some, think about what you must do so that you will be prepared.

1. ____ Are you aware of how to create effective relationships with elected officials?

2. ____ Are you aware of how to write effective letters to elected officials?

3. ____ Are you aware of how to write effective letters to the editor of your local newspaper?

4. ____ Are you aware of how to create an effective meeting with elected officials?

5. ___ Are you keeping up with current events and know what is going on in your community and in the world?

6. ___ Are you modeling good citizenship for your students?

7. ___ Are you taking effective political actions on behalf of your students?

Endnotes

1. Kauchak, D. P., & Eggen, P. D. (2007). *Learning and teaching: Research-based methods* (pp. 215–216). Boston: Pearson/Allyn & Bacon.
2. Zukergood, D. (1994). The meanings student teachers give to student feedback. Dissertation, Syracuse University.
3. Savage, T. V., & Armstrong, D. G. (2004). *Effective teaching in elementary social studies* (pp. 52–58). Upper Saddle River, New Jersey: Pearson/Merrill/Prentice Hall.

WEEK SEVEN

"The task of the excellent teacher is to stimulate "apparently ordinary" people to unusual effort. The tough problem is not in identifying winners: it is in making winners out of ordinary people."

K. PATRICIA CROSS

Day 1: My Last Week/Time to Fly or Time to Die!
— Feeling Successful, Classroom Management, Teacher Issues (Confidence and Attitude)

Day 2: Living in the City?
— Dealing with Doubt, Teacher Issues (Philosophy)

Day 3: Student Feedback Rocks!
— Listening to Students, Teaching Methods, Student Feedback, Teacher-Student Relationships, Constructivist Teaching

Day 4: Final Observation/Miss B at the Plate—Bases Loaded, Two Out, Full Count
— Being Observed, Being a Reflective Practitioner, Teacher Issues (Confidence and Attitude)

Day 5: My Last Day of Student Teaching
— Being a Reflective Practitioner

Discussion Starters for Week Seven
Professor Z's Student Teaching Checklist

Topics Discussed This Week

In this chapter, you will learn

1. How to develop a powerful and positive attitude towards classroom management.
2. How to decide whether to teach and live in an urban area.
3. The importance of student feedback.
4. How students believe they learn best.
5. More tips on how to succeed in student teaching.
6. The importance of learning about the community you are teaching in.
7. How to create a vision for your future classroom.
8. New methods of classroom management.
9. The merits of using student feedback to improve instruction.
10. More dos and don'ts for being observed by your college supervisor and cooperating teacher.

DAY 1

From: Anne Marie Bettencourt

To: Professor Z

Subject: Week 7, Day 1—My Last Week/Time to Fly or Time to Die!

This is it! It's the last week of my practicum. This week, I start giving my classes back to Mr. B, much to my chagrin. But as it comes to an end, I am amazed at what I have learned in these last six weeks in the same class, with the same students and the same teacher. God bless the brutally honest, no-holds-barred people of the world because those are the ones who encourage people to do their best and take a close look inside themselves. If this were "American Idol," you and Mr. B would be the Simon Cowells of the teaching world.

Mr. B told me today, "You have made massive improvements. Your objectives are clear, you are on time to class, and you have a command of your class that is much better than even a week ago."

Yup! I agree because I feel it now. I know I have said it before, but I have never felt it to this degree. I can say something to a student and in my head go, "Nope, shouldn't have done that," or "Ohhhh, she SO gets detention for that one!" And then, my mouth opens and I say, "Detention. Tomorrow. If you can't make it, no worries! I'll just write you up," instead of, "If you do that again, I am going to give you detention."

Nope, they get one warning and I'll be damned if they don't receive a consequence for having the audacity to do it again and have me catch them. What was I thinking a few weeks ago? Warnings. Another warning. No, I really mean it this time. I can almost see the wheels turning in their minds going, "Oh yeah, I can get away with ANYTHING!" Hrmph.

"Four weeks ago you were whining," Mr. B stated. Four weeks ago if he had said that, I would have gone home crying. Today, I just laughed and nodded. Yes, yes I was. I made every excuse in the book for why I couldn't discipline them, couldn't gain command of my class. I was new at this, and I was afraid. Mr. B's style didn't seem to work for me back then (let me tell you, I am more like him now than I thought!).

Student teachers need a military boot camp instructor standing beside them going, "Suck it up cupcake, go teach that class!" or "If you let Wilson walk on you one more time you are giving me 50!" In boot camp, there is no "try." There is just "do." Anything else is unacceptable.

Student teachers have so many insecurities about being new, like what the students think, that it gets in the way of them actually becoming good teachers. It's like we have this miniature person from the negative part of our brain sitting on our shoulder saying, "Look at them glaring at you. Clearly you can't do your job. See that kid over there looking bored? That means your lesson STINKS! Go home. They hate you. Clearly this is not your field."

Then the boot camp instructor walks up and glares down the mini-me barking, "Maggot! We like glares. We live for confronting students and pushing them to do their best! 'I can't' is not a phrase we utter around here! Do they SCARE you? I can take on any student and make them succeed." Yeah, that's what we need.

Somewhere along my student teaching (and by somewhere I mean like the last week or so) I learned to say to mini-me, "Shut up. I can do this. I'll prove it." And whenever I start to let the "I can'ts" get in my head, I have to pause and literally say out loud (under my breath of course), "Thanks for sharing, tell someone who cares," and continue with my work. Clearly, attitude is 80% of the battle. And mine has sucked for much of the time I have been here.

I used to love school. I did my best work because I enjoyed it. I liked the challenge of coming up with something stellar. Lately, in my courses, it has been "OK, paper due at 4. I can start at 2 and it will be OK." I stopped doing things well because people settled for less than my best. I could take it easy, not work hard, and I'd still get the same grade (A) as when I was working my butt off.

When I did my best work, it was because someone saw that I could do better and let me know it. Now, if I am a graduate student thinking this, what on earth are my high school students thinking? Duh, ladies and gentlemen. As an adult, I need to give myself a pep talk and say, "Listen, you *know* you can do better than this, so stop pulling this crap and do it." As teachers, we cannot be afraid to tell our kids the same thing. Who cares if they glare? If glaring equals success, then glare away. We can have an "Ugliest Mug" contest while writing essays.

~ Anne Marie

PS: Thanks for the "being powerful" spiel Professor Z. Between you and Mr. B, I think it is starting to work! Perhaps I can get more lessons on shutting myself up again? :-)

From: Professor Z

To: Anne Marie Bettencourt

Subject: Week 7, Day 1—My Last Week/Time to Fly or Time to Die!

Dear Anne Marie,

No Paula Abduls in this crowd! Only Simon Cowells (Yechh—another lousy sign of the times—when we look at Simon as a powerful person!). Again, you had me laughing, crying, and everything in between. This one definitely goes into "the book."

Mr. B was right. You are certainly not acting out of the same parts of that brain of yours that you were a few weeks ago. You are accessing and acting out of that powerful part etc., the part that knows you are a good teacher if only you listen to the powerful voices in your head instead of the wimpy ones. It is a major breakthrough and one that you need to keep accessing over and over again. The negative voices will only be there if you resist them. There is a saying "What you resist will persist." I think your method is a good one—acknowledging them and saying, "Thanks for sharing but I'm doing something else."

Regarding my "being powerful *spiel*," I sold myself on you right from the start when I saw you teach and got to know more about your attitudes and philosophy towards teaching. My goal was to help you become a great teacher. I wanted you to know I believed in you. I wanted to push you hard and not settle for you being just an "OK" teacher. As I keep saying, we have too many "OK" teachers out there already and don't need more of them.

I look to see whether you might be one of those teachers in whose class I would someday want my daughter. Yes, I sold myself on you and didn't let you take yourself down when it would have been easy for you to do so. Like any coach, my job is to help prop you up when you are falling. I am SO proud of who you are becoming as a teacher!

I also want to applaud you for creating an extraordinary working relationship with Mr. B. This is so important! He seems to be giving you enough room to navigate by yourself but is also keeping a close eye on you and providing you with good feedback. Furthermore, he seems like a good role model.

On occasion, the matchup between the student teacher and the cooperating teacher is not a good one. The cooperating teacher will complain to me about the student teacher and the student teacher will complain about the cooperating teacher. While a three-way meeting sometimes pulls them back together, you were able to create a great relationship with Mr. B and it has made this experience an exceptional one. Congratulations!

.... **MINI TIP** ....
Creating a powerful working relationship with your cooperating teacher is very important in having a successful student teaching experience. See *How to Work Effectively with Your Cooperating Teacher* in today's Tips, Strategies, and Relevant Data section.

I'm looking forward to our final observation. Did we make a date for this yet? I am running out of times!

Have a great night!

Prof Z

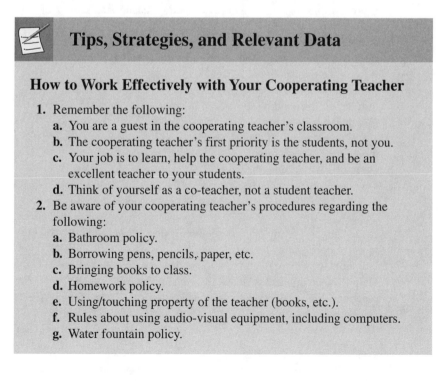

Tips, Strategies, and Relevant Data

How to Work Effectively with Your Cooperating Teacher

1. Remember the following:
   a. You are a guest in the cooperating teacher's classroom.
   b. The cooperating teacher's first priority is the students, not you.
   c. Your job is to learn, help the cooperating teacher, and be an excellent teacher to your students.
   d. Think of yourself as a co-teacher, not a student teacher.
2. Be aware of your cooperating teacher's procedures regarding the following:
   a. Bathroom policy.
   b. Borrowing pens, pencils, paper, etc.
   c. Bringing books to class.
   d. Homework policy.
   e. Using/touching property of the teacher (books, etc.).
   f. Rules about using audio-visual equipment, including computers.
   g. Water fountain policy.

    h. Routine for cleaning up at the end of class and waiting for dismissal.

    i. Talking in class.

    j. Raising hands to respond to teacher questions.

    k. Gum chewing.

    l. Clothing policy (hats, hoods, etc.).

    m. Seating policy.

    n. How to enter the room.

    o. What to do before class starts.

    p. What to do when the bell rings to start class.

    q. Procedures for asking questions.

    r. Procedures for missed work.

    s. What to do when the student is late or misses class.

    t. Keeping attendance/grades.

    u. Behavior during announcements.

    v. Fire drill policy.

3. Do the following:

    a. Act professionally at all times. You represent not only yourself, but your school and your cooperating teacher.

    b. Be early for school each day. Show that you are eager to be there and prepared for your classes.

    c. If you will be absent, call your cooperating teacher and send in all lesson plans.

    d. Dress professionally.

    e. Be proactive. Look at what needs to be done and do it, particularly if it will help the cooperating teacher.

    f. "Champion" the teacher. If you are going to say anything about him or her, it should be something positive.

4. Do *not* do the following:

    a. Do not speak critically about your cooperating teacher to anyone in the building at any time.

    b. Do not be late to school or class.

    c. Do not put the cooperating teacher on the spot in class or in a meeting by asking a question he or she might not be able to answer.

    d. Do not engage in any conversation with students about their gripes with the cooperating teacher.

    e. Do not leave school the minute the bell rings at the end of the day. Help to clean up, discuss plans for the next day, and attend meetings. Show the cooperating teacher that student teaching is a top priority for you.

DAY 2

From: Anne Marie Bettencourt

To: Professor Z

Subject: Week 7, Day 2—Living in the City?

I have not been able to sleep well since James Duncan-Andrade's lecture last week titled "Wankstas, Gangstas, and Riders: Effective Methods of Urban Teaching." It was an excellent lecture. He is Latino, and he spoke straight from his experience of growing up in the "hood." He is a doctoral student, so he provided statistics, examples, and theory to back up his ideas. He was also a teacher and basketball coach for ten years in an urban school, so he could provide very concrete pictures of effective urban education as well—a first in my book of all the seminars and lectures I have been to.

But he said something that made me think long and hard over the past week. "The most effective teachers who teach in the hood like the hood, or spend all their time there so they may as well live in the hood." The reason being, it gave you "street credit" with the students—the students who got shot at, did the shooting, and woke up to the gunshots, the ones most people call "throwaways." It made perfect sense to me. Who is going to sit and listen to you talk about "the real world" if your version is Beverly Hills and the students' world is straight out of *Cops?* Translated into a bigger picture, he was saying that, the best teachers live in the communities where they teach. Then they can have a shared experience with their students, and get to know the community. No kidding. It makes perfect sense.

Then it hit me. I hate the city. I don't want to live in the "hood". I hate rap. And I want a family—one that doesn't wake up to gunshots. I don't want to worry about my kids being shot at, or getting jumped, or stabbed, or our house broken into at 3 AM. Theoretically I could teach urban kids and live in the suburbs or a rural area. Lots of teachers do. But then again, James said the *most* effective teachers, the *best* teachers . . . so are these suburbanites the most effective? If we are striving to revolutionize education and make it realistic to our students, to connect it to their lives, I would say "No" to those teachers. Sure, they have an idea what these kids' lives might be like, but having an idea and actually living that reality are two very different things.

This translates into why I can't sleep: Maybe I am not meant to teach urban kids. I love them to pieces. I have fun with them. My lessons are creative and engaging. But if I want to do them justice and truly get them out from under, then I should make myself a part of their community, and I don't really want to do that. It would require me to be someone I am not, which would lead to feeling bitter and having that "I did this for you, you owe me" attitude. And this is the *wrong* attitude to have as a teacher!

I don't want to buy hip hop records because that would mean having to listen to them to create lessons. Let me repeat, I *hate* hip hop and rap music. Now, this would not have been a big deal if I hadn't spent my entire college career believing that I was going to rock the urban spectrum and be an awesome urban teacher.

I wanted to teach urban kids (and still do) because I know there is a severe shortage of "good" teachers for them out there. I love their energy, their passion, and their up-front attitudes about life. I also see possibilities in them that I think other people skim over. I wanted to show them that I expected better of them than they often did of themselves. I wanted to walk into their city—their lives—and show them that there could be more to their lives than housing projects, gangs, drugs, and becoming a mother at age 15. I never had a plan B because I never thought I would need one. I need one.

At first, panic set in. "I can't teach! I can't teach! Oh my god. That's it. The world is over. I may as well give up and throw in the educational towel. If I can't teach urban kids, I am screwed." Then the Anne Marie that is positive, the newly improved Anne Marie said, "Now wait a minute. Instead of thinking of what I can't do, what about what I *can* do."

I love the outdoors, I love the country, wide-open spaces, and I am still very passionate about teaching and issues of oppression. So, why can't I move into a community that I actually *enjoy* being in, and work from there? Every community has issues. There is no perfect community. So I tend to think now that no matter where I go, I can teach something that is valuable. There is oppression in *all* schools. Suburban kids have to deal with oppression even though they may have way more privilege than most. They need to know about their privileges and how others don't have them. They need to look at their stereotypes and biases and how they may inadvertently be helping to keep oppression in its place by keeping things the way they are and not doing anything about it. Rural kids can have just about as crappy an education as urban kids.

But I am still stuck and slightly saddened. Perhaps South Central LA isn't for me, but maybe there is a city out there I would like. After all, not all urban kids live on blocks that get shot up every night. That's a stereotype too. So maybe I am not ready to move into a "war zone," but perhaps there is an area of a city that I like. As my student teaching comes to an end, I am really thinking about what I want to do, and where I see myself in a few years. The more I think, the less I see the concrete jungle as my home. Have I finalized anything yet? No, and this is why I am losing sleep (not a good thing at the end of the semester)!

~ Anne Marie

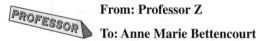

From: Professor Z

To: Anne Marie Bettencourt

Subject: Week 7, Day 2—Living in the City?

Dear Anne Marie,

Again, I am truly moved by your passion for teaching. Now that it is your last week, I want to remind you again to be saving things for your portfolio, which will be needed to get you that job, wherever it may be. Make sure you have taken some photographs of your room, of your students working (if allowed by the school district), and of you teaching the class. Make sure you have examples of student work, samples of lesson plans, assessments, activities, etc.

.... **MINI TIP** ....
While you are student teaching, you should be gathering artifacts for your portfolio. See *How to Create a Teaching Portfolio* in today's Tips, Strategies, and Relevant Data section.

Regarding where you will be looking to teach, it is true that not everybody is cut out to be Jonathan Kozol. And while I agree with Duncan-Andrade on many points, I also think there is a world of good a teacher from the burbs can bring to urban kids. Some people say that you need to be a football player to coach a football team. Yet, some of our most successful coaches never played a game in their lives. Some, including myself, say that you shouldn't teach in a college education department if you haven't taught in the public schools. Professor J has only taught one year in a public school. Yet, he seems to be doing an excellent job teaching prospective teachers. Duncan-Andrade has his opinion. So do I. So do you. I wouldn't let this one guy's opinion rock your world.

Prof Z

Tips, Strategies, and Relevant Data

How to Create a Teaching Portfolio

Now that you are near the end of your student teaching experience, you will need to continue to gather documents and other materials to create a professional portfolio to show prospective employers. Keep in mind that your portfolio may be read by principals, teachers, parents, and even students who are on the search committee. Therefore, you want to present yourself as professional, and showcase your best work.

What you should include in your portfolio depends on the situation. Portfolios should be designed to show prospective employers that there is a match between their needs and what you can provide. For example, if there is an advertisement for a teaching position and the school is looking for a teacher who is qualified in a particular subject, has expertise in a specific area, has a particular teaching philosophy, or has special qualifications, then the portfolio should target these areas.

Another way of organizing your portfolio is to do so according to state or federal standards. For example, if you are looking for a teaching job in the state of Massachusetts, your portfolio might be arranged according to each of the state standards for teachers:

- Plans curriculum and instruction.
- Delivers effective instruction.
- Manages classroom climate and operation.
- Promotes equity.
- Meets professional responsibilities.

For each of these, you would include photos, samples of student work, examples of lessons, forms of assessment, letters to and from parents, evaluations from supervisors, and so forth.

In general, a standard portfolio will include

1. A clean, professional resume (no more than two pages long).
2. A copy of your college transcript (assuming you had good grades).
3. Letters of reference accounting for your experiences working with students, taking on leadership roles and participating in other activities. Three letters would be appropriate.
4. Examples of one or two written lesson plans.
5. Examples of an assignment, including students' work that resulted from that assignment.
6. Photos displaying special class activities or school events in which you have participated.

7. An example of your writing, perhaps from an assignment, or something you've included in your journal that demonstrates your own philosophy about student learning.

In most cases, you will use your portfolio during an interview. It is sometimes easy to anticipate what questions will be asked of you during the interview, particularly if there is a job posting that says what they are looking for. You can bet that many of the questions will be about these topics. That is why you should arrange your portfolio around them. The portfolio should be used to document and support things you say during the interview. For example, if the search committee asks about your philosophy of teaching, you might tell them your philosophy, but then refer to the portfolio item to back up what you say. If you say you are a constructivist teacher, open the portfolio to a lesson that demonstrates how you apply constructivism in your teaching. Then show examples of student work, photos of the students working on the project, and assessments of the students' work.

If you are one of the final candidates for a position, you may be asked to leave your portfolio with the search committee. I recommend that you write a cover letter and leave it in the portfolio. In your cover letter, make it clear why you think there is a "marriage" between what the school is looking for and what you can provide.

Show them that you have researched the school and are aware of their mission, their programs, and other basic information. Have them see how much you want to work with them. Show them how you can contribute to their program. The cover letter should be no longer than one to two pages.

Good luck!

DAY 3

From: Anne Marie Bettencourt

To: Professor Z

Subject: Week 7, Day 3—Student Feedback Rocks!

Thanks for the information on creating a portfolio. Not surprisingly, I am a little behind schedule in putting my portfolio together, and I appreciate the push! I'm also trying to put together a resume. Do you have any samples of resumes I could look at?

Well, last week you wrote about the importance of getting student feedback. And boy did I get lots of feedback today! And it confirmed a lot of what I believed about teaching and student learning!

I am realizing that some of my best ideas come from the kids, and more often than not, I get these ideas when I am keeping one of them after school and talking about their classes. Today it came from Alia. In my class, she is doing well. Half of that success I attribute to her brains and the other half to the fact that, in all truthfulness, my last six weeks could have had more rigor to the course. But in Chinese and math, Alia is not doing so well and she informed me that she is getting suspended for three days. This inevitably leads to a sigh from me and then a talk. "Alia, do you want to go to college?" "Yeah Miss, I want to be a nurse." "And do you think you are on a college path right now, young lady?" "Sometimes Miss, but class is boring!"

Now usually teachers take that comment and snap, "Well, once you show me you can do the things I give you, then I'll make it harder for you!" But I said, "OK, Alia, why is class boring?" And then it all came out. . . .

"Miss it isn't so much what we learn, it's HOW we learn," she complained. "In math, the teacher just stands up in front of the class and writes notes on the board, and nobody in the class gets it, and he just keeps going so nobody knows what they are doing, except for like two people, so I hate it." OK, that to me makes perfect sense. I would also hate something if I had no idea what I was doing. Hence my extreme dislike of chemistry! This is followed by, "Oh and in my other class, he doesn't really have control. Well he kind of does, but really he lets the kids talk, so we don't learn much, and it's boring." Again, I think most of us would find it hard to work or learn with a party going on in a three-foot radius of our learning environment.

"OK Alia, so how would you want to learn?" (At this point, I am taking mental notes in my head and thanking GOD she didn't finish her essay in class on time or else I would not be having this talk with her). "OK, Miss, like what we do, like that game you played for the Harlem Renaissance? (Meaning—My nerf ball basketball review.) Like, we don't have to play games all the time, but just not lecturing all the time, writing essays all the time, and just reading." I nod.

"So, do you get why you are learning this stuff?" "No, Miss! I don't see why we would learn Shakespeare at all. I really don't see the point. What does this have to do with me being a nurse?"

Hrmm, she had me there. Now, I don't believe that EVERYTHING has to relate all the time directly to a student's career goal, and I do think you can learn an appreciation of things outside your subject matter (hence my fondness for a liberal arts education). But I DO think the student has to see a reason for learning it, period.

"So, would you be more interested if English were more geared to the 'real world' and you saw the point in all this reading and writing?" "Yeah, definitely." That led to a conversation about Shakespeare's ability to peg human characteristics of people and how people have set his plays in modern times, because he was so good at noticing people's character traits.

I went home and surfed the net and found the MET. It's a school based in Providence with no grades, no tests, no classes, and 120 students. That's right, I said a school. The students spend their time in the real world with mentors, internships, and advisors, creating portfolios that are reviewed every 9 weeks. Their experiential learning is grounded by the school's five guiding principles of what students must know how to do: Communication, Empirical Reasoning, Personal Qualities, Quantitative Reasoning, and Social Reasoning. Using their internship as their base, the students work with their advisor and mentor to design their coursework based on those five principals. The great thing is that 80% go to college and are passing all the state tests. If you Google "Big Picture" schools, you can see for yourself.

This was what Alia was talking about. So, I stuck to my agenda: how to make English more effective and relevant. Immediately, I came up with some ideas. The students could work in teams, over 8 weeks, to pick a topic, pose a problem, and develop an action plan to solve it. I was thinking I wanted problems related to their communities. Then, they could read books about how those problems were dealt with in the past and how they are dealt with in other countries, states, cities, etc. A variety of writing would be involved, from editorials, to research papers, to posters.

Students would learn how to solve problems, work together, and develop a model for a real problem that they would plan on implementing. If 8 weeks was not enough, then 16 weeks. Each student would focus on two projects a year that engaged him/her, yet employed useful writing and reading skills, and critical thinking. I could bring in speakers to talk about these topics, and send students out to sites to interview people about their problem. The only problem is that I am essentially creating my own curriculum, which ought to be interesting my first few years of teaching. But hey, all my skills are backed by state standards, and we would still be reading a variety of literature, so really, is it all that bad?

As you can see, I am very excited to start teaching, and very thankful that I got to talk to Alia, who clearly had some very important things to say. If only teachers would take more time to listen to their students!

While I am trying to avoid making this a bigger deal than it is, I am definitely nervous and excited about my final observation tomorrow. I know I have blown my first two chances. I know I have two strikes against me. But I also have a confidence that I did not have before. I feel in charge. I feel like my classes ARE my classes. So, I am nervous but confident. I'll see you tomorrow!

~ Anne Marie

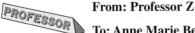

From: Professor Z

To: Anne Marie Bettencourt

Subject: Week 7, Day 3—Student Feedback Rocks!

Dear Anne Marie,

I spend a lot of time getting input from my students. In fact, I think I told you that I now collect feedback at the end of *every* class. The good ideas that I get from my students go right into improving that lesson for next year. Many of them truly *do* know what they need to succeed, and our job is to try to give that to them whenever possible. I do not think I would collect feedback at the high school level after every lesson, but I would certainly consider doing it after every unit.

> .... **MINI TIP** ....
> Get student feedback after you teach a unit. Then use that feedback to revise, refine, and improve the unit for next year.

There is one thing missing from the equation dealing with Alia. I think it is also important for her to look at her role/responsibility in the matter. It is just *too* easy to blame everything on boring teachers. Being a parent of a 17-year-old, I can look back and say that the best thing I ever taught her was that she needs to take responsibility for her life. She can blame whatever she wants on whomever she wants, but it is still *her* life and it is she who will have to live with the consequences. Somehow, my daughter caught on to this at an early age. When she fails a test, she realizes that this will affect *her* college chances. When *she* doesn't practice her field hockey, *she* realizes this will affect *her* playing. If she were to lie to us and lose our trust, it is *her* problem that she will have to live with.

Alia still is young and not fully mature at this point. What can *she* do to get herself motivated? What can *she* do to make a difference with other teachers besides you? Does she know how to give feedback to teachers in a way that tells them how to better teach her without offending them? By simply blaming the teachers for not getting good grades, and not going to college, she still doesn't go to college. She still suffers. She needs to stop feeling powerless about this and get off her butt and do something. I think you might be able to coach her on this.

What do you think?

By the way, I am sending you some information on resumes for you to look at.

.... **MINI TIP** ....
Be sure to put together a well-written resume by the end of your student teaching experience. It will be used for getting a teaching job. See *How to Write a Resume* in today's Tips, Strategies, and Relevant Data section.

Prof Z

PS: I am looking forward to our final observation tomorrow. You seem to be in an excellent mental space for it. Do what you know is right. Don't just try to please me. Teach a good class that will be relevant to your students. Make a difference in their lives. Teach them something they have never known before. And don't forget to have fun!

Tips, Strategies, and Relevant Data

How to Write a Resume

To get hired for a teaching position, you will need to have a resume that shows a prospective employer your educational background and degrees earned, your professional experiences, related activities, a professional objective, and your philosophy on teaching and learning.

Things to consider when writing your resume:

1. This resume will reflect who you are as a professional teacher, so it should be clearly written, neat, and well organized.
2. Start from the most recent experiences and work backwards.
3. Organize your resume by sections (education, teaching experiences, related work experiences, and special interests or talents).
4. Be truthful about your past experiences and accomplishments.
5. Include a list of references at the end.
6. Your resume should always be sent with a cover letter to the person responsible for the search to fill the position. Try to find out the name of this person if you can.
7. Make sure that you proofread all of your materials that you submit. There should be no spelling or grammatical errors.

DAY 4

From: Anne Marie Bettencourt

To: Professor Z

Subject: Week 7, Day 4—Final Observation/Miss B at the Plate—Bases Loaded, Two Out, Full Count

"You did not hit a home run with me," says Prof Z.

"Oh God, I knew I did something wrong!" I thought as I sat in front of Prof Z and Mr. B for our final observation post-conference. In my head I was going over and over everything I did. I couldn't see it. Where did I make a mistake? Should I not have brought the pear into class to eat? Should I have sent Warren out of the room instead of keeping him in? Did I walk around too much?

I looked at Prof Z's face, waiting to hear what I call "The Litany." Each observation works the same: I teach and Prof Z sits in the back scribbling furiously the whole time, and I pretend not to notice and ignore my sweating palms and racing heart. After it's all done, Mr. B, Prof Z, and I sit down and I do a lot of the talking. I say how the lesson went, how the students were, how I was in terms of my teaching skills, positives, negatives, and so forth. Then Mr. B puts in his two cents.

Then last but not least comes Prof Z with his pages and pages of notes on legal paper.

Usually I end up crying during or after the session because Prof Z leaves no thought unsaid, and no corners cut. He is a no-bull type of guy. In the long run, I am grateful for it, but at the time, I was making up new lyrics to "99 Bottles of Beer on the Wall" that go like this: "99 Comments from Prof Z on the wall, 99 comments by Prof Z, you cross one out, then you pout, 98 comments from Prof Z on the wall. . . ."

I am not kidding here. I have had shorter sermons at Catholic Mass! So here I am, my last shot at proving to him that I am this great teacher that I have been promising him he would see by the end of my practicum, and I am sitting here thinking, "I blew it. I can't teach. It's done." So I look up at Prof Z, waiting to hear the end of those words, "Well, you didn't hit a home run with me . . . ."

He looks down at his notes then up at me with the perfect poker face and says, "You hit a grand slam today," and he breaks into a gigantic grin. This is that moment that never happens except in fairy tales. It's when the princess gets the prince. It's when Charlie gets the golden ticket to the Chocolate Factory. I think I leaned over to pick up my jaw from the floor, and then it stretched into this loose, goofy grin. "Really?" is all I can stutter.

"Absolutely. That was great! Now I would put my daughter in your class." That was the comment of all comments. If Prof Z would put his daughter in your class, you have to be one hell of a teacher. And he told me flat out after our second observation that "maybe in a couple of years I would put her there, but not right now." I was grinning, Mr. B was grinning. Prof Z was grinning. We all looked like wonderful idiots.

I FELT it today too. I felt it all come together. I damn well should have because I spent four hours in the library last night planning this lesson, typing up sheets and directions, and thinking out every possible "what if . . ." scenario. I planned which students would be in groups. I planned my skills first and then decided how I would have them demonstrate those skills.

I must have looked absurd to anyone walking by me at the table gnawing my pen to pieces muttering to myself as I was flipping through *Romeo and Juliet.* "Hrmm, OK-OK, let's have them analyze some characters . . . OK-OK, how about they do this by comparing quotes to song lyrics; OH, I LIKE THAT (scribble scribble) . . . OK now I don't want Quan with Warren so he will be put over there (scratch out a student's name, swear silently, write in another name) . . . I am going to get Prof Z tomorrow. This is going to be fool-proof . . ." and on and on.

I spent my entire lunch period setting up the class, going over notes, making sure everything was in place before he walked in. Then I said to myself, "This is *my* class. He is a visitor. Run my class the way I've been doing it these past weeks. *My* classroom. *My* kids. Let's do it." Then the bell rang, Prof Z walked in, and it began.

It was fun. I joked; I laughed; we tossed a volleyball around (my students love throwing things, why not use it to my advantage, right?), then they did IT. They got into groups; they debated; they argued, and they were brilliant. And they did it all on their own. I merely walked around listening, nudging here and there, and keeping general order. I wasn't the "sage on the stage" I was the "guide on the side."

It was all about my kids. And THAT is apparently what magnificent teaching is all about. I was so proud of them I wanted to yell and hug them and cry, "YES!" But I refrained. Those were my students— my creative geniuses, my jokesters, and the kids I will miss most when I leave this school. It took me my entire practicum to get there, but I finally achieved what I had been striving for so hard—complete and utter success and control of my class. I DID IT!!!!!!!!!!!!

At the end of the day, I got into my car, pausing before I put the key in the ignition. I looked out at the fields where the kids were practicing their various after-school sports. I watched the girls throw softballs to one another in the bright daylight. I went back in my mind to images of me crying at my desk after a bad class, laughing at one of Wilson's random jokes to sidetrack me, and the panic I felt while trying to plan lessons, get in midterm grades, and finish a lengthy paper for my own graduate classes.

Teaching is definitely a lot of work. But I know now that I can do it, and do it well. But this is only the beginning. There are teaching jobs to acquire, faculty to love and hate, school politics to navigate, and a school of my own to build. As hard as this was, I know if I REALLY want to be good, it is going to get a lot harder.

Laughter from the field echoed over to the open window of my car. I glanced in its direction and smiled. I thought, "BRING IT ON" as I put the car in drive and headed out of the parking lot.

When I got home, I looked again at Prof Z's written comments on my Final Observation Form. He had written:

"Overall—The light bulb has gone on! The teacher has seen the light. The teacher has decided that the room belongs to her and the only way that students will learn anything is if the room belongs to her. The Jekyll/Hyde teacher is GONE!

"There is a very different feel to what I am experiencing today than at the last observation. Last time, there was a sense of futility—an attitude that there is 'nothing I can do.' Today, the teacher was in charge. Most importantly, the students knew it! Congratulations on a tremendous breakthrough.

"This was a blow-me-out-of-the-water lesson. It was meticulously planned. It hit on the strengths of the students, it was fun, creative, involved many types of critical thinking, hits on many of the multiple intelligences, and covers the material of *Romeo and Juliet*. Wow!

"Bottom line: this was not a home run. It was a grand slam! Congratulations on a job very well done. Congratulations on taking back YOUR classroom. Once it is yours, you can then make it the student's as well!"

~ Anne Marie

PROFESSOR

From: Professor Z

To: Anne Marie Bettencourt

Subject: Week 7, Day 4—Final Observation/Miss B at the Plate—Bases Loaded, Two Out, Full Count

Dear Anne Marie,

Yes, you really showed me the Anne Marie I knew was always in there. The secret: You did a great job planning this lesson. Good planning is the lifeblood of good teaching. Teachers who are good planners will be much better than those who attempt to wing each lesson. This is particularly true with new teachers.

.... **MINI TIP** ....
The better you are at planning, the more likely it is that you will be more effective as a teacher.

I call a really well-planned lesson a "monkey lesson." It is planned so well that a monkey could teach it! This wasn't really a "monkey lesson" in the sense that it required some excellent teaching skills, but it was so well planned that you only had to follow the plan to ensure success! You are getting a good sense of all the things to take into consideration when planning a lesson (all your "what if" scenarios, etc.). And you anticipated them perfectly today. It all fell into place.

You *owned* your classroom today. It was *yours*. You *made* it be the way *you* wanted it to be. That's what a good teacher does and that is what you did. It took some time to get where you wanted to be, but you have gotten there. There will be setbacks. There will be days when you won't be able to find the time to create lessons as well thought out as this one. But as you go on, you will accumulate all the lessons from the year before and have more time to create new ones. The pressure will be off because of the work you did the previous year.

My goal is to have every lesson be a great one. In time, this is an achievable goal. It may not happen in your first two years, but it is certainly achievable after that. And with your wisdom, your passion and your love for your students, you are going to be one of those teachers who will be an earth mover, a transformer of children, otherwise known as a great teacher.

And yes, I would put my daughter in your class in a heartbeat! Welcome to the profession!

Prof Z

PS: Now that you have passed your last major student teaching hurdle, it is time for you to start looking for a teaching job for next year. I know you have been gathering materials for your portfolio. It is now time to pull them together.

.... **MINI TIP** ....
Begin preparing for getting a teaching job while you are still student teaching. See *How to Prepare for Getting a Teaching Job* in today's Tips, Strategies, and Relevant Data section.

Tips, Strategies, and Relevant Data

How to Prepare for Getting a Teaching Job

There are many things you can do to prepare for getting a teaching job while you are still student teaching:

1. *Ask for Letters of Recommendation from Various Sources*
   a. *Cooperating Teacher*—This is the person who has seen you teach most often and probably knows your strengths and weaknesses

better than anyone. Therefore, prospective employers will give tremendous weight to the recommendations of your cooperating teacher. Likewise, if you do not get a letter of recommendation from your cooperating teacher, this could serve as a red flag to prospective employers.

b. *College Supervisor*—Most college supervisors will have a good idea of your strengths and weaknesses and are an important source of information to prospective employers. Since they work with many local schools, college supervisors know many of the administrators and teachers there and can be of tremendous assistance in helping you get a job at one of these schools.

c. *School Principal or Assistant Principal*—Before you end your student teaching placement, ask the school principal to come in and observe you teach. There is a good chance that he/she will say yes, particularly if he/she has heard good things about you from your cooperating teacher. School principals are always looking for good teachers because they never know when a teacher will leave. A good letter of recommendation from a principal will send a strong positive message to a prospective employer. Plus, principals talk to each other frequently and may just recommend you to another principal who is looking for the right teacher for their school.

d. *College Professors*—Letters of recommendation from college professors are probably not as critical as the first three listed because most of your college professors have never seen you teach. However, if you took a leadership position in some capacity in the class, your teacher may have an opportunity to write about skills that would support your ability to teach. It is sometimes suggested to use college professors who have not seen you teach as character references.

2. *Revise and Update Your Resume*—Include items in your resume that make you stand out from the crowd. Make your resume visually appealing. If you created, led, or joined any education projects as a student; worked with kids as a camp counselor; or participated in any other child-related activities, include these in your resume. If you were a member of any honor society or service organization, list it as well. Be sure to include your accomplishments as a student teacher. Include any outside activities like coaching, helping with the school play, or any other clubs you might have assisted with.

3. *Substitute Teach*—Becoming a substitute teacher, particularly in a district in which you may want to teach, is a great idea because it gives teachers and administrators an opportunity to get to know you and see your strengths as a teacher. When you substitute, try to handle as many discipline problems as possible on your own. Again, if you are interested in teaching in that school, invite the principal to observe you. Principals like to hire people they already know personally and who have shown that they can be effective teachers. They know that if you can handle substituting for others, it is likely you will be able to handle your own class.

4. *Make Sure You Have Completed All Your Assignments for Student Teaching*—Make sure all of your journals, self-evaluations, unit plans, video assignments and evaluations, and portfolios have been sent in. Your cooperating teacher, professors, or college supervisors should not have to remind you. This is the time to show that you are a professional and can be counted on to be reliable.

5. *Begin Searching for Job Openings*—When you know what town or city you would like to teach in, let people know that you are hoping to work there. Use your network of friends, relatives, and teaching friends. You would be surprised at how fast word of mouth travels. Check the newspapers, find out as much as you can about the school, and make contact with the school if you are still interested. Just sending in a resume is not usually an effective way of getting a job. Deliver your resume and cover letter in person, if possible.

6. *Be Prompt in Following Through with Information Requested by the School*—Do not worry if you do not have all the documentation asked for if you are still finishing your student teaching. Principals will understand that your documentation may not be available until student teaching is completed.

7. *Practice Being Interviewed*—Do mock interviews with others in which you make good connections between what the school is looking for and what you can provide for them. Remember that attitude and personality counts. Be enthusiastic, professional, positive, and confident. It is okay to show that you have a sense of humor as long as it is done appropriately.

8. *Create a Teaching Portfolio*—Use the portfolio in the interviews to back up what you are saying. Providing visuals will give prospective employers a better view of who you are as a teacher. Some schools will like seeing the hard copy of your portfolio and others may ask for an e-portfolio on a disc.

DAY 5

From: Anne Marie Bettencourt

To: Professor Z

Subject: Week 7, Day 5—My Last Day of Student Teaching

Well, it is all over. Each of my classes gave me a send off I will never forget. Of course, being the creative, dynamic teacher that I am, I also had something for my C and E period classes. I wrote poems for each of the classes talking about each student and what I had learned from them over the course of the student teaching experience, which of course, made them laugh. Then Jeremy and the rest of C period almost made me cry. He wrote a note to me thanking me for teaching him and saying that he was going to miss me next year . . . and every single kid came up and hugged me good-bye. Quan even gave me THREE hugs! Mr. B whipped out the digital camera and took pictures of me with my classes and also handed me the gift.

"I have never seen a turnaround such as yours," he said in his usual nonchalant tone as I walked into his office at the end of the day. "Usually when classroom management is bad in student teachers, it stays bad. You have done things that no other student teacher has done, and have certainly raised the bar for future ones in my classroom!"

I was stunned. Mr. B is not the kind to dish out compliments (he usually errs more on the critical side). He also handed me a wrapped package and said, "Every teacher needs a sense of humor and some creativity. I know you will figure out how to use this in your classroom." It was a collection of images from a popular comic strip. I laughed, and flipped through it, and ideas already began to zip through my head.

It was sad leaving. I felt a little twinge in my heart similar to graduation day, when you know you are leaving friends behind, but also know that you made some killer memories and that the future holds even greater possibilities. Ralph Waldo Emerson once said, "Go where there is no path, and blaze a trail." I had blazed my trail, and it was time to seek out another one to explore. And if I get lost, well, I always have that comic book to make me laugh along the way!

I figured since we are taught that good teachers are constantly reflecting on their practice, I would reflect on my entire practicum experience. At our last seminar, we got some Dos and Don'ts of

Student Teaching, which was really helpful at the END of our experience (;-) . . . but I digress. Looking them over, I decided to come
up with a few I didn't see on the list, and then mention the ones
that really stick out as, "Oh, definitely tell all the newbies this one."

1. Be visible. Be involved. At first, I showed up at school about 15
minutes before my first class to allow for "prep" time. First of all,
that is never enough prep time when teachers are fighting over
copiers that don't work and you can't find the papers you swore
were in the second drawer yesterday. Elves move things at night
and break the copiers. Trust me on this one. Get to school a good
30 minutes prior to the first bell.

Now this is the tough part. You have to stay after school too.
I mean after 2:30 and the detention bell. Plan on 3:30-ish, minimum.
Students will pick up on the fact that you hang out after school and
will drop by, announced or not. This is the best time to get to know
the kids. They get one-on-one attention, and if they don't need help
with work, you can talk with them about their life, the lousy Yankees, or how late they stay up watching siblings or doing mom's
hair. This effort carries over into class. I can tell you that I get better work out of Christy since we've played tennis together and that
Alicia is more apt to call me for essay help since our talks after
school. This is "time on learning" because the kids are learning that
you care and you are learning that their life does not revolve around
passing your tests and being in awe over the Harlem Renaissance.

Go to their activities. Your students will remember this and see
that you care about them. Go to plays. Go to games. Do whatever
you can. It gives you a chance to see your students outside the academic setting. It lets them know that you are interested in things
other than your subject matter and getting them to class on time
(though these are important, too).

2. Beware the Teacher's Lounge! I won't tell you not to go there,
because I have met some great friends and gotten great ideas for
class in there. But I will tell you that you have to filter what you
hear. More often than not it is filled with negative thoughts and
comments about kids. "They won't do this. They won't do that. You
will rarely hear, "Gee, I should have done this, and perhaps Johnny
would have paid more attention," or "I am going to try something
new other than dittos and see if the class likes it or not."

True story: One afternoon in the teacher's room, I was listening
to teachers complain about new student teachers sending failing
students on field trips and then watched as those same teachers
SIGNED the slip giving the students permission to go and then

remarked, "They'll never make it to college anyway, so they might as well use it as a day to skip." Wow! A+ for high expectations there.

I did meet a couple of teachers who love kids, and they invited me to watch them teach anytime. This is always a good sign, by the way. Mark those teachers with a star. So, admittedly, I will go into the teacher's room, but I realize that I have control over the attitude that I choose to take with me.

3. Pay attention to the difficult students. If I have failed at anything this semester, it has been that I have not tried hard enough with my difficult students. I will honestly say that there were days when I prayed that they had in-house suspension because class was so much more peaceful without them (although I have a guilty feeling about this).

In my defense, I have attempted to pull in students for individual conferences and made phone calls home, but I typically gave up after one or two tries. This is an absolute no. Clearly, those students who were testing me won, because I did what they expected me to—it got rough; I made a noble attempt; it didn't work; so I walked away like everyone else. I could have made more phone calls, spoken with guidance counselors, and taken more time with them after school. In reality, you can't save everyone and for your effort to work, the student has to be willing to work with you. But by all means don't give up after one or two phone calls.

4. Plan skills first, activities second. I planned really creative lessons this semester. They painted, they rapped, and they acted. And as a result, their writing skills did not improve a smidge. By the way, I teach English. Mr. B helped me to recognize that while creative activities are awesome, you have to anchor them to skills and content.

I used to plan like this: "OK, I want to hold a debate . . . OK-OK, what can we hold a debate on . . . OK-OK, now what standards are these in the Frameworks?" This is what we call poor planning. My last lesson, which was awesome, interactive, higher order, and creative, was planned the CORRECT way. I sat down and thought, "OK, what do I want them to practice today . . . OK, writing metaphors (jot down on notepad), analyzing characters using textual evidence (more scribbling)" (notice skills first here). Then, once I had a few skills, I worked on the type of activities I wanted, including group, pairs, or singles. Then I focused on *how* I would know that the students could do this. What would they be able to do? From that, came THE GREAT LESSON. (I am certain it will make it into the Student Teaching Hall of Fame.) Don't ever, EVER focus on lesson planning around an activity. Skills first! Trust me, the activities will come on their own, but you have to know *what* you want them to do, and then *how* you will know they can do it before any learning takes place.

5. Be a reporter and ask questions and solicit feedback. I learned so many things from so many teachers and students this semester, and half of them were not from my own students and my supervising teacher. If there are after-school activities, go to them and talk to people—the coaches, the kids, the parents. If you have a question about something, ASK! And if you want advice . . . ASK! Too many of my student teacher peers did a lot of wondering but not a whole lot of finding out. I used my time around teachers to the fullest by asking, "What do you do when a student does . . ." and "How do you grade essays? When do you make a phone call home?" I got GREAT ideas from the history teachers, and a few from foreign language teachers, but you have to open your mouth.

An addendum to that rule, however, is to realize that you are new, and know nothing. The quickest way to turn a teacher off from talking to you is to respond to their advice with, "Oh, I would never do it that way," or "Well, in my methods classes, we are told that that method is obsolete."

There is a big difference between the bubble that is the college coursework and the actual classroom, which these teachers have been in for years. When a teacher is telling you something, and you disagree, either say, "Thank you" and keep your opinions to yourself or use very judicious phrasing. A simple, "OK . . . well why do you do it that way?" said in an inquisitive, not demeaning or rude tone, will get you answers. Whatever opinions you have of these teachers and their methods, this is *their* school, and you are not only new, you are also temporary and trying to get a job. And they form just as many opinions while talking to you as you do them. Keep this in mind.

6. Rethink what *urban* actually means. So many teachers go into urban schools with scenes from *Dangerous Minds* playing in their heads—students throwing paper balls at the teacher, jeering at her, walking out of class. That is rare, and usually only happens to teachers that the students despise. Will one or two walk out occasionally? Sure. But overall, urban has more to do with the socioeconomic status, diversity, and home life of our students than with the violent rap they are given.

Our school had no metal detectors, few fights (given the large student population and overcrowding), and few incidents of guns, bombs, or knives. When I say I work with "urban" kids, I often get a raised eyebrow, "Wow! I could never do that; they're tough! You must have so much patience."

They have this "Did they eat you alive?" attitude. This one makes me laugh. Eat me alive? What are they, cannibals? Most often they are starved for any type of affection, positive attention, and assistance. When they see that you aren't going anywhere, they not only respect you but become extremely protective of you.

Also, don't underestimate the intelligence of these kids. Think about their street smarts—they navigate complicated bus systems, take care of younger siblings, often work a job until late at night, and still manage to show up at school every day. This is in spite of knowing that the school is sub-par, that some teachers hate them, that the classrooms are packed, and that they may not even have paper to do their work that day. When it snows, those kids don't have jackets or gloves, but they show up at school after hoofing it in three feet of snow.

I am not the one with patience. These kids are. Once, after some of my students gave a talk at my college about racism in education, one of the undergraduate college students commented, "Wow, they're a lot smarter than I thought they would be." I resisted the urge to punch him in the face, realizing that his only image might be what he saw on BET television or heard on the radio.

Urban does not equal violence. Urban, in our city, usually means not having toilet paper in the bathrooms and having cracked ceilings. It means students eating one meal a day, coming to and from Puerto Rico, and changing schools every few months. And it means students whose teachers gave up on teaching them how to read, so they are struggling with the work. But urban also means shouts of, "What up, Ms. Bizzle!", daily hugs, high fives, good natured laughter, students coming after school for help with essays, students reading in the library during lunch, and students showing up at your class early in the morning or late in the day because your classroom is better than their house, the block, or anywhere else they could be. Urban equals an inner strength and a bond of trust between peers and teachers that I do not hear about from suburban teachers. Urban is not *Eight Mile*. It is going the extra mile, and getting a note at the end of the year for your efforts. So go. Teach. Students are waiting for you!

I am sure I can think of more, but right now, I am having separation anxiety and am off to observe Mr. B teach and finish up some last-minute activities at the school. Besides James McBride is coming tomorrow, and I have to collect permission slips so we can go to his reading tomorrow. (See # 1 on this list). :-)

~ Anne Marie

PROFESSOR

From: Professor Z

To: Anne Marie Bettencourt

Subject: Week 7, Day 5—My Last Day of Student Teaching

Dear Anne Marie,

First off, watch what you say about those "lousy" Yankees!☺

Seriously, I love your new list of "Dos and Don'ts for Urban Teaching." Newbies in urban schools will certainly benefit from these, as will students who are teaching in rural and suburban schools. Your description of urban schools was an excellent counterpoint to the stereotypical image that many student teachers have.

Your ideas addressed many of the issues I was dealing with when I did my student teaching. I wish I had acquired your insights back then. I know that it took me a few years of teaching to really feel that I was able to put in the effort of reaching *all* of my students. For the first two years of teaching, I remember that *my* survival was the goal. But after I reached a certain level of teaching proficiency and was secure about my survival, I was able to spend more time trying to reach each student. I wasn't always successful, but at least I was clear that it really was my job to reach *every* student, no matter how easy or hard it was to do so. This was a major breakthrough for me.

Another idea you made clear was that many of the problems faced by urban school teachers can be found in *all* schools. Yes, there are certainly important differences accentuated by low socio-economic status and the effects of racism, but many of the problems *are* similar. *All* kids want to be liked, respected, nurtured, and challenged. You just never know which key will "open up" each student. There lies the challenge of teaching!

A good example: Remember that class I told you about during my first year of teaching. It was right after lunch and destroying me every day? It was the one where the principal took eleven of the worst kids out of the class, and I taught them during my lunch period.

It just so happened that the teachers would go to a local restaurant/bar every Friday after work for a few beers. I was with them one day and needed to go to the bathroom. In order to get to the bathroom, you had to walk through the game room, where there was a pool table. A whole bunch of my students from the "roughing up" class were there playing pool. When they saw me, they sort of laughed and said, "Hey, Mr. Z, do you want to play a game of pool?"

I went over to the table and told them I was terrible at pool. I proceeded to hold the cue stick backwards, acting as if I didn't know what I was doing. They all laughed. So I asked them to show me how to play. What they didn't know was that I had spent a good deal of time during college making money on pool. I was a decent hustler. Needless to say, they *"showed"* me how to hold a stick and how to break.

I broke and then "ran the table." By the time I sunk the last ball, their mouths were so wide open they could barely speak! I thanked them for teaching me how to play so well. Not only did my discipline problems nearly disappear, the students seemed to be more eager to learn from me! The story was around the school by second period that next Monday. So, you never know what it will take.

So this is it! You are done! I want to tell you that supervising you was unlike any other student I have ever had. Nobody has ever done such an in-depth job on their journals as you have. And I have never spent so much time responding! The truth is, I enjoyed every minute of it. I truly appreciated the trust you showed in me by being so honest about both your successes and your failures. Many students try to hide their failures from me. Not you!

I think this says a lot about your commitment to teaching—the fact that you sincerely discussed your weak areas so that you could grow as a teacher. I applaud you for that and for overcoming your fears and acting out of your desire to be a great teacher. Well done!

I was looking over some of your earliest journal entries and laughed about how far you have come during this semester! Whew! It is not like you won't have new issues to contend with next year when you have your own classroom. Teaching takes time to master. But you will! I am quite certain of it.

I actually started laughing at some of the comments you made in some of your older journals and realized again what a fine writer you are! You need to write a book some day! In fact, if it is okay with you, I would love to share some of these journals with future classes so they can see what a good journal looks like and what a true reflective practitioner does. How's this for an idea—maybe we should turn this into a book!

What do you think?

Prof Z

✎ Tips, Strategies, and Relevant Data

How to Become More Involved in the Teaching Profession

Now that you are done with your student teaching, it is time to get more involved in your new profession even before you get your first teaching job. There are many ways to do this.

1. *Read all you can about teaching issues.* Read as many books as you can that will give you ideas to use in the classroom. Subscribe to educational magazines and journals.
2. *Take courses.* Many states require a master's degree after you receive your initial certification. Begin this as soon as you can. It may be wise

to leave the most demanding classes for later and take the less demanding courses now so you can spend more time on your actual teaching. Take courses that will be useful to you as a new teacher.

3. *Join professional teacher organizations.* Each subject area has local, state, regional, or national organizations. These organizations can provide a tremendous support to new teachers by supplying teaching materials, journal articles, conferences, websites, etc. that will help you grow as a teacher. Some of these organizations are listed at the end of this section.

4. *Present at local, state, regional, and national conferences.* You might want to begin by being a co-presenter with someone who is experienced in this. Then, begin to submit your own proposals in areas of teaching where you feel you have something to contribute to others.

5. *Apply for grants.* There is a tremendous amount of grant money out there to help you improve your own knowledge and skills as well as to obtain needed materials for your classroom. Learn how to fill out grant proposals from someone who has done it before.

6. *Find a mentor.* It is always good to have a mentor/coach. Ask a teacher you respect and trust to be your mentor. Observe his/her classes. Ask them questions about difficult situations you've experienced. Have them observe you teach and ask for their feedback.

Professional Organizations You Should Join

For Social Studies:

The National Council for the Social Studies—*www.ncss.org*

For Reading/Language Arts:

The National Council of Teachers of English—*www.ncte.org*

For Science:

The National Science Teachers Association—*www.nsta.org*

For Math:

The National Council of Teachers of Mathematics—*www.nctm.org*

Other:

The Forum For Education & Democracy—*www.forumforeducation.org*

Magazines You Should Read

Rethinking Our Schools—www.rethinkingschools.org
The Radical Teacher—www.radicalteacher.org
The Forum Newsletter—www.forumforeducation.org

Discussion Starters for Week Seven

1. To what degree do you agree or disagree with Miss B that each student teacher should have the equivalent of a boot camp instructor to toughen them up?

2. Should teachers in urban schools live in the city in which they teach? Explain.

3. What ideas do you have about making your subject relevant to the students and creating lessons that are based on real world issues?

4. What might be the advantages of working at a school like the MET? Disadvantages?

5. To what degree do you agree or disagree with Professor Z that Alia was not taking responsibility for her life? Explain.

6. To what degree do you agree or disagree with Professor Z that "planning is the lifeblood of good teaching"?

7. What do you think were the key reasons why Miss B was able to get to the point she did by the end of the book?

8. What teaching strategies do you intend to use to create your "laboratory of learning"?

9. Do you think Professor Z is fair to judge student teachers by whether he would eventually want to put his daughter in their class? What criteria would you use?

10. With which of Miss B's list of dos and don'ts do you agree? Disagree? Why?

☑ Professor Z's Student Teaching Checklist

Post-Student Teaching Activities: Think about each of these questions. Take appropriate actions when necessary.

1. ___ Did you send thank you letters to your cooperating teacher and other appropriate staff members?

2. ___ Did you request recommendations, if appropriate, from your cooperating teacher, supervisor and any other appropriate person?

3. ___ Did you update your resume?

4. ___ Did you coordinate your teaching portfolio?

5. ___ Did you file all of your lessons in a way that you can retrieve them easily?

6. ___ Did you make notes on each of your lessons and unit plans so that they will be improved upon the next time you use them?

7. ___ Did you return any materials you borrowed from your cooperating teacher or college supervisor?

8. ___ Did you complete all college assignments for your student teaching experience?

EPILOGUE

One year later ...

June 25, 2007

Hey Professor Z,

Whew! It's the end of my first year with my own classroom. I am officially a "real" teacher of seventh-grade English. No more graduate classes, no seminars, and no back-up teacher to keep an eye on me in the classroom.

I guess my student teaching experience made an impression on me, though, because I thought of you as I was reading through my students' end-of-the-year essays. I had them reflect on the year and tell me (1) One thing they liked about my class, (2) One thing they didn't like, and (3) One thing I do that I should improve upon for next year's students. Since you have permanently brainwashed me about reflecting, here are some of the things I have learned this year that might be of interest to new student teachers.

For my first year, I think I did pretty well. The vice principal and principal are in my corner 100 percent. My department head calls me the "middle child" because he "doesn't have to worry about me" as he does about some of the other English teachers in the building. The real kicker (this will make you really proud) is that the vice principal wants me to teach classroom management strategies to the other teachers! HAH!

Enough compliments. There is always room for improvement. So, as a tribute to you and Mr. B, here is a summary of the things I learned during my student teaching placement that were most helpful for my first year of teaching. So, here it is, **Miss B's Top Ten Teaching Tips for the Practicum/First Year Teacher:**

1. Routines, Policies, and Procedures + Consistency = Success and Less Stress

Of all the things I did, maintaining consistent classroom procedures helped me the most. My vice principal mentioned one day that of all her seventh-grade teachers, I had the most consistent routines and procedures. She credited my relatively few classroom management problems to my consistent structure and policies. I agreed. My class *was* orderly. Students had easy access to the pencil sharpener, crates holding their journals, the trash, and a stapler, resulting in minimal distractions to their peers. I could get to anyone's desk in milliseconds.

Second, I had a list of five expectations that I had posted above my chalkboard, in addition to the procedures our team had set up, which were also posted on a board. Anytime a student tried something out of line or challenged my reasoning, I simply pointed to an expectation or a rule and followed it with, "Dude, you know the drill. That's not how this class rolls." And, *poof,* there might be some minor grumbling, but no major disruptions.

My classroom has an agenda of what we are doing each day, a "homework corner" listing the night's homework, and an "objective corner" stating in simple terms what skills they must master by the end of class that day. We always start off with a warm up (usually a journal entry), then a mini-lesson or homework check, and then our major activity, followed by a homework assignment. I had procedures for everything including how students were chosen to share their journal entries, how they passed in journals, where papers went for homework, and how I wanted essays stapled. It worked like a charm because if I was absent, my kids automatically retrieved their journals, knew how to share responses and knew where to look for the night's homework.

Finally, I was consistent with everything. If one student got lunch detention for chewing gum, every student got lunch detention for chewing gum. Sometimes I announced to the class that I was changing a rule. I always told them the reasoning for my decisions. They understood that most of the time the class was a democracy, but I was the President and I could "veto" at will. "All sales were final" in *my* store! There would be no bartering for consequences if you broke a rule. The consequences were the consequences, period!

2. Demonstrate to Students That You Care About Them as People

This will solve 98% of your discipline issues. Professor Z, if you stress anything to your students, emphasize this. I learned this during my student teaching and it has worked wonders for me this year.

I had one student who was being extremely defiant with me for a good three months. But I kept asking her if she was OK and telling her I cared, even when she yelled at me, "Stop asking me that! I don't want you to care about me!"

One day, the student came to me in angry tears. I sat on the floor while she sat on a bench and ranted about me. I listened, and listened, until she blurted out the real reasons for her defiance, which had nothing to do with me, and everything to do with her home. I listened and hugged her, and *poof!* No more problems. In fact, in her end-of-the-year essay she wrote, "Ms. B's my Batman and I'm her Robin—she cared about me even when I didn't want her to."

I once showed up at a baseball game to a chorus of "Ms. B's here!" and parents saying, "Yeah the boys were talking all day about you showing up and were worried that you wouldn't come." Kids run up to me in the hallway asking, "Did you see the play last night? Wasn't it awesome?"

When I take in interest in students' lives, I notice a distinct difference in the way they act in the classroom. I have shown them that I truly care, and that I respect and value their different talents. Hence, they respect me and listen to what I have to say to them during class time. It's that personal connection that allows me to have an "off" day or teach a not-so-fun lesson, and still have their attention. It also allows them to take risks academically with me. I can raise the bar with my students because we have become a team, and together, we can accomplish our goals. Finally, knowing their interests makes it so much easier to relate my lessons to their lives.

3. Secretary and Custodian Appreciation Day Is Every Day

Believe it or not, the school secretary is the eyes and ears of the school. In our building she also happens to be in charge of the laptop cart keys and is the person who assigns teachers to cover classes. I have made sure from day one that I *always* say good morning to her and I am *always* polite and courteous. As a result, I get first pick of the classes I want to cover, and because she works closely with the principal, I have been recommended to participate in grants and workshops for when a select few are chosen.

So many teachers overlook the importance of the custodians and the school secretaries. Don't! You will regret it if something breaks in your classroom, a locker gets jammed, or you need a favor down the road. Trust me, eventually you will need a favor. While the principal and vice principals are in charge of the school, the secretary and custodians know everything about the building and the people in it. For a first year teacher, this comes in very handy.

4. Plan, and Then Plan Some More

I mentioned earlier that 98% of your discipline problems can be avoided by building relationships with your students. Well, the other 2% usually is covered by great planning. My department head once told me, "You have no idea how many teachers come in to this building and don't have a clue what they are doing until five minutes before the students walk in!" We often get surprise walk-through visits from our vice principal and principal. They have told me that by just walking past a classroom, they can tell which teachers have planned lessons and consistent routines, and which teachers do not.

I have adopted the mantra that teaching is really easy if you are horrible at it. Horrible teachers don't plan. Good teachers know the importance of planning, both for themselves and for their kids. Your students want and need structure, regardless of age or environment. This is especially true for kids who come from families where structure is lacking or not there at all. The school may be the only predictable, safe spot they are in all day. The best way to make your kids feel safe is to have consistent routines, connect to students as people, and plan your lessons in advance!

Granted, once in a while a lesson that I have "winged" will turn out better than the lesson I planned, but usually this is not the case. There are many things that a first year teacher faces, so don't add "unplanned chaos" to your list. Do lesson plans a week in advance. Whether you have to do this or not, I think it is a great idea to have an overview of your week, month, and unit.

My biggest mistake when I was student teaching was spending all my time thinking of all the cool, outside-the-box activities I could be doing with my students. What I should have been doing was looking at my unit and listing the objectives. You should ask yourself, "At the end of all this, what do students need to 'get' out of it?"

After determining my specific objectives, I print out a calendar of the month and sketch out my goals for each week in pencil. I can erase and readjust if I need to, but now I can quickly glance at the calendar and know what I want to accomplish. What do I want my students to learn at the end of the day? From there, I create the daily lesson plans. It's very difficult to plan lessons when you aren't sure what you want the students to learn!

Another thing I do is always have a good answer to the question, "Why?" Students will always ask, "Why are we learning this?" Answering "Because it's in the curriculum" or "Because you have to" is not going to win you points. I have learned to answer with examples of how they will use the skills they will be learning in their lives.

I point out that they are learning to become better communicators so that their voices can be heard and people can understand them. I show them that they are learning different ways to express themselves in real world situations that will help them get what they want out of life. If that doesn't work, I tell the students that they enter school with a toolbox, and as teachers, we fill it with all kinds of tips, tricks, and tools for being successful in the world. Will every tool be used in every job? Of course not, but at least it is there if they need it! Sometimes I throw the question back on the students and ask them, "Why do you think you might need to know grammar, or be able to recognize a theme?" Usually they come up with things I've never thought of, and they have answered their own question.

Well-planned lessons allow you to anticipate all the worst case scenarios and provide a means to avoid them. They also allow you to deal with the unpredictables—fire drills, assemblies, and fights—with a lot less stress because you have your day laid out. You can communicate your plan to your students and work around the rest. Tell teachers to jot notes on their lesson plans throughout the day. Ask yourself, "Does the lesson need changes? Were there things I forgot to consider?"

Perhaps a student made a comment that gave you a great idea. I always print out a copy of my lesson and scribble the heck out of it. They don't have to be long, just little tidbits that will be useful if you teach the same material next year or do a similar lesson down the road. At day's end, I can look back at what I did and adjust my plans for the next day. If something bombs, well, welcome to the world of teaching! You'll know where things broke down and be able to adjust for it next time.

5. Keep Discipline Problems Between You and the Student as Much as Possible

New teachers need to realize three things. First, you are dealing with a child, a teenager, a mini-adult. If they are yelling, don't yell back. If they insult you, don't fling a witty insult back. You are the adult, so act like it. You would be amazed at the classrooms I walk by where I hear screaming, sarcastic teachers who are waiting to throw a kid out and then call the principal and tell her that the student walked out of class. Many students come from environments where yelling is the norm. They are pros at dealing with this and will do anything to ramp up a situation because they know they can get you to look like an idiot. Don't let them take you there.

Second, we all need "chill-out" time. If a student is raging mad, they get a couple of options with me. They can take a five-minute breather in the hallway, or they can write in their journal, disregarding the day's topic and just sounding off. Occasionally, a student can write me a note and tell me they are having a bad day, so their participation might be minimal.

I always give the student a way out. If they refuse, they can make up the time after school the next day. I've had students tell me, "Ms. B, my butt is killing me from these chairs. Do you mind if I stand and do this work?" I say, "Go right ahead." Consider your ultimate goal: to get the student to learn and participate in class that day.

Third, give yourself some space. If you piss off a student so that they can't learn, you have defeated your own goal, and just made life harder for yourself. If you are at the point where you just might want to commit homicide, it's okay to tell the student in a calm voice, "Listen, I know we are both angry right now, so let's chill out, and come back to this later. I definitely want to fix this, but I know right now, when we are both mad, is not the time." And if they mutter, let them mutter. THEY ARE KIDS. It is their job to try to piss you off, remember?

Fourth, students don't want to hate you or have you hate them. Most of the time, the blowups have nothing to do with you. They've had a rough time at home, a student has insulted them, or they have walked in in a bad mood. It's not about you! So, if I can't pull them into the hallway for a quick chat during class, I make an appointment with them during lunch, after school, or during tomorrow's class. My students know I *want* them in my class, and I want them to work. It's MY class, so sending them right to the vice principal is not a good idea. If I keep sending them out, the students will come to believe that I can't control my class. Worse, they would see that I really don't want to deal with them.

6. Come Early, Stay Late

The "come early" part should be obvious. You don't want to be rushing into your classroom ten minutes before your students get there. If I have everything all set for the day, I can chat with other teachers or grade some papers (English teachers ALWAYS have papers to grade!). The stay late part is where it gets interesting. This is good one-to-one time, or one-to-three time with your students. You can chat with them, help with homework, or just be a listener.

I've had students stay after school that I could have sworn hated my class. It turns out they hated home or the outside world even more than my class. For some students that really needed extra help, I've stayed as late as 6 PM working with them. Sometimes

I hold study parties after school to teach kids how to study for spelling or grammar quizzes.

At our school, we have one required late day a week. But one late day per week won't cut it with your kids. Most kids have sports teams, church, or babysitting jobs and need you to be flexible. I stay late at least three days a week. I wait one hour, and if no one shows up, then I leave. But in that hour, I can adjust plans for the next day, call parents, or fix bulletin boards so I am still productive with or without students.

When students are there, you will be amazed at how much they want to talk with you about life and their interests. Listen to them. I have gained much appreciation for what my students do outside of school, and it becomes useful material for relating my subject to their lives or just gaining their respect. Students who have boasted about their cooking have brought in dishes for the class. And often I find that students will work harder for me because I took the time to take an interest in them.

Teachers laugh at me when I tell them that I went to students' plays, ball games, or other activities. However, I have almost no behavior problems with those students, and they work harder because we are a little bit tighter than the other teachers. They know that I know and appreciate their lives out of school. Besides, it's fun when you are teaching to be able to relate their interests to your lesson. Kids will often complain, "I don't know what to write," so I will say, "Well, you play baseball, right? So why don't you think of different ways to look at the game," or "You know that dance you went to this weekend? Maybe your character could be a dance, and. . . ." and the eyes light up and the ideas start flowing. After-school and outside of school time gives you and your students new perspectives on each other that enrich classroom time.

7. Give Students Options!

Regardless of the age group, kids are capable of making decisions. Even at the camp I work at in the summer, the five- and six-year-olds can decide what games they want to play, and whether or not they want milk with lunch. When you give students options, you let them become part of the learning process, which in turn, gets them more invested in learning, because they think they came up with the great idea in the first place.

When I assign essays, I give a topic, and then let students branch off of it. For tests, I give several essay questions and ask the students to answer two of them. The skills are the same, but the students get to choose how to demonstrate the skills. When we draft or take notes, some students use our school's "graphapillar," some make charts, and others draw boxes instead of circles.

I don't care as long as the student is brainstorming and the method works for him/her. If their method isn't working, then I step in and offer some additional ideas. Mandated curriculum can limit the options that your students have, what books to read or what concepts to learn, for example, but even within those limitations, you can build choices into your lessons.

8. Three Heads Are Better Than One, Most of the Time

Silence does not equal learning. Students really do learn more when they are allowed to bounce ideas off each other and help each other out. There are a few tricks to doing group work, most of which are learned by trial and error. You just have to plan as best you can and see what happens.

Many teachers believe that you should never let kids pick the groups they work in. Hogwash. Don't *always* let the kids pick their own groups, but if you are dealing with students who are afraid to take academic risks, start off by letting them choose partners they are comfortable with. Warn them that if they are not on task, then you will pick the partner, and it's not up for debate.

Also, this is not the time for you to sit behind your desk and ignore the class. Kids will have questions, get off task, and get stuck, so you will need to walk around the classroom the whole time. Yes, the whole time. Most group work fails because the teacher disappears, and the kids figure out that they don't really have to be on task because no one is checking up on them.

Groups work if you have to produce a final product of some sort. For longer projects, I have the kids keep work logs with the date and what each person did that day. I tell the kids I will factor that into their individual grade. I give two grades—a group grade, and an individual grade based on what I see, on the work logs, and on the peer feedback sheets that students fill out at the end of a project. I tell the kids that it's easy for the group to get an A and a student to get an F for doing nada.

The result is the ideal method for teaching! You teach a concept and then the kids work in groups to practice the concept and learn from each other. Who ends up doing most of the work? The students. Who ends up learning the most? The students! Swallow your pride and realize that you as glorious teacher-preacher is not what it's about.

9. You Are Not Going to Become the Perfect Teacher Your First Year!

If there is one thing I value from my student teaching experience, it was the chance to try new ideas. Sometimes I would be successful, and sometimes I would fail. Failure is just part of the game. We can learn some of our biggest lessons from our failures. Humility is a great teacher. If you let it, it teaches you again and again how to become a better teacher.

As a first-year teacher, you learn to cultivate humility. It doesn't mean you fear your students or lack faith in your lessons. What it means is you approach each lesson trying your best, with an open heart. If it works, it's a joy. If not, remember, this is your first year! Use the failure to learn how you can improve next time.

This is where your student teaching experience comes in handy in at least two ways. First, it teaches you to cultivate self-reflection. Never stop that—it is a technique you will use the rest of your teaching life.

Second, use your student teaching experience to try new methods and ideas! You'll never have quite the same opportunity again. If student teaching is like walking the high wire, your cooperating teacher and supervisor are the big cushion underneath. Use them to break your falls.

When you teach your first year, the cushion is not quite the same. You have to start building your *own* cushion! How do you do that? The first step is to remember, "I'm not going to be perfect all the time." Be kind to yourself, then be humble. Let the humility trigger all the great self-reflection techniques you learned during your practicum. I guess if learning is a lifelong process, so is learning to teach.

10. Have Fun!

I saved this for last, because it is the most important. I see so many teachers who are burnt out and jaded, and who don't enjoy their classes or their subjects anymore. I tell everyone I know that I love what I do. And I do! My principal was shocked that I only called in sick one day this year (compared to the ten plus days for many of our staff). I told her it's because I love my job.

Why do I love my job so much? We have *fun* in my class. Kids tell stories, do imitations of me, share hilarious journals, and mix it up. We put on doctor's gloves and operate on teddy bear patients to learn "syntax surgery" and we play "Party Quirks" from *Whose Line Is It Anyway?* to learn how to dramatize a text. My students repeatedly told me that my class was their favorite, despite the fact that they also told me I give the most and hardest work. You don't have to sacrifice learning to have fun.

And while not all learning has to be fun, most of it should be. I will often bust out laughing at a student's shirt (my favorites are "Come Back When You're Hot" and "Really, Really, Really Ridiculously Good Looking"). I have to push myself out of my comfort zone sometimes and do something off the wall. Remember, you are asking your students to take risks, so you as a teacher should be willing to take some, too. Teach on the opposite side of the room. Stand on your desk to make an important point. Throw a Koosh ball around when you want answers to questions. (This won big points this year.) Whatever you do, love it, and love the students.

Well Professor Z, that's all I have for now. I know I worry a lot about whether I have done a good job. But really, all I have to do is look to my students for the answer. They've grown into strong writers, and decent people to boot. The kids keep asking me to teach eighth grade next year and move up with them. They tell me they will visit me next year (harass me might be a better term).

As I mentioned before, one girl wrote of me, "Ms. B is my Robin and I am her Batman. She cared about me even when I didn't want her to. She believed in me when I didn't believe in myself. She is one person who has changed my life." So, I can't ask for much more. I mean, who else gets a classroom full of superheroes for students? And I am lucky enough to be the sidekick! I just ride the cool sidecar and put my superheroes in the middle of the action.

And *that* is my first-year experience in a nutshell.

Have a great summer!

~ Anne Marie aka "Miss B," "French Fry," "Miss!"

In June, 2007, after completing her first year of teaching, Anne Marie was nominated for the Springfield, Massachusetts, New Teacher of the Year.